The Old Testament
in Early Christianity

Canon and Interpretation
in the Light
of Modern Research

E. Earle Ellis

BAKER BOOK HOUSE
Grand Rapids, Michigan 49516

Copyright © 1991 by J. C. B. Mohr (Paul Siebeck)
First published in 1991 by J. C. B. Mohr (Paul Siebeck)
(Wissenschaftliche Untersuchungen zum Neuen Testament, vol. 54)
Baker Book House edition published in 1992
by arrangement with J. C. B. Mohr (Paul Siebeck)

Library of Congress Cataloging-in-Publication Data

Ellis, E. Earle (Edward Earle)
   The Old Testament in early Christianity : canon and interpretation
in the light of modern research / by E. Earle Ellis.
        p.   cm.
   Includes bibliographical references and indexes.
   ISBN 0-8010-3217-2
   1. Bible. O.T.—Canon. 2. Bible. N.T.—Relation to the Old
Testament. 3. Bible. O.T.—Criticism, interpretation, etc.—History—
Early church, ca. 30–600. 4. Typology (Theology)
I. Title.
BS1135.E44   1992
221.6—dc20   91-48112

Printed in the United States of America

For

Jerry Hawthorne

Christian Brother
Valued Friend
Pleasant Sparring Partner

Contents

I. The Old Testament Canon in the Early Church

II. Old Testament Quotations in the New:
A Brief History of the Research

III. Biblical Interpretation in the New Testament Church

Appendix I: Jesus and his Bible

Appendix II: Typological Interpretation – and its Rivals

Preface

The present volume is a revision and expansion of essays that have appeared separately in an earlier form.[1] To the editors and publishers of those volumes a word of deep appreciation is especially due and here gratefully given.

The chapters and appendices of the present book develop a theme that has had a continuing place in my thinking and writing since my doctoral dissertation at the University of Edinburgh.[2] While my mind has changed in some respects and, I hope, my understanding deepened, I remain convinced that the use of the Old Testament by the New Testament writers is the primary key to their theology and, thus, to the message of God that they taught the early church and that they continue to teach the church today.

I have dedicated this volume to a friend of almost forty years, who lives with his Bible and whose grace and integrity exemplify the best in Christian character.

I am most grateful to Professors Martin Hengel and Otfried Hofius and to the publisher, Georg Siebeck, for accepting the manuscript for the *WUNT* series. Also, I wish to express my appreciation to the many colleagues and students whose queries and comments have made this a better book. I want to thank especially my assistants, David Edwards, who prepared the indices, and Tom Hood; and my secretary, Mrs. Vicki Barrs, whose patience and commitment to the task have been more than any writer has a right to expect.

Southwestern Baptist Seminary, Lent 1990   E. Earle Ellis

---

[1] Chapters 1 and 3 first appeared in *Compendia Rerum Judaicarum ad Novum Testamentum*, ed. S. Safrai et al., Assen: Van Gorkum Publishers, 1974–, II, 1 (*Mikra*, edd. M.J. Mulder and H. Sysling), 653–724. Chapter 2 was published in *International Standard Bible Encyclopedia*, 4 vols., ed. G.W. Bromiley, Grand Rapids: Eerdmans Publishing Co., [2]1979–88, IV, 18–25. Appendix I was published in the *Criswell Theological Review* 3.2 (1989), 341–351. Appendix II appeared as the Foreword to L. Goppelt, *TYPOS. The Typological Interpretation of the Old Testament in the New*, Grand Rapids: Eerdmans Publishing Co., 1982, ix–xx.

[2] E.E. Ellis, *Paul's Use of the Old Testament*, Grand Rapids [5]1991 ([1]1957).

Abbreviations

ANF	*The Ante-Nicene Fathers*, 10 vols., edd. A. Roberts and J. Donaldson, Grand Rapids 1951 (c. 1885).
ARN	*Abot de Rabbi Nathan*
Ant.	Josephus, *Antiquities*
ATR	*Anglican Theological Review*
BASOR	*Bulletin of the American Society of Oriental Research*
Bib	*Biblica*
BJRL	*Bulletin of the John Rylands Library*
B. T.	*Babylonian Talmud*
BTB	*Biblical Theology Bulletin*
Bib Sac	*Bibliotheca Sacra*
BZ	*Biblische Zeitschrift*
c.	Circa = about; contra
CAH	*Cambridge Ancient History*, 12 vols., ed. S. A. Cook et al., Cambridge 1925–1939
CBQ	*Catholic Biblical Quarterly*
CJT	*Canadian Journal of Theology*
Compendia	*Compendia Rerum Judaicarum ad Novum Testamentum* edd. S. Safrai et al., Assen 1974–
DCB	*A Dictionary of Christian Biography*, 4 vols., edd. W. Smith and H. Wace, London 1877–87
DBS	*Dictionnaire de la Bible, Supplément*, ed. Louis Pirot, Paris 1928–
EB	*Encyclopedia Biblica*, 4 vols., ed. T. K. Cheyne, London 1899–1903
EJ	*Encyclopaedia Judaica*, 16 vols., ed. C. Roth, New York 1971
Est Bib	*Estudios Biblicos*
ET	English Text (Translation)
ET	*Expository Times*
GT	German Text (Translation)
GTJ	*Grace Theological Journal*
HDB	*Dictionary of the Bible*, 5 vols., ed. J. Hastings, Edinburgh 1898–1904
HE	Eusebius, *Historia Ecclesiastica*
HUCA	*Hebrew Union College Annual*
IDB	*Interpreters Dictionary of the Bible*, 4 vols., ed. G. A. Buttrick, New York 1962
IDBS	*Interpreters Dictionary of the Bible Supplement*, ed. K. Krim, Nashville 1976
IEJ	*Israel Exploration Journal*
IMJ	*The Israel Museum Journal*
Int	*Interpretation*
ISBE[2]	*International Standard Bible Encyclopedia*, 4 vols., ed. G. W. Bromiley, Grand Rapids [2]1979–88

JBL	*Journal of Biblical Literature*
JBR	*Journal of Bible and Religion*
JE	*The Jewish Encyclopedia*, 12 vols., ed. I. Singer, New York 1901
JETS	*Journal of the Evangelical Theological Society*
JNES	*The Journal of Near Eastern Studies*
JQR	*Jewish Quarterly Review*
JSJ	*Journal for the Study of Judaism*
JSS	*Journal of Semitic Studies*
JSNT	*Journal for the Study of the New Testament*
JSOT	*Journal for the Study of the Old Testament*
JTS	*Journal of Theological Studies*
JTSA	*Journal of Theology for Southern Africa*
JTVI	*Journal of the Transactions of the Victoria Institute*
KD	*Kerygma und Dogma*
LCL	*Loeb Classical Library*
LXX	The Septuagint
M.	*Mishnah*
MPG	*Patrologia Graeca*, 162 vols., ed. J. P. Migne, Paris 1857–66
MT	Masoretic Text
n	note
NKJV	New King James Version
NT	*Novum Testamentum*
NTS	*New Testament Studies*
Neot	*Neotestamentica*
PAAJR	*Proceedings of the American Academy of Jewish Research*
P. T.	*Palestinian Talmud (= Jerusalem Talmud)*
PTR	*Princeton Theological Review*
Q	Non-Markan traditions common to Matthew and Luke
RB	*Revue Biblique*
RGG³	*Religion in Geschichte und Gegenwart*, 7 vols., ed. K. Galling, Tübingen ³1957–65.
RHE	*Revue d'Histoire Ecclésiastique*
RHPR	*Revue d'Histoire et de Philosophie Religieuses*
RQ	*Revue de Qumran*
RSV	Revised Standard Version
Sales	*Salesianum*
SJT	*Scottish Journal of Theology*
ST	*Studia Theologica*
SVT	*Supplements to Vetus Testamentum*
T.	*Tosefta*
TB	*Tyndale Bulletin*
TDNT	*Theological Dictionary of the New Testament*, 10 vols., ed. G. Kittel, tr. G. W. Bromiley, Grand Rapids 1964–76
TDOT	*Theological Dictionary of the Old Testament*, ed. G. J. Botterweck, tr. J. T. Willis, Grand Rapids 1974–
TLZ	*Theologische Literaturzeitung*
TU	*Texte und Untersuchungen*
VT	*Vetus Testamentum*
WTJ	*Westminister Theological Journal*

WUNT	*Wissenschaftliche Untersuchungen zum Neuen Testament*
WW	*Wirkendes Wort*
ZNTW	*Zeitschrift für die neutestamentliche Wissenschaft*
ZTK	*Zeitschrift für Theologie und Kirche*
†	date of death

I

The Old Testament Canon
in the Early Church

Introduction

The term κανών, from which the English word 'canon' is derived, means 'a measuring stick' and is first used for biblical writings in the fourth or perhaps third century A.D.[1] Cognate forms[2] and similar terms such as 'covenantal books' (ἐνδιαθήκοι βίβλοι)[3] also were employed. At the beginning of the church, however, other terminology was current: Scripture (γραφή),[4] the Law, the Law and the Prophets,[5] the Old Covenant,[6] Moses and all the Prophets,[7] the Law of Moses and the Prophets and Psalms.[8] Verbal formulas were also employed: God said, he says (or said; λέγει, φησίν), Scripture says, Isaiah says, Moses wrote, as it is written.[9] These expressions signified an appeal to divine authority and most, if not all, correspond to designations for the Old Testament that were current in the wider community of Judaism.

---

[1] Amphilocius, *Iambi ad Seleucum* 319 (*MPG* 37, 1598A); Eusebius *HE* 6, 25, 3; Athanasius, *de decretis nicaenae* 18 (*MPG* 25, 456A). The expression, ὁ λόγος τοῦ προφη-τικοῦ, often translated 'the doctrine of the prophetic rule,' may in the third century (?) Clementine Homilies (2, 15, end = *MPG* 2, 85C) refer to Scripture as such.

[2] Origen, *Prol. in Cant.* 36, end *(canonicus)*; *Comm. in Mt* on Mt 23:37–39 *(canonizo)* and on Mt 24:23–28 *(canonicus)*. On the term cf. T. Zahn, *Grundriß der Geschichte des neutestamentlichen Kanons*, Leipzig ²1904, 1–14; B.F. Westcott, *A General Survey of the History of the Canon of the New Testament*, London ⁷1896, 512–519. In the New Testament κανών is used of a prescribed standard of conduct (II Cor 10:13, 15f.; cf. Phil 3:16) or belief (Gal 6:16).

[3] Origen, *Comm. in Pss* 1 (Introduction); in Eusebius *HE* 6, 25, 1; cf. 3, 3, 1.

[4] E.g. Jn 13:18; Gal 3:8. B.B. Warfield ('Scripture,' *A Dictionary of Christ and the Gospels*, 2 vols., ed. J. Hastings, Edinburgh 1924, II, 585) considered the anarthrous use to refer to a known, 'unitary written authority,' i.e. the Scripture as a whole. Cf. II Tim 3:16; II Pet 1:20.

[5] E.g. I Cor 14:21 (Isa 28:11f.); Jn 10:34 (Ps 82:6); Mt 7:12.

[6] II Cor 3:14f; cf. I Macc 1:56f.: 'the books of the law... [and] a book of the covenant.'

[7] Lk 24:27; cf. Jn 1:45; Acts 26:22.

[8] Lk 24:44.

[9] E.g. II Cor 6:2, 16; Heb 1:5; 8:5,8; Rom 11:2; 10:20; Mk 12:19; II Cor 8:15. On the formulas introducing scriptural citations in the New Testament cf. E.E. Ellis, *Paul's Use of the Old Testament*, Grand Rapids ⁵1991, 22–25, 48f.; J.A. Fitzmyer, '... Quotations in Qumran and the New Testament,' *NTS* 7 (1960–61), 299–305.

New Testament writers reflect their viewpoint not only by their formulas of quotation but also by their understanding of prophecy. They consider the prophet to be 'a man of the Spirit' (Hos 9:7; cf. I Cor 14:37) and the Holy Spirit to be the spirit of prophecy (Acts 2:17).[10] Thus, they equate the Scriptures, even those specifically classified as 'the Law' or 'the Writings', with 'the Prophets' (Acts 26:27) or with the teaching of prophets and, consequently, regard the canonical books as inspired by God. Their attitude toward the prophetic and, therefore, the divine origin of Scripture is nowhere better summarized than in II Tim 3:16 and II Pet 1:21:

'All Scripture is inspired by God (γραφὴ θεόπνευστος) and profitable for teaching...'
'No prophecy was ever produced (ἠνέχθη) by the will of man but, being carried along by the Holy Spirit, men spoke from God.'

With variations in nuance other writers express the same conviction about the prophetic character of Scripture, and they all reflect the attitude of Judaism as a whole. Josephus, for example, limits the canon of Scripture not only to prophets but to a particular succession of prophets, and Philo describes the Scripture virtually as an emanation of the prophetic spirit. Similarly, rabbinic writings state that the departure of the Holy Spirit, presumably the spirit of prophecy, brought the giving of canonical prophecy to an end.[11]

Nevertheless, not all prophetic words or writings were included in the received Scriptures. This is recognized in the Old Testament, in Josephus, and in the New Testament. In I Sam 10:10 certain prophecies remain unrecorded. For Josephus prophecy is a continuing phenomenon and a number of first-century figures are identified as prophets even though, on principle, any writings of such persons would be excluded from canonical Scripture.[12] In early Christianity there were also writing prophets, some of whose 'scriptures' illumined the church (Rom 16:26) and were some-

---

[10] Cf. (H.L. Strack and) P. Billerbeck, *Kommentar zum Neuen Testament*, 4 vols., München 1922–28, II, 127–134. For a theory of uninspired 'canonical' books in rabbinic Judaism cf. S.Z. Leiman, *The Canonization of Hebrew Scripture*, Hamden CT 1976, 127–131.

[11] E.g. *B.T. Sota* 48b; cf. Billerbeck (note 10), I, 127; IV, 435–450; cf. Philo, *Vita Mos.* 2, 188–191. See R.T. Beckwith, *The Old Testament Canon of the New Testament Church*, London 1986, 63–71; Leiman (note 10), 30–34, 66, 129ff.

[12] Josephus, *Ant.* 13, 311ff.; 15, 373–379; *idem.*, *War* 6, 286; 6, 300–309.

times incorporated into the New Testament canon.[13] For the most part these inspired writings, including some writings of apostles (I Cor 5:9), apparently did not enjoy a continuing authoritative use and were allowed to perish. That is, while canonical Scripture was regarded as prophetic, prophetic writing did not necessarily become canonical. This was true both for the prophetic word in ancient Israel and for that in the apostolic church.[14]

The writings to which Jesus and his messianic community appeal as a divine sanction for their message were well-known and were evidently recognized by them and their Jewish hearers not only as *divinely inspired* but also as the *continuing, normative authority* for the faith and life of the people of God. It is with this twofold attribution that these writings can be said to constitute a *canonical authority*.[15] At the same time the NT writers, and Jesus as he is represented by them, not only alter the texts of these canonical books when they cite them[16] but also occasionally quote in the same manner other Jewish writings[17] that were never recognized by the church or the synagogue to have a fixed and abiding, i.e. canonical authority.[18] Thus is posed the problem of the canon in the early church. To address it one must examine (1) the canon of the church in its relationship to the canon of Judaism and (2) the rationale by which canonical and non-canonical writings could be similarly used but nevertheless distinguished.

---

[13] E.g. I Cor 14:33–36, 37; Eph 5:14; II Tim 3:1–5; Jas 4:5. Cf. E.E. Ellis, 'Traditions in the Pastoral Epistles,' *Early Jewish and Christian Exegesis*, ed. C.A. Evans, Atlanta GA 1987, 237–253 = *The Making of the New Testament Documents*, Tübingen 1992, forthcoming.

[14] The same attitude was present in the patristic church. See below, 33f.

[15] J.A. Sanders (*Torah and Canon*, Philadelphia 1972, 91; in *Magnalia Dei*, ed. F.M. Cross, Garden City NY 1976, 551) somewhat similarly notes the threefold requirement in Judaism for the canonical status of a writing: divine authority, a fixed and invariable acceptance and adaptability. *Pace* Sanders, an 'adapted' scripture continued to have authority only if the adaptor was also recognized to have prophetic gifts and status. Cf. also G.W. Anderson, 'Canonical and Non-Canonical,' *The Cambridge History of the Bible, Vol. I*, ed. P.R. Ackroyd and C.F. Evans, Cambridge 1970, 117f.; Beckwith (note 11), 63–71.

[16] E.g. Matt 2:23; John 7:38; I Cor 2:9; 15:45; Gal 4:22. The citations in Luke 11:49–51, Eph 5:14 and Jas 4:5 (γραφή) appear to be from Christian prophetic writings.

[17] E.g. in Jude 9, 14f. Regarding the number of apocryphal quotations A. Oepke ('κρύπτω,' *TDNT* 3 [1965/1938], 987–992) concludes that 'in the New Testament [they] prove to be very small, though one can hardly deny them altogether' (992).

[18] For the same practices among Jewish and patristic writers see below.

The Determination of the Canon

Witnesses: The First Century and Earlier

With its recognition of the books of the New Testament alongside those of the Old Testament, the church departed decisively from the canon of Judaism.[19] But with regard to the Old Testament it appears to have remained in conscious and intentional accord with the Jewish community.

1. Early Christian writings reveal no trace of friction with other Jewish groups about which books carried divine authority. This remains the case in the second century even in Justin's *Dialogue with Trypho the Jew*, where any such divergence might be expected to surface.[20]

2. When the later Diaspora, now mainly gentile, church was uncertain about the precise extent of the Old Testament books, it sought an answer from Jewish or Jewish-Christian communities in Palestine.[21]

3. In what has been termed 'the crisis of the Old Testament canon,'[22] the second-century church raised questions, in fact, not about the authority of the Old Testament but about its interpretation and

4. the heretic Marcion, who rejected the Old Testament, represented an aberration in Christian practice that was uncharacteristic even of the heretical movements.[23]

---

[19] Although dated, Westcott (note 2) and T. Zahn, *Geschichte des neutestamentlichen Kanons*, 2 vols., Erlangen 1888–92, remain the best and most comprehensive studies. More recently, cf. B. M. Metzger, *The Canon of the New Testament*, Oxford 1987, and from a Lutheran perspective, cf. H. von Campenhausen, *The Formation of the Christian Bible*, London 1972. Zahn has much information on the Old Testament canon as well, as does the excellent survey of B. F. Westcott, *The Bible in the Church*, Grand Rapids 1979 (1864).

[20] The only differences cited are certain passages in the books of the Septuagint said to have been deleted from the Hebrew texts by the rabbis. Cf. Justin, *Dial.* 71–73.

[21] E. g. Melito in the second century, Origen in the third and Jerome in the fourth. See below, 10f., 16f., 31 ff.

[22] By von Campenhausen (note 19), 62–102: 'Before Marcion there were hardly any "anti-biblical gnostics" in the strict sense. The view which dominated earlier scholarship, that "the gnosis" had more or less rejected the Old Testament from the start, is no longer tenable...' (75). 'In general what [the ecclesiastical polemicists] condemn in the gnostics is not the rejection but the arbitrary exegesis of holy scripture...' (76).

[23] On Marcion's rejection of the Old Testament cf. Irenaeus, (*adv. Haer.* 1, 29, 1; 1,

5. Admittedly, parts of the church later gave canonical status to certain Jewish apocryphal books. But this appears to have been the outgrowth of a popular and unreflective use of these writings, a case of custom triumphing over judgement.

These observations must now be supported by a more detailed consideration of the historical witnesses[24] to the canon in the early church and in the Judaism that gave it birth.

Josephus

Witnesses to the biblical canon at the beginning of the present era appear in Jewish and Christian sources. Most explicit is the Jewish historian Josephus:[25]

'Our books, that are justly accredited (τὰ δικαίως πεπιστευμένα), are but two and twenty, and contain the record of all time... Five are of Moses [and] thirteen [of] the Prophets... who wrote the history of the events of their own times... The remaining four (αἱ λοιπαὶ τέσσαρες) contain hymns to God and precepts for the conduct of human life. After Artaxerxes (c. 400 B.C.)... the [writings] have not been deemed worthy of equal credit... because of the failure of the exact succession of the prophets... Although a long time has passed no one has ventured to

---

27, 2) and Tertullian (*adv. Marc.* 1, 2; 4, 1). For the Gnostics' use of the Old Testament cf. R. M. Wilson, 'The Gnostics and the Old Testament,' *International Colloquium on Gnosticism*, ed. G. Widengren, Stockholm 1977, 164–168; the index of passages in W. Foerster ed., *Die Gnosis*, 2 vols., Zurich 1971 (ET: Oxford 1972–1974, II, 350–352): Of some 300 Old Testament citations about forty percent are from Gen 1–6.

[24] See also R. T. Beckwith, 'The Formation of the Hebrew Bible,' *Compendia*, II, 1 (1988), 51–58.

[25] Probably the books of our present Old Testament: the Pentateuch (5); Joshua, Judges-Ruth, Samuel, Kings, Chronicles, Ezra-Nehemiah, Esther, Isaiah, Jeremiah-Lamentations, Ezekiel, Daniel, the Twelve Minor Prophets, Job (13); Psalms Proverbs, Ecclesiastes, Song of Songs (4). A couple of passages in Josephus support this reconstruction. In *Ant.* 5, 318–337 the story of Ruth follows Judges and is dated on the basis of that combination; in *Ant.* 10, 78 Lamentations is regarded as Jeremiah's book; in *Ant.* 10, 267 f. Daniel is identified as one of the prophets. The same order of the books (5 + 13 + 4) is given by the fourth-century Father, Rufinus († 410), in *Exposito Symboli* 35 f. Cf. H. E. Ryle, *The Canon of the Old Testament*, London ²1909, 229; see note 88. It is uncertain whether Josephus is referring to Artaxerxes I († 425 B.C.), Artaxerxes II († 359 B.C.), or to Xerxes († 465 B.C.). Like the Septuagint, he also used the name Artaxerxes for Ahasuerus (*Ant.* 11, 184; cf. Esther 1:1). For IV Ezra (14:45 f.; c. A. D. 100), as for Josephus, writings after the time of Ezra are not placed in the canonical Scriptures. Cf. also *T. Sota* 13:3.

add, to remove or to alter by one syllable[26] [those Scriptures]. Rather every Jew... regards them as the decrees of God (θεοῦ δόγματα)... and is willing if need be to die for them.'[27]

Such is the view of Josephus. As we hope to show, it represents not just the views of his own religious party, the Pharisees, but the attitude of first-century Judaism as a whole.

Philo

A second Jewish witness, who wrote in the early part of the first century, is the Alexandrian philosopher Philo. Although he is less specific than Josephus, he is in substantial agreement with him. Of the books of Moses Philo states,

'[The Jews] have not altered even a single word of what had been written by him [who gave them their laws] but would rather endure to die ten thousand times than yield to any persuasion contrary to his laws and customs.'[28]

To underscore the Bible-centered character of the Therapeutae, an Essene-like Jewish community in Egypt, Philo comments:

'[They take into their study rooms nothing] but the laws, the oracles uttered by the prophets, and hymns and the other [books] (ἀλλὰ νόμους καὶ λόγια θεσπισθέντα διὰ προφητῶν καὶ ὕμνους καὶ τὰ ἄλλα) that foster and perfect knowledge and piety.'

That the reference is to the sacred writings commonly received in Judaism and excludes the books of the sect seems to be clear from Philo's following words:

In addition to the Holy Scriptures (τοῖς ἱεροῖς γράμμασι), i.e. the ancestral philoso-

---

[26] Cf. Deut 4:2; Matt 5:17ff.; Rev. 22:18f.; I QS 1:1–3; 8:22. Like the biblical writers, Josephus is speaking of the divine authority and inviolability of the books and not of the Jewish use of other writings nor of translation variants or midrashic elaborations upon or within the received books. Of the latter practices he was not uninformed or disapproving as the proem to his *Antiquities* and his use of I Esdras (*Ant.* 10, 68–80; 11, 33–158) and of Greek additions to Esther show (*Ant.* 11, 216–83). But see H. B. Swete, *An Introduction to the Old Testament in Greek*, Cambridge [2]1914, 266f.

[27] Josephus, *c. Apion.* 1, 38–42, also cited in Eusebius, *HE* 3, 10, 1–5; cf. Josephus, *Ant.* 10, 35 where Isaiah and twelve other prophets appear to refer to the thirteen 'prophetic' books.

[28] A fragment from Philo's *Hypothetica* (6, 9) preserved in Eusebius, *Praep. Evang.* 8, 6f.; 8, 11. As is the case with Josephus, the statement is hyperbolic and should not be literally pressed. Nevertheless, it accurately witnesses to the sanctity accorded the Scriptures in first-century Judaism.

phy (πάτριον φιλοσοφίαν), 'they have writings of men of old, the founders of their way of thinking...'[29]

The remarkably similar descriptions of the Scripture in Philo and Josephus are significant. They show that, as far as those two scholars represent them, Jewish communities in Palestine, Rome and Alexandria agreed in identifying their sacred writings with a definite number of books, ordered sequentially into three (or four) divisions: laws, prophecies or oracles, hymns and the rest. A tripartite division of Scripture, not unlike that of Josephus and Philo, is also attributed to Jesus in Luke 24:44: 'the law of Moses and the prophets and psalms.'[30]

Ben Sira (Sirach)

This tripartite division of the Bible was not the creation of first-century Judaism, for it has a precedent at Qumran and in the prologue attached in Alexandria to the Greek translation (c. 132 B.C.) of Ben Sira, a Hebrew work originating in Palestine in the early second century B.C. The translator observes that

'My grandfather Jesus [devoted himself] to the law and the prophets and the other ancestral books (τοῦ νόμου καὶ τῶν προφητῶν καὶ τῶν ἄλλων πατρίων βιβλίων). [In Greek translation] not only this work but even the law itself and the prophecies and the rest of the books (αὐτὸς ὁ νόμος καὶ αἱ προφητεῖαι καὶ τὰ λοιπὰ τῶν βιβλίων) differ not a little [from the original].'

As the prologue shows, already in the late second century B.C., and probably two generations earlier, certain sacred books had a canonical status. That is, they constituted a definite and identifiable collection with a continuing, normative authoriy distinguished from that of other religious writings. They had already been translated into Greek and, like the Holy Scriptures known to Philo and Josephus, they were divided into three parts: the law, the prophets and the other books. It is possible that,

---

[29] Philo, *De Vita Contemplativa* 1 f., 25, 28 f. Here there seem to be four divisions of canonical books: laws, oracles, hymns and the rest. But since Josephus subdivides his third division into 'hymns and precepts', the difference may be more apparent than real. But see F.H. Colson et al., *Philo (LCL)*, 12 vols., London 1929–53, IX, 520; Beckwith (note 11), 117.

[30] Since the Psalms stand at the beginning of the Hagiographa in some Hebrew manuscripts and are a part of the title (ὕμνους καὶ τὰ ἄλλα) of the Hagiographa in Philo, they may represent the third division of the Old Testament canon in Luke. Cf. also Luke 24:27. For a somewhat similar division in a Jewish writing cf. II Macc 2:13.

since the individual books are not named, those in the canon of one writer were not identical with those of the others. However, they are designated by very similar expressions and are apparently well-known works requiring no enumeration. In the absence of contrary historical evidence the twenty-two books mentioned by Josephus and perhaps earlier in Jub 2:23 may, with some probability, be presumed to be the sacred books of Philo and Ben Sira as well.

Qumran

In an epistle from Qumran dated c. 150 B. C. the Scriptures also appear to be classified in three (or four) divisions:[31]

'For on account of [these things] we have [written] for you that you may perceive in the book of Moses [and in the words of the pro]phets and in Davi[d and in the words of the days (= Chronicles)] from generation to generation.'

Only in the second century A. D., when uncertainty existed about their number or order, are the books of the Old Testament listed by name. We may now turn to these later testimonies.

Witnesses: The Second and Third Centuries

Melito

The two principal witnesses to the state of the Old Testament canon in the second century are the Babylonian Talmud tractate Baba Batra and Melito, bishop of Sardis. Melito, answering an inquiry concerning the 'number' and the 'order' of 'the old books' (τῶν παλαιῶν βιβλίων), writes the following words (c. A. D. 170):

... When I came to the East and reached the place where these things were preached and done, and learned accurately the books of the Old Testament (τὰ τῆς παλαιᾶς διαθήκης βιβλία), I set down the facts... These are their names: Of Moses five, Genesis, Exodus, Numbers, Leviticus, Deuteronomy; Joshua son of

---

[31] 4Q MMT *(Miqsat Ma'aśe haTorah)* B, II, 9ff. The piece will be published by E. Qimron and J. Strugnell. Cf. E. Qimron and J. Strugnell, 'An Unpublished Halachic Letter from Qumran,' *IMJ* 4 (Spring 1985), 9–12. Otherwise: N. Golb, 'Khirbet Qumran and the Manuscripts of the Judean Wilderness,' *JNES* 49 (1990), 103–114, who dates MMT to c. A. D. 70 (111) and rejects the sectarian origin of the Dead Sea Scrolls generally (113n).

Nun, Judges, Ruth, four of Kingdoms, two of Chronicles, the Psalms of David, Solomon's Proverbs or Wisdom (ἡ καὶ σοφία), Ecclesiastes, Song of Songs, Job; of the Prophets: Isaiah, Jeremiah, the Twelve [Minor Prophets] in one book, Daniel, Ezekiel, Esdras.[32]

In the light of some subsequent catalogues given below, it is apparent that this enumeration includes Samuel within Kings, Lamentations under Jeremiah and identifies Ezra-Nehemiah as Esdras; Solomon's 'Wisdom' is in all likelihood an alternative designation for Proverbs.[33] If so, this list conforms to the present Old Testament with the exception of Esther, which was apparently omitted, either by accident or by design.[34]

Melito's canon represents the Old Testament as it was received in certain Palestinian Jewish and/or Jewish-Christian circles in the second century. Apart from Esther it presumably contained the same books as the canon of Josephus. It also has three divisions, with the first and third designated 'Of Moses' and 'Of the prophets.' However, it differs in the numbering since Samuel and Kings are counted as four, Judges-Ruth as two and Chronicles as two, to give a canon of twenty-five books. In this respect, in the books within each division and in sequence it conforms more closely than Josephus to Codex B of the Septuagint and has the following order: Law (5), Histories (9) and Poetry (5), Prophets (6). It is also closer to the Septuagint in the titles of the books.

Since both the Septuagint (Greek) version of the Old Testament and a Hebrew recension with a Septuagint text-form were already in use in first-century Palestine, the divisions and sequence represented by later codices of the Septuagint such as Codex B may also have been known. At least, Melito's canon, chronologically speaking, has as good a claim to represent an accepted Jewish order as does the rabbinic arrangement that one first encounters also in a second century document, a baraita of the Babylo-

---

[32] Eusebius, *HE* 4, 26, 13f. If Melito's reference to a trip was literary convention, as A. D. Nock ('The Apocryphal Gospels,' *JTS* 11 [1960], 63–70, 63f.) thought, he in any case identifies Palestine as the source of his information.

[33] According to Eusebius (*HE* 4, 22, 9) this designation for Proverbs was common in the second century.

[34] Cf. Ryle (note 25), 214–218, 229ff. In other lists Ἐσθήρ follows Ἔσδρας and, if this was the case in Melito's catalogue, it may have been omitted by a scribe inadvertently or because of a confusion of names. A parallel for this is offered by Origen's list of Old Testament books which omits the Twelve Minor Prophets. However, of the twenty-two Old Testament books only Esther is lacking at Qumran, and the biblical status of Esther was questioned by some rabbis (cf. Leiman [note 10], 200 n. 634) and by a few Christian writers. Therefore, it is possible if not probable that the book was not recognized as Scripture by Melito's informants. Cf. *B. T. Sanhedrin* 100a.

nian Talmud. It is reasonable to suppose that the canonical lists of both the rabbis and of Melito represent revisions of an older order or orders to which Josephus, Philo, Qumran and Ben Sira bear witness.[35]

Baba Batra

A tradition in the Babylonian Talmud tractate *Baba Batra* (14b) reads:

'Our rabbis taught that the order of the Prophets is Joshua, Judges, Samuel, Kings, Jeremiah, Ezekiel, Isaiah, the Twelve [Minor Prophets]... The order of the Hagiographa is Ruth, Psalms, Job, Proverbs, Ecclesiastes, Song of Songs, Lamentations, Daniel, Esther, Ezra, Chronicles.'[36]

The section is introduced by the formula, 'our rabbis taught,' which identifies it as a baraita and thereby probably dates it before A.D. 200.[37] It appears to represent the accepted limits and divisions of the sacred Scriptures among (some) second-century rabbinic schools. With a few variations in the divisions of the canon and in the sequence of certain books, i.e. Isaiah, Ruth, Song of Songs, Esther, it agrees with the subsequent form of the Hebrew (masoretic) Bible received and used in Judaism. Since the Pentateuch is presupposed, it reflects a canon of twenty-four books:[38] Law or *Torah* (5), Prophets or *Nebiim* (8), Writings or *Ketubim* (11).

---

[35] On the background of the text-types underlying the Septuagint and Masoretic texts cf. *The Canon and the Masorah of the Hebrew Bible*, ed. S.Z. Leiman, New York 1974, 327–333 (= W.F. Albright, *BASOR* 140, 1955), 334–348 (= F.M. Cross, *IEJ* 16, 1966, 81–95), 833–869 (H.M. Orlinsky).

[36] The order of the Hagiographa is meant to be chronological with the possible exception of Job. Ruth is attributed to Samuel; Proverbs, Ecclesiastes, Song of Songs to Solomon; Lamentations to Jeremiah; Daniel is from the Exile; Esther, Ezra and Chronicles are post-Exilic. Cf. C.D. Ginsburg, *Introduction to the Massoretico-Critical Edition of the Hebrew Bible*, New York 1966 (1897), 1–8; Billerbeck (note 10), IV, 415–434.

[37] For the most part the *baraita* sections of the Talmud originated in the Tannaitic period (i.e. pre-A.D. 200) but were not included in the collection of Tannaitic traditions, the Mishnah. Cf. *EJ* IV, 189–193.

[38] Cf. The *Gospel of Thomas* 52: 'Twenty-four prophets spoke in Israel and all of them spoke in you'. Some manuscripts of IV Ezra 14:44–46 (c. A.D. 100) may imply a canon of twenty-four books (and seventy apocryphal books), but others give a different numbering. Some manuscripts of the masoretic Bible have four divisions: Pentateuch, Megillot (Ruth, Song of Songs, Lamentations, Ecclesiastes, Esther), Prophets, Hagiographa. Cf. Ryle (note 25), 250–261; Ginsburg (note 36), 3. On the possible origins of an 'ordering' of the individual canonical books cf. Leiman (note 10), 162 n. 258, 202 n. 644, and Beckwith (note 11), 181–234.

It is significant that the baraita is concerned not with the *identity* of the canonical books but with their *order*. That is, it suggests no controversy about the *limits* of the canon, but it may reflect a situation in which there were uncertainties or divergent traditions among the Jews about the sequence and divisions of the canon, for example, which books belonged among the Prophets and which among the Writings. The kinds of variations from the rabbinic order given in the baraita occur in the canons of Josephus and Melito and in the Hebrew Bible known to later Christian writers.

Origen

While still at Alexandria, and therefore before A.D. 231, the eminent biblical scholar Origen (c. A.D. 185–254) wrote an exposition of Psalm 1 in which he included 'a catalogue of the sacred scriptures of the Old Testament' (τῶν ἱερῶν γραφῶν τῆς παλαιᾶς διαθήκης καταλόγου). He comments that 'there are twenty-two canonical books (ἐνδιαθήκους βίβλους) as the Hebrews tradition them, the same as the number of the letters of their alphabet.' He proceeds to give the titles in Greek, followed by a transliteration of the Hebrew names:

Genesis, Exodus, Leviticus, Numbers, Deuteronomy, Joshua, Judges-Ruth, Kingdoms (1, 2) [= Samuel], Kingdoms (3, 4), Chronicles (1, 2), Esdras (1, 2) [= Ezra-Nehemiah], Psalms, Proverbs, Ecclesiastes, Song of Songs, Isaiah, Jeremiah-Lamentations-Letter, Daniel, Ezekiel, Job, Esther.

In conclusion Origen states, 'And outside of these are the Maccabees, which are entitled Sarbethsabaniel'.[39]

The account, also preserved by Eusebius,[40] gives only twenty-one books, and it is evident that the Twelve (Minor Prophets) has been accidentally omitted by a scribe. Like Melito, Origen employs Septuagint titles and roughly follows the Septuagint sequence of Law, Histories, Poetry and Prophecies. However, he goes beyond Melito in several important respects: (1) He sets the Septuagint titles beside those of the Hebrew books and gives a more specific listing. (2) He considers (elsewhere) the problem of differences between the Hebrew and Septuagint texts and (3)

---

[39] Perhaps, 'the book *(sefer)* of the house *(beth)* of *Sabaniel*, i.e. of the Maccabees. On the problem cf. F.M. Abel, *Les Livres des Maccabees*, Paris 1949, iv f.; M. Alon, *Jews, Judaism and the Classical World*, Jerusalem 1977, 8f.; Leiman (note 10), 159 n. 229; H.W. Attridge, 'Historiography,' *Compendia* II, 2 (1984), 171 n. 39.

[40] Eusebius, *HE* 6, 24, 2; 6, 25, 1f.

introduces a (?Jewish) practice whereby religious books 'outside of these' canonical writings, but nevertheless useful to the people of God, may be regarded as a kind of appendix to the canon. Let us consider these points in detail.

1. Origen transcribes the Hebrew names and details those books, usually divided in the Septuagint, that appear 'in one [book]' in the Hebrew canon known to him. Of the six such books – Samuel, Kings, Chronicles, Judges-Ruth, Jeremiah-Lamentations-Letter, Ezra – the last three are of special interest.

a. As Jerome later states explicitly,[41] the combined and separate disposition of Ruth and Lamentations accounts not only for their different classification, respectively, among the Prophets *(Nebiim)* or among the Hagiographa *(Ketubim)* but also for the different number of books in the Hebrew canon of Josephus, Origen, Epiphanius and Jerome (twenty-two books) and in the list of *B. T. Baba Batra* 14 b, other rabbinic traditions and the masoretic Bible (twenty-four books).

b. The 'Letter' attached to Jeremiah in Origen's list refers either to Baruch[42] or to the Letter of Jeremiah. While the latter was originally written in Greek, Baruch may have existed in Hebrew and may therefore be the 'Letter' referred to here. In support of this supposition the Greek text of (parts of) Baruch manifests signs of a Hebrew original[43] and, according to the fourth-century *Apostolic Constitutions* (5,20), Baruch was read by certain Jews on the Day of Atonement. Furthermore, a reference to the Letter of Jeremiah is virtually excluded by the following considerations: Origen had the Hebrew Scriptures in his possession and presup-

---

[41] In *Prologus Galeatus* ('the Helmeted Prologue'), which was the preface to Jerome's Latin translation of the Old Testament. The Prologue stands before Samuel and Kings, the first books that Jerome translated, and notes that, while the Jewish canon ordinarily had twenty-two books, some *(nonnulli)* Jews count Ruth and Lamentations separately, giving a canon of twenty-four books. For the text cf. B. Fischer, ed., *Biblia Sacra iuxta Vulgatam Versionem*, 2 vols., Stuttgart 1969, I, 364 ff.; for the ET cf. P. Schaff and H. Wace, edd., *Nicene and Post-Nicene Fathers, Second Series*, 14 vols., Grand Rapids 1961 (1900), VI, 489 f. For rabbinic witnesses to a canon of 24 books cf. Leiman (note 10), 53–56.

[42] So, Ryle (note 25), 218 f.; G. Wildeboer, *The Canon of the Old Testament*, London 1895, 79. Both Baruch and the Letter are referred to as 'epistles' in Epiphanius, *Panarion* 8, 6; *De Mens. et Pond.* 5. Cf. the discussion in A. C. Sundberg, *The Old Testament of the Early Church*, Cambridge MA 1964, 75–77. See note 68.

[43] Cf. Swete (note 26), 275 f. So for Baruch 1:1–3:8, E. Tov, *The Septuagint Translation of Jeremiah and Baruch*, Missoula 1976, 170.

posed a knowledge of them in his commentaries and his Hexapla. Even though he defended some Septuagint additions, for example, to Daniel, he was quite aware of the different readings 'in their [Hebrew] copies (ἀντι-γράφοις) and 'in our [Septuagint] books'.[44] It is, therefore, difficult to suppose that Origen here added a *Septuagint* appendix, whether Baruch or the Letter of Jeremiah, and then explicitly identified the whole with the *Hebrew* book Jeremiah. Either 'the Letter' is a Baruch appendix to Jeremiah in the Hebrew Bible known and used by Origen, or it is a scribal gloss on Origen's list.

Several items of evidence favour the latter alternative, that is, a scribal gloss, as the most satisfactory resolution of the problem.

(1) Jerome states that the Hebrews 'neither read nor possess' *(nec legitur, nec habetur)* Baruch, and Epiphanius excludes both Baruch and the Letter of Jeremiah from the canon of the Hebrews,[45] as does rabbinic tradition. Thus, the isolated comment that certain Jews read Baruch *(Apostolic Constitutions* 5, 20) applies at most to a local phenomenon, if it is not completely without historical worth.

(2) When other fourth century lists combine either the Letter of Jeremiah[46] or both the Letter and Baruch with the book of Jeremiah, they apparently reflect the content of Greek and Latin Bibles currently in use. This usage might have given occasion for a scribe to alter Origen's list accordingly.

(3) Scribal 'mending' of texts to conform them to current usage is not unknown elsewhere, and it may well account for the addition of the Letter to Jeremiah-Lamentations.

c. In Septuagint manuscripts now extant, all considerably later than Origen, the Hebrew 'double' book Ezra-Nehemiah is placed in one book under the title II Esdras and is preceded by a book entitled I Esdras, a Greek paraphrase or midrash of parts of Chronicles and Ezra-Nehemiah.[47] In Origen's canon the two Greek books called Esdras are

---

[44] *Ad Africanum* 5; on different readings cf. *Ad Afr.* 2; 5 (in Daniel); 3f. (in Genesis, Esther, Job, Jeremiah). See note 50. On Origen's possession of Hebrew Scriptures cf. Eusebius, *HE* 6, 16,1.

[45] Jerome's prologue to Jeremiah in his Vulgate; Epiphanius, *De Mens. et Pond.* 5.

[46] Hilary, *Prol. in Libr. Pss.* See note 85.

[47] The two books are apparently parallel translations of (Chronicles and) the Hebrew Ezra, Greek I Esdras more paraphrastic or midrashic and Ezra-Nehemiah more literal, somewhat analogous to the Septuagintal and Theodotionic translations of Daniel. Cf. Swete (note 26), 265 ff.; S. Jellicoe, *The Septuagint and Modern Study,*

said to be 'in one' book, *viz.* Ezra, in his Hebrew Bible. For reasons given above in the matter of the Letter, Origens's two books of Esdras refer in all likelihood not to the two Septuagint books of those names but to the books of Ezra and Nehemiah, books that were 'one' in the Hebrew Bible but were separated in some Septuagint codices of that period.[48] In the case of readers whose Septuagint copies contained I Esdras (alongside Ezra-Nehemiah), Origen's statement may have been misunderstood and interpreted to mean that I Esdras was part of the Hebrew canon. Indeed, this apparent terminological confusion may have promoted the canonical status later accorded I Esdras although the major influence to that end seems to have been the inclusion of the work in some early Septuagint codices (e. g. Vaticanus, Alexandrinus). In any case the misunderstanding can hardly be charged to Origen.[49]

2. If the above reasoning is correct, Origen's canon agrees in content with that of *B. T. Baba Batra* (14 b) and, with the exception of Esther, of Melito. His defense of the Septuagint additions to Daniel, i. e. Susanna,[50] does not represent a different judgement about *the books* that belong in the canon. Rather, as the context makes evident, it concerns *variant readings and diverse content* within a commonly received book of the Hebrew canon. Like Justin (*Dial.* 71–73), Origen suspects that the texts of the rabbis may have been tampered with. Of course he could not know, as we today know from the library at Qumran, that the Septuagint text-type does have a Hebrew *Vorlage* that in some respects is superior to the masoretic text.[51] He was

---

Oxford 1968, 290–294. An apocalyptic book, IV Esdras = IV Ezra, is also sometimes called II Esdras.

[48] Jerome, *Prologus in Libro Regum* (= *Prologus Galeatus*). Cf. *Biblia* (note 41), I, 365:... 'Ezra, which is itself similarly divided into two books in the Greek and Latin [Bibles].'

[49] *Pace* Zahn (note 19), II, 331.

[50] Origen, *Ad Africanum* 9: The Hebrew copies lack the Septuagint readings because the elders 'hid from the knowledge of the people' passages that might bring discredit on them, e. g. the story of Susanna. Some of the passages 'have been preserved in their non-canonical writings' (ἀποκρύφοις). For an English translation of *Ad Africanum* cf. A. Roberts and J. Donaldson, edd., *Ante-Nicene Fathers*, 10 vols., Grand Rapids 1956 (1885), IV, 386–392.

[51] Cf. Tov (note 43), 168; Cross (note 35): The biblical manuscripts from Qumran reflect a plurality of text-types including that of the Septuagint. In some instances 'the Septuagint faithfully reflects a conservative Hebrew textual family. On the contrary, the Proto-Masoretic and Masoretic family is marked by editorial reworking and conflation...' (82). The (traditional) view that the masoretic text was 'standard' and all the others 'vulgar' cannot explain the data (91 ff.).

influenced substantially by a natural preference for the traditional 'Christian' Septuagint Bible. But for him it was a textual and doctrinal rather than a canonical preference and, as his compilation of the Hexapla shows, it was not maintained uncritically.[52]

The canonical list of Origen, which presents the books 'as the Hebrews tradition them,' is not inconsistent with his defense of Septuagint text-forms, and it is a most significant witness to the church's canon in the early third century. A hundred years later it is recorded by Eusebius because he, at least, views it as Origen's own conviction about the books that the church should acknowledge. Since Origen's translator and admirer Rufinus endorses a similar list, we may consider it very probable that Eusebius has represented the matter correctly.

3. Like other patristic writers, Origen cites writings outside his 'canonical books' with formulas that also introduce quotations from the canon.[53] He appears to be the first, however, to enunciate a principle to distinguish, in their employment and in their authority, writings that are *canonical* from writings that are *useful* for the church. In his commentary on Matthew he states,

'It is of great virtue to hear and fulfil that which is said, "Prove all things; hold fast to that which is good" (I Thess 5:21). Nevertheless, for the sake of those who... cannot discern... and guard themselves carefully so as to hold that which is true and yet "avoid every kind of evil" (I Thess 5:22), no one ought to use for the confirmation of doctrine any books that are outside the canonical Scriptures' *(canonizatas scripturas)*.[54]

---

[52] Cf. Swete (note 26), 480f. for Origen's criticims of certain Septuagint readings. Cf. N. R. M. de Lange, *Origen and the Jews*, Cambridge 1976, 50f.

[53] E. g. I Enoch in *De Principiis* 4, 35 ('he says'). In the context Origen, like Jude, views I Enoch as a prophecy. However, in *Contra Celsum* 5, 54 he states that Enoch does not generally circulate at all (οὐ πάνυ) in the churches as divine (θεῖα). In *Ad Africanum* 13 Origen comments that 'since the churches use Tobit,' he can adduce it to rebut an argument of Africanus. But the qualification is hardly an affirmation of the canonicity of Tobit, and it may indicate the opposite. Professor Wiles' conclusion that Origen's usage 'is a case of having it both ways' and of citing the apocryphal writings used by the church 'as authoritatively as any other part of the Old Testament' seems doubtful to me. Cf. M. F. Wiles, 'Origen as Biblical Scholar,' *The Cambridge History* (note 15), 456.

[54] Origen, *Comm. in Matt.* 28 (on Matt. 23:37–39), extant only in the Latin translation of Rufinus. The reference may be primarily to New Testament apocrypha, but it is equally applicable to the Old; cf. Westcott (note 19), 136f. The Latin *canonizatus* probably translates ἐνδιαθήκος ('covenantal'), a term that Origen uses elsewhere for 'canonical' books. In 117 (on Matt 27:3–10) Origen distinguishes quotations found in

This distinction, which is elaborated in the following century by a number of Christian writers, is similar to and appears to rest upon earlier Jewish practice.[55] It is implicitly ascribed to the Jews by Origen himself when, in his catalogue, the Maccabees are mentioned along with but 'outside of' the canonical books of the Hebrews. It also seems to be presupposed by Josephus, who excluded from the canon writings after Ezra as 'not worthy of equal credit' but nevertheless employed them in constructing his *Antiquities* of the Jews.[56] The distinction is present, moreover, in Philo's comment, given above, on the Holy Scriptures and the sectarian writings of the Therapeutae.

Somewhat different but perhaps not without similarity to Origen's conception are the Qumran writings, Ben Sira and the rabbinic literature. In his prologue the translator of Ben Sira sets his volume apart from writings that had normative authority in Judaism, and yet he clearly regards it as a useful supplement, i.e. 'a further help.' On a different level the rabbis contrast the 'oral law' (*B. T. Shabbat* 31 a) or 'traditions of the elders' (cf. Matt 15:2) with the written Torah. But they consider the oral law as embodied in the Talmud to be the authoritative interpretation of the Torah and also cite Ben Sira, a book never received as canonical, with formulas ordinarily used for canonical writings.[57] As we hope to show below, the conception that *Holy Scripture can be supplemented* is significant not only for understanding the patristic church's authoritative use of

---

a 'standard book' *(regulari libro)* or 'public books' *(publicis libris)* from those in a 'secret book' *(libro secreto)*, i.e. the *Apocalypse of Elijah* and the *Book of Jannes and Jambres*.

[55] See note 50. When in *Ad Africanum* 13 Origen states that the Jews neither *use* Tobit and Judith nor *have* them in the Hebrew apocrypha (ἀποκρύφοις Ἑβραϊστί), he implies that the Jews had a twofold classification (at least) of religious writings. This seems to be confirmed by the 'kind of intermediate holiness' that is ascribed in rabbinic literature to Ben Sira and, at the same time, the condemnation of the (?public) reading of 'outside books'; cf. M. Haran, 'Problems of Canonization', *Tarbiz* 25 (1955–56), 245; IV Ezra 14:45f. See also M. Gilbert, 'Wisdom Literature,' *Compendia* II, 2 (1984), 300–301; *M. Sanhedrin* 10:1.

[56] See note 26. Cf. Josephus, *Ant.* 12 and 13 passim (I Macc).

[57] In *B. T. Berakot* 48 a, Sirach 11:1 is combined with Prov 4:8 and introduced with the formula, 'as it is written'; in *B. T. Baba Kamma* 92 b, Sirach 13:15 is introduced with the formula, 'as written in the Hagiographa.' But cf. *T. Yadayim* 2:13: 'Ben Sira and all the books written from that time on do not defile the hands,' i.e. are not canonical. Some rabbis forbade Ben Sira to be read (*B. T. Sanhedrin* 100 b) or classified it as apocryphal (*P. T. Sanhedrin* 10:1[28 a]). Cf. *B. T. Hagigah* 13 a; *Erubim* 54 a; *Yebamot* 63 b. On the status of Ben Sira in the Pharisaic-rabbinic tradition, see Beckwith (note 24), 68–73; idem (note 11), 377–380.

approved Jewish apocrypha and of post-apostolic Christian writings but also for the process of canonization itself.

The Fourth Century: Custom Versus Judgement

In the fourth century the canon of the Old Testament posed an increasing problem for the church. Divided by a conscious and widening gap were the scholarly judgements on the canon and the popular usage of the church. The scholarly attitude was often expressed in explicit catalogues and was most clearly defined in the writings of Jerome. The popular conception was reflected in the (greater number of) books contained in many Greek and Latin Bibles and by the quotations of various writers.

There was, moreover, a different perception of the canon in the East and in the West. Especially in Africa, the church appears to have used indiscriminately the additional books of the Old Latin codices that were taken over from the Septuagint. The church in the East was more influenced by leaders who knew the Hebrew Bible (e. g. Origen, Jerome) or at least knew of a Hebrew canon to which their own should be subject.

Canonical Lists in the Eastern Church

As was true earlier, the compilers of fourth-century canonical lists[58] were for the most part writers of the Eastern church. Early in the century[59] Eusebius († c. 339), bishop of Caesarea, included in his *Church History* the canonical statement of Josephus and the catalogues of Melito and Origen. He thus conveyed his own conviction that the Old Testament to be received by the church was the twenty-two books of the Hebrew Bible.

Other fourth-century Fathers imply or expressly mention a second order of useful books outside the canonical twenty-two, but they are chiefly concerned to make known the limits of the canon in order to protect the believers from the dangerous influence of heretical writings. Cyril,

---

[58] Zahn (note 19, II, 172–259) gives most of the texts. The lists are conveniently tabulated by Swete (note 26), 203–214, and Sundberg (note 42), 58 f.

[59] The tenth book of his *History*, added in the third edition and dedicated to Paulinus of Tyre (*HE* 10,1,2) upon the consecration of the basilica there, can be dated to A. D. 317. Cf. Eusebius, *The Ecclesiastical History*, ed. K. Lake, 2 vols., London 1953, I, xx.

bishop of Jerusalem, writing his *Catechetical Lectures*[60] about the middle of the century, exhorts the catechumens as follows:

'Read the divine Scriptures (θείας γραφάς), these twenty-two books of the Old Testament (παλαιᾶς διαθήκης) that were translated by the seventy-two translators (33)... [For] the translation of the divine Scriptures that were spoken in the Holy Spirit was accomplished through the Holy Spirit. Read their twenty-two books but have nothing to do with the apocryphal writings (ἀπόκρυφα). Study diligently only these that we also read with confident authority (μετὰ παρρησίας) in the church. [For] much wiser and holier than you were the apostles and ancient bishops who led the church and handed down these books' (34f.).

Cyril proceeds to tabulate the books in three divisions: twelve historical, five poetic and five prophetic.[61] It is not certain whether I–II Esdras, 'reckoned [by the Hebrews] as one', refers to Ezra-Nehemiah, as seems probable, or includes I Esdras. 'Baruch and Lamentations and Epistle', appended to Jeremiah, clearly represent an accommodation to the contents of (Cyril's) Septuagint; and other books may implicitly comprehend the Septuagint additions. After enumerating the New Testament books, Cyril concludes:

'Let all the rest be placed outside [the canon] in a second rank[62] (ἐν δευτέρῳ). And whatever books are not read in churches, neither should you read them in private...' (36).

Cyril makes his strict injunction against reading apocryphal books in the context of opposing the heretical Manicheans.[63] Yet, addressing the same hearers, he himself cites works that he excludes from the canon in a manner somewhat similar to his citations of Scripture.[64] It is probable, then, that in the conclusion quoted above, Cyril has in view three classes

---

[60] Cyril, *Catech.* 4, 33–36, a section with the title, 'Concerning the Divine Scriptures.' For the English translation cf. *Nicene Fathers* (note 41), VII, 26 ff.; Zahn (note 19, II, 172) dates it to A. D. 348.

[61] Cyril, *Catech.* 4,35: Genesis, Exodus, Leviticus, Numbers, Deuteronomy, Joshua, Judges-Ruth, Kingdoms (1, 2), Kingdoms (3, 4), Chronicles (1, 2), Esdras (1, 2), Esther; Job, Psalms, Proverbs, Ecclesiastes, Song of Songs; Twelve [Minor Prophets], Isaiah, Jeremiah-Baruch-Lamentations-Epistle, Ezekiel, Daniel.

[62] Cyril, *Catech.* 4, 36. ET in *Nicene Fathers* (note 41), VII, 28; Westcott (note 19), 169.

[63] In *Catech.* 4, 36; 6, 31 Cyril ascribes the 'pseudepigraphal' *Gospel of Thomas* to the Manicheans; 4, 34 appears to have in view the Marcionites also.

[64] Cyril, *Catech.* 9, 2; 9, 16 (Wisdom of Solomon) and 6, 4; 11, 19; 22, 8 (Ben Sira). However, they are not cited as Scripture or, for the most part, with introductory formulas used to introduce canonical Scripture.

of writings: the canonical books, the books of 'second rank' (that also may be read or cited in churches) and the heretical apocrypha.

In his *Easter Letter* (A. D. 367) Athanasius, bishop of Alexandria, makes this threefold classification explicit: canonical books, books read in church (especially) to catechumens, rejected heretical writings. Like Cyril, Athanasius also writes in the context of opposing the 'apocrypha' that some heretics sought 'to mix... with the inspired Scripture' (θεοπνεύστῳ γραφῇ). With respect to approved but non-canonical books, he writes:[65]

'But for the sake of greater exactness I add this also, writing under obligation, as it were. There are other books besides these, indeed not received as canonical but having been appointed (τετυπωμένα) by the Fathers to be read to those just approaching [the faith] and wishing to be instructed in the word of godliness: Wisdom of Solomon, Wisdom of Sirach [= Ben Sira], Esther, Judith, Tobit, the Didache and the Shepherd [of Hermas]. Nevertheless, my brothers, neither among those that are received as canonical nor among those that are read is there mention of any of the apocryphal books; they rather are the imagination (ἐπίνοια) of heretics, who indeed write them whenever they wish...'

Canonical catalogues from Asia Minor during the mid-fourth century[66] show a similar concern to guard the readers from the dangers of 'strange books', and they have virtually the same content as the canons of Cyril and Athanasius.

Epiphanius († 404), bishop of Salamis (= Constantia), does not at first impression appear to be a very reliable witness. He is obsessed with

---

[65] Athanasius, *Easter Letter* 39. ET in *Nicene Fathers* (note 41), IV, 551 f.: Genesis, Exodus, Leviticus, Numbers, Deuteronomy, Joshua, Judges, Ruth, Kingdoms (1, 2), Kingdoms (3, 4), Chronicles (1, 2), Esra (1, 2), Psalms, Proverbs, Ecclesiastes, Song of Songs, Job; Twelve [Minor Prophets], Isaiah, Jeremiah-Baruch-Lamentations-Epistle, Ezekiel, Daniel. Esther is omitted, but by a separation of Judges and Ruth a twenty-two book total is maintained.

[66] (1) Gregory Nazianzus (*Carmen* 1, 12), bishop of Constantinople, who, like Cyril, follows an arrangement of 12 historical, 5 poetic and 5 prophetic books; he counts Judges and Ruth separately and omits Esther. (2) Amphilochius, cited by Gregory (*Carmen* 2, 8, 264–288), indicates no double books and employs no number analogies; he concludes that 'some add Esther.' Both lists, given in verse, are intended to guard the reader from the danger of heretical books. Gregory draws an analogy with the twenty-two letters of the Hebrew alphabet. Neither mentions any books appended to Jeremiah. (3) The synod of Laodicea (c. A.D. 360) which, in its canon 59, restricted readings in church to 'the canonical books of the New and Old Testament,' was apparently the first *ecclesiastical* action giving the canonical books a special and exclusive authority. The list of books itself (canon 60), agreeing with Cyril except for the position of Esther and Job, is a later appendage. Cf. Zahn (note 19), II, 193–202; Swete (note 26), 209.

number analogies,[67] is incessantly repetitive and rather absent-minded and gives three canonical catalogues that do not entirely agree.[68] However, the differences in the lists are more apparent than real; and the writer's wooden, repetitive style and candid 'after-thought' qualifications suggest a severely honest, if dogmatic temperament.[69] Moreover, Epiphanius had a knowledge of Hebrew and had independent Jewish traditions, i. e. a catalogue of canonical books, that he carefully transliterated for his readers.[70] His comment on the list in *Panarion* or *Haereses* 8, 6 (A. D. 376) is, therefore, of considerable importance:

'These are the twenty-seven books given by God to the Jews. But they are to be counted as twenty-two, the number of the Hebrew letters, since ten books are doubled and reckoned as five...[71] There are also two other books near to them in

[67] Epiphanius, *De Mens. et Pond.* 22 f. E. g. there are twenty-two generations from Adam to the twelve patriarchs, therefore there are twenty-two Hebrew letters 'from Aleph to Tau'. The Jews have twenty-two canonical books – 'there being twenty-seven but counted as twenty-two' – with five double books, just as there are twenty-two Hebrew letters with five double letters. There are twenty-two works of God in creation and twenty-two sectaria (pints) in a modius (peck), just as there are twenty-two letters and twenty-two sacred books. In *De Mens. et Pond.* 4 he arranges the Old Testament into four pentateuchs – Law, Poets, Holy Writings, Prophets – plus two other books (Ezra, Esther).

[68] In the *Panarion*, i. e. *Haer.* 8, 6 (= 1, 1, 9 [6]) Epiphanius agrees with Cyril in the content though not in the sequence of books. In *De Mens. et Pond.* 4 f. and 22–24, written some fifteen years later, he gives a different sequence and does not mention the additions to Jeremiah. However, Epiphanius (*De Mens. et Pond.* 5) explains that he includes the additions with the book of Jeremiah 'though the Epistles [of Baruch and the Letter] are not included by the Hebrews: they join to Jeremiah only the book of Lamentations.'

[69] Zahn (note 19, II, 222, 224) is certainly mistaken in supposing that Epiphanius wants to 'smuggle in' the Septuagint (apocryphal) books while professing to adhere to the twenty-two books of the Hebrew canon. For Epiphanius is at pains to single out the 'useful and beneficial' apocryphal books of Wisdom and Ben Sira from the canonical twenty-two and to explain that he includes the 'Letters' appended to Jeremiah while the Hebrews do not.

[70] Epiphanius, *De Mens. et Pond.* 23. It is not derived from Origen; J. P. Audet ('A Hebrew-Aramaic List of Books of the Old Testament in Greek Transcription,' *JTS* 1 [1950], 135–154) relates it to the list in the Bryennios manuscript (photograph in J. B. Lightfoot, *The Apostolic Fathers*, 3 vols. in 5, London ²1889–90, I, 1, 474) whose source he dates to the first or early second century. The 27 books of the Bryennios canon are Genesis, Exodus, Leviticus, Joshua, Deuteronomy, Numbers, Ruth, Job, Judges, Psalms, Kings (1, 2, 3, 4), Chronicles (1, 2), Proverbs, Ecclesiastes, Song of Songs, Jeremiah, Twelve (Minor Prophets), Isaiah, Ezekiel, Daniel, Esdras (1, 2), Esther.

[71] From *De Mens. et Pond.* 4 it becomes clear that the double books are Judges-Ruth, I–II Chronicles, I–II Kingdoms (= Samuel), III–IV Kingdoms, and I–II Esdras which 'also is counted as one'. Jeremiah-Lamentations-Letter-Baruch is counted as

substance (ἀμφιλέκτῳ), the Wisdom of Sirach and the Wisdom of Solomon, besides some other apocryphal (ἐναποκρύφων) books. All these holy books (ἱεραὶ βίβλιοι) also taught Judaism the things kept by the law until the coming of our Lord Jesus Christ.'

His distinction between the canonical (ῥητά, ἐνδιάθετα) and the apocryphal books is stated more precisely in *De Mensuris et Ponderibus* 4.

In these passages Epiphanius, a disciple of Athanasius, agrees with the Alexandrian in identifying two classes of books that are read in the church. Unlike Athanasius, he names the second class 'apocrypha' and, similar to Augustine (*De Doct. Christ.* 2, 12 f.), can regard both as 'holy books' or 'divine writings' (*Haer.* 76, 1). That the 'apocrypha' have no special connection with his Old Testament is evident also from the fact that he (again like Athanasius) can mention them, *viz.* Wisdom and Ben Sira, after the New Testament books.

In conclusion, among the fourth-century writers of Asia Minor, Palestine and Egypt[72] the scholarly judgement of the Eastern church is intelligible and relatively consistent, and it rests upon appeal to ancient Christian tradition. It is divided only on the sequence and numbering of the books and on the inclusion of Esther, which were points at issue already in Judaism. It departs from the rabbinic determinations only with respect to the Septuagint additions to Jeremiah and (apparently) to other books, seemingly content to follow the conviction of earlier Christian scholars, for example, Justin and Origen, that the masoretic rather than the Septuagint text was defective.

At the same time these writers were quite prepared to recognize certain extra-canonical works as a second rank of holy books, to cite them authoritatively[73] and to include them in the same volume with canonical

---

one among the twenty-seven and, therefore, is not a double book. In *De Mens. et Pond.* 23 Epiphanius is not embarrassed to admit that, beyond the five double books, 'there is also another little book called Kinot' (= Lamentations) joined to Jeremiah. This shows that he is not a prisoner to his number analogies.

[72] The judgement of the fourth-century Syrian church is less clear. The *Apostolic Constitutions* (2, 57, 2), extant in Syriac, gives the groupings of Old Testament books without naming them all individually. The Syriac Old Testament, that is, the Peshitta, may be Jewish in origin (cf. P.B. Dirksen, 'The Old Testament Peshitta,' *Compendia* II, 1 [1988], 262 f.). Apparently at the beginning it contained only the books of the masoretic canon. But by the fourth century it, like the Septuagint, had added apocryphal books, books that also were being cited as 'Scripture.' Cf. Jellicoe (note 47), 246–249; C. van Puyvelde in *DBS* 6 (1960), 836; Zahn (note 19), II, 227 ff.

[73] E.g. Gregory Nazianzus, *Orat.* 29, 16 f.: 'from the divine oracles,' followed by a score of biblical passages and one apocryphal saying (Wisdom 7:26); 45:15: 'the

Scripture.[74] In this matter also they followed ancient practice. However, while they were able to differentiate the two kinds of holy books, the popular mind of the church increasingly mixed and confused them.

The popular attitude posed a danger not only for the integrity of the canon received from Judaism but also for the canonical principle itself. It was challenged and resisted by one man above all, who in spite of many faults was 'the great representative of Western learning, its true head and glory, and the rich source from which almost all critical knowledge of Holy Scripture in the Latin Churches was drawn for almost ten centuries.'[75] In his historical knowledge, his scholarship and industry he can be compared in the ancient church only with Origen, and in his judgement on the canon he was unsurpassed. The man was Jerome. He can be best understood in the light of the general situation in the Western church of his time.

The Western Church: Hilary and Rufinus

The church in the West produced no list of Old Testament canonical books before the fourth century. As its Bible it had the Old Latin version(s) and the Septuagint from which it was translated,[76] both of which mixed together rather indiscriminately canonical and other ancient Jewish religious books. The Latin church, which by the fourth century was the church throughout the West, was separated by language and custom,

---

Scripture,' referring to phrases from Judith 5:6 and Ps 138:9. Among earlier writers cf. Barn 4:3: 'concerning which it is written, as Enoch says' (I Enoch?); 16:5: 'the Scripture says' (I Enoch 89:56?); Hermas, *Vis.* 2, 3, 4: 'as it is written in Eldad and Modad'; Clement Alexandrinus, *Strom.* 1, 21: 'for it is written in Esdras' (I Esdras 6–7?); Origen, *Luke: Homily* 3: 'the Scripture promised' (Wisdom 1:2); Cyprian, *Epistulae* 73 (74), 9: 'as it is written' (I Esdras 4:38–40); Irenaeus, *Haer.* 4, 20, 2: 'Well did the Scripture say' (Hermas, *Mand.* 1, 1). See notes 64, 102.

[74] The fourth-century Septuagint codices, Sinaiticus and Vaticanus, both contain the apocryphal books of Wisdom, Ben Sira, Tobit and Judith. Vaticanus also has Greek I Esdras; Sinaiticus, I and IV Maccabees. The Septuagint apparently had this inclusive character from the beginning of its codex form, i.e. in the second or early third century. Cf. Swete (note 26), 265–288.

[75] Westcott (note 19), 180f.

[76] But see Jellicoe (note 47), 251. H.F.D. Sparks ('The Latin Bible,' *The Bible in its Ancient and English Versions*, ed. H.W. Robinson, London [2]1954 [1940], 102f.) calls attention to Jewish (-Christian) influences in the 'haphazard and gradual' process of translation. J. Cantera ('Puntos de contacto...,' *Seferad* 25 [1965], 223–240) finds that the Old Latin has points of contact with the targum and with the Peshitta and that it probably has a targumic origin. Cf. B. Kedar, 'The Latin Translations,' *Compendia* II, 1 (1988), 308–311.

even more than the Greek church, from its Jewish origins. In its popular expression, at least, it regarded its version of the Old Testament as 'the Bible' and resisted or accepted only reluctantly and gradually even the new Latin translation of Jerome.[77]

This state of affairs is reflected by the *Mommsen Catalogue*, which was probably composed in North Africa in A.D. 359.[78] In its Old Testament list it numbers the apocryphal books of I and II Maccabees, Tobit, Judith, and perhaps (under the title 'Solomon') Ben Sira and Wisdom. At the conclusion it compares the twenty-four 'canonical books' with the twenty-four elders of Revelation (4:4). However, the total can be reconciled with the enumerated books only by arbitrary combinations and appears to be a number, traditional in some circles of the Western church,[79] that has been gratuitously appended to a list with which it has no essential connection. Like certain Greek and Latin biblical codices, the Mommsen Catalogue appears to represent not a critical opinion but a popular usage with which the traditional twenty-four books were then identified. It indicates a changed situation from the early third-century African church where Tertullian, in deference to the Hebrew Bible, qualified his use of I Enoch with the comment that it was 'not admitted into the Jewish ark.'[80]

Two other sources, that at first look promising, prove to be of little help in determining the canon used in the West. Philaster († 397), bishop of Brescia in Italy, states with reference to the Old Testament that 'nothing

---

[77] For Augustine's reservations cf. *De Civ. Dei* 18, 43. See also Augustine, *Letters* 71, 5 (cf. *DCB* III, 45), where it is related that a North African congregation loudly corrected its bishop when he, reading Jerome's translation, differed from the traditional wording.

[78] On the provenance cf. Zahn (note 19), II, 154f. It is also known as the Cheltenham List from the place where one of the two extant manuscripts was found. It is reproduced and evaluated by Zahn (note 19), II, 143–156, 1007–1012. Cf. also W. Sanday, *Studia Biblica III*, ed. S. R. Driver, Oxford 1891, 217–303. The Old Testament books are Genesis, Exodus, Numbers, Leviticus, Deuteronomy, Joshua, Judges, Ruth, I Kingdoms, II Kingdoms, III Kingdoms, IV Kingdoms, Chronicles (I, II), Maccabees (I, II), Job, Tobit, Esther, Judith, Psalms, Solomon, Major Prophets (4): Isaiah, Jeremiah, Daniel, Ezekiel; Prophets (12).

[79] A total of twenty-four books is mentioned also by Hilary *(Prol. in Libr. Pss.)*, who compares it to the twenty-four letters of the Greek alphabet; by Victorinus of Pettau († 304, *Comm. on Apcl.* 4:6,8 cited in Zahn, note 19, II, 338); and by ps-Tertullian (= ? Commodian, c. A.D. 250), *Poem against Marcion* 4, 251–265 *(Ante-Nicene Fathers* [note 50], IV, 160). Jerome, in the *Prologus Galeatus*, states that some Jews count twenty-four books in their canon; the twenty-four count in the West also probably had its origin in Jewish tradition or usage.

[80] Tertullian, *De Cult. Faem.* 1, 3; cf. Epiphanius, *De Mens. et Pond.* 4.

else ought to be read in the catholic church but the law and the prophets...'[81] But he does not identify the books. Equally unhelpful is the *Decretum Gelasianum*,[82] which is usually attributed to Gelasius, bishop of Rome from A.D. 492–496, but in some manuscripts is credited to the Roman bishop Damasus († 384). Its second section contains an Old Testament catalogue including apocryphal books that, in the opinion of some scholars, represents a canon promulgated by Damasus at the council of Rome in A.D. 382. However, Epiphanius, who participated in the council, had only a few years before endorsed a canon limited to the twenty-two books of the Hebrew Bible, and he would not likely have joined in commending as divine Scripture 'which the universal catholic church receives'[83] books that he had earlier set apart as apocrypha. More significantly, the *Decretum* is extant only in a later compilation of mixed vintage, and it is impossible to say what the list may have looked like in an original fourth-century document if, in fact, such a document ever existed. The list cannot, therefore, be regarded as a reliable witness to the canon received in the West in the fourth century.[84]

At about the time that the Mommsen Catalogue appeared in North Africa, Hilary († 367), bishop of Poitiers in Gaul, published a canon of the Old Testament in the prologue to his commentary on the Psalms.[85] It consists of the twenty-two books of the Hebrew Bible and of our present Old Testament although some books, like Jeremiah, may represent the longer Septuagint text-forms. Apparently influenced by the catalogues of the Greek church, it represents the canon that was also accepted by some

---

[81] Philaster, *Treatise on Heresies* 88 (c. A.D. 385). Cf. Zahn (note 19), II, 237.

[82] Cf. E. von. Dobschütz, ed., *Das Decretum Gelasianum* (*TU* 38, 4), Leipzig 1912, who gives the text (24–26) and concludes (348–351) that it is a private work, compiled in Italy in the sixth century.

[83] *Decretum Gelasianum* 2, Title: *'quid universalis catholica recipiat ecclesia.'* Cf. Zahn (note 19), II, 261n.; von Dobschütz (note 82), 24. Apocryphal books included in the list are Wisdom, Ben Sira, Tobit, I Greek Esdras, Judith, I–II Maccabees.

[84] Otherwise: E. Schwartz, 'Zum Decretum Gelasianum,' *ZNTW* 29 (1930), 168; C.H. Turner, 'Latin Lists of the Canonical Books,' *JTS* 1 (1900), 554f.; Zahn (note 19), II, 259–267. The supposition of H.H. Howorth, 'The Influence of St. Jerome...,' *JTS* 10 (1909), 481–496, followed by Sundberg (note 42, 148f.), that Jerome accepted the canonicity of the apocrypha at the Council and later changed his opinion, only adds conjecture to conjecture.

[85] Hilary, *Comm. in Pss.*, Preface 15: Moses (5), Joshua, Judges-Ruth, Kingdoms (1, 2), Kingdoms (3, 4), Chronicles (1, 2), Ezra [= Ezra-Nehemiah], Psalms; Solomon: Proverbs, Ecclesiastes, Song of Songs; Twelve [Minor] Prophets, Isaiah, Jeremiah-Lamentations-Letter, Daniel, Ezekiel, Job, Esther.

churches and/or teachers in the West. For it concludes with the comment that some 'by adding Tobit and Judith count twenty-four books.' This alludes to a tendency in the West, observable in the Mommsen Catalogue, to accommodate a traditional twenty-four book count to the popular use of apocryphal writings.

Rufinus († 410), presbyter of Aquileia in northeast Italy, who had long known Hilary's views,[86] set forth the same canonical standard in that country that Hilary had published in France.[87] He presents a list that in two respects is remarkable. Like the lists of the Greek Fathers generally, it limits the Old Testament books to the twenty-two books of the Hebrew canon. But unlike any known Christian catalogue, it follows a sequence like that of Josephus three centuries before: Law (5) + Prophets (13) + Hymns and precepts (4).[88] In this respect Rufinus does not follow Origen but, since he appeals to the 'records of the fathers' *(ex patrum monumentis)*, he presumably received the sequence from a Christian tradition. Possibly he deduced it from the account of Josephus found in Eusebius, but more likely he found it elsewhere.

Like several Eastern writers, Rufinus distinguished three classes of 'scriptures:' canonical, ecclesiastical and apocryphal. He placed the ecclesiastical writings – Wisdom, Ben Sira, Tobit, Judith, Maccabees – after the list of Old Testament and New Testament books, thereby avoiding any implication that they belonged to his canonical Old Testament, and he stated that they were not to be used as authority 'for the confirmation of doctrine' *(ex his fidei confirmandam)*. He designated as apocrypha those books that were explicitly excluded from the churches' corporate life and worship. His repeated references to 'the fathers' or 'the ancients' as the transmitters of the canon show that he derived his understanding of the matter not from popular usage but from traditional

---

[86] Jerome, *Epistulae* 5, 2: '[Send] me Hilary's commentary on the Psalms... which I copied for [Rufinus] at Trêves...'

[87] Rufinus, *Exposito Symboli* 34 (36). Rufinus can elsewhere defend the Septuagint additions, e.g. to Daniel *(Apol.* 2, 35). But this is more a textual than a canonical question, as it was also for Origen and for Cyril.

[88] *Ibid.* 35f. (37f.): Five of Moses: Genesis, Exodus, Leviticus, Numbers, Deuteronomy; Joshua, Judges-Ruth, Kingdoms (4) 'which the Hebrew count as two,' Chronicles, Esdras (2) 'which (the Hebrews) count as one,' Esther; of the Prophets: Isaiah, Jeremiah, Ezekiel, Daniel, Twelve [Minor] Prophets, Job; Psalms, Three of Solomon: Proverbs, Ecclesiastes, Song of Songs. Unlike Josephus, there is no demarcation between a second and third division of the canon. For the text cf. Zahn (note 19), II, 240–244; for an English translation, Rufinus, *Commentary on the Apostles' Creed*, ed. J. N. D. Kelly *(Ancient Christian Writers* 20), Westminster MD 1955.

authorities such as Cyril (whom he must have met in Jerusalem), Origen and other Fathers whose writings he had read. Rufinus gives the impression that he was not so much opposing a different canon currently advocated in Italy as clarifying uncertain distinctions between canonical and uncanonical books, distinctions that had been preserved among the Greek theologians but were less clearly perceived among the churches of the West.

Augustine

Of the three Western witnesses to the Old Testament canon discussed above – the Mommsen Catalogue from North Africa, Hilary in Gaul and Rufinus in Italy – only the first identifies apocryphal writings as canonical. These testimonies probably reflect in substantial measure the differing regional attitudes of the Latin church in the latter half of the fourth century. The churches of Italy and Gaul, which had been served by prominent Greek-speaking writers until the beginning of the third century, remained undecided or, at least, of two minds on the question of the canon. On the other hand the churches in North Africa, which from the beginning of the third century exercised an increasingly important role in Western Christianity, had apparently reached a settled acceptance of apocryphal writings and received them at full parity with the other Scriptures.

The North African attitude received an official standing in the canon promulgated at the council of Hippo (A.D. 393) and was reaffirmed by two councils at Carthage (A.D. 397, 419).[89] These resolutions, which rested on no appeal to ancient patristic authority and which apparently reflected only the consensus of contemporary usage in Africa, drew no distinction between canonical and ecclesiastical, i.e. apocryphal writings. Both classes were equated under the dictum, 'Nothing shall be read in church under the name of divine Scriptures except canonical Scriptures.'

---

[89] For the text and the problem of interpolation cf. Zahn (note 19), II, 246–259. For the Old Testament the councils approved the following 'canonical scriptures': Genesis, Exodus, Leviticus, Numbers, Deuteronomy, Joshua, Judges, Ruth, Kingdoms (4), Chronicles (2), Job, Psalter, Solomon (5), Twelve [Minor] Prophets, Isaiah, Jeremiah, Daniel, Ezekiel, Tobit, Judith, Esther, Esdras (2). A concluding instruction of the Council of A.D. 397 that the transpontine (Roman) church be consulted for a confirmation of the approved canon apparently did not achieve its desired end, for in the renewed affirmation in A.D. 419 the confirmation of Boniface bishop of Rome 'and other bishops of those parts' is again requested.

At these provincial assemblies Augustine, bishop of Hippo († 430), exercised an influential role, and his name was largely responsible for the far-reaching influence of their decisions.[90] Yet, unlike the councils, the bishop himself did not make an unqualified equation of canonical and apocryphal books. Before his conversion Augustine was for some years an adherent of Manicheism, a sect that was then active in North Africa and that made use of heretical apocrypha to promote its teachings among the Christians. This context best explains both Augustine's concern to circumscribe the writings used in the churches and, at the same time, his relative lack of interest in distinguishing among them the books 'accepted by all catholic churches' from those 'not accepted by all.'[91] In the first half of his treatise *On Christian Doctrine*, written soon after the council of Hippo, he draws this distinction[92] and proceeds to list the 'whole canon of scriptures.' Within the Old Testament section he names a number of apocryphal books with the concluding comment, 'The authority of the Old Testament is restricted *(terminatur)* to these forty-four books.'[93]

Like Epiphanius, Augustine used the term 'divine scriptures' of a broad category of religious writings of which the 'canonical scriptures' formed only a part and, among the canonical, he distinguished between universally accepted and disputed books.[94] Thus, he appears to recognize a three-fold classification of religious writings common in the East and sometimes known there as canonical, ecclesiastical and apocryphal. But he termed the first two classes 'canonical', apparently held the distinction

---

[90] As the survey by Westcott (note 19, 191–291) shows, even in the Middle Ages the canonical parity of the apocrypha was by no means universally acknowledged.

[91] Cf. Westcott (note 19), 185.

[92] Augustine, *De Doct. Chris.* 2, 12.

[93] *Ibid.* 2, 13: Five of Moses:..., Joshua, Judges, Ruth, Kingdoms (4), Chronicles (2), Job, Tobit, Esther, Judith, Maccabees (2), Esdras (2); the Prophets: Psalms, Three of Solomon: Proverbs, Song of Songs, Ecclesiastes; Wisdom, Ecclesiasticus [= Ben Sira]; Twelve [Minor] Prophets: Hosea, Joel, Amos, Obadiah, Jonah, Micah, Nahum, Habakkuk, Zephaniah, Haggai, Zechariah, Malachi; Four Major Prophets: Isaiah, Jeremiah, Daniel, Ezekiel.

[94] Cf. Augustine, *De Civ. Dei*: Although 'some writings left by Enoch... were divinely inspired..., [they] were omitted from the canon of scripture... of the Hebrew people' (15, 23). 'Three books [of Solomon]... were received as of canonical authority, Proverbs, Ecclesiastes and Song of Songs;' two others, Wisdom and Ecclesiasticus, 'are not his but the church of old, especially the Western, received them into authority...' (17, 20). The books of Maccabees are not recognized by the Jews as canonical, but 'the church accepts [them] as canonical because they record the great and heroic sufferings of certain martyrs' (18, 36). Cf. Augustine, *On the Soul* 3, 2: 'Scripture has spoken' (Wis 1:5).

between them rather lightly and, in any case, failed to impress it upon his readers and upon the North African councils. Furthermore, apparently reluctant to offend popular piety,[95] Augustine preferred to rely on the traditional usage of the churches and on patristic citations to establish the limits of the canon. He displays little knowledge of the Fathers' express canonical statements. For a more acute perception of the issues involved, one must turn to Jerome who, though he lacked the theological creativity of Augustine, was in matters of church history better informed and in spite of a certain narrowness was on this issue gifted with a more critical faculty.

Jerome

Jerome of Bethlehem (c. A.D. 331–420)[96] was born of Christian parents in Dalmatia (= Yugoslavia) near Aquileia in northeast Italy. After his conversion and baptism as a student in Rome, he mastered Greek, travelled in Gaul and returned to Aquileia (c. A.D. 370). In 374 he journeyed to Syria where he adopted a monastic lifestyle, learned Hebrew[97] and was ordained a presbyter. After a brief return to Rome in 382 in the service of the Roman bishop Damasus, he went back to the East and in 386 settled in Bethlehem where until his death he lived in a cell, taught the Scriptures and continually devoted himself to study and to writing.

Jerome began his great work of biblical translation with a Latin rendering from the Septuagint but became convinced, largely by the use of Origen's Hexapla and his own knowledge of Hebrew, that the extant Greek version, no less than the Latin, suffered from many inaccuracies. Like Cyril, he still viewed the original work of the Septuagint as inspired[98] but decided soon after his return to the East to start afresh with a translation directly from the Hebrew text, whose reliability he apparently did not question.

---

[95] Cf. Augustine, *Epistulae* 82, 35 (end); *De Civ. Dei* 18, 43.

[96] Following J. N. D. Kelly, *Jerome*, London 1975, 337 ff. Cf. also W. H. Fremantle, 'Jerome,' *DCB* III, 29–50.

[97] Jerome, *Epistulae* 18, 10; 125, 12. According to Rufinus (*Apol.* 2, 9) Jerome also did not know Greek before his conversion.

[98] Cf. the preface to his translation of Chronicles from the Hexaplaric Septuagint (cited by Swete, note 26, 101 f.). However, citing Josephus, Jerome appears to restrict the original Septuagint to the Pentateuch (Preface to the *Book on Hebrew Questions*; cf. *Comm. in Ezek.* 2, 5, 12). Cyril restricted it to the twenty-two books of the Hebrew canon. Later (*Apol.* 2, 25) Jerome rejected the inspiration of the Seventy.

The relationship between Jerome's preference for the Hebrew text and his commitment to the Jewish canon is not entirely clear. The Jewish canon of twenty-two or twenty-four books was followed by some in the West and was known to Jerome very early in his Christian life if not from the beginning:

1. While in Gaul he copied for Rufinus Hilary's commentary on the Psalms with its canonical catalogue.

2. He began the study of Hebrew during his first sojourn in the East, some years before his interest in biblical translation. This indicates an implicit recognition of the priority of the Hebrew Bible.

Jerome's translation of certain works of Eusebius and Origen at this time shows the impression that the Greek writers had made upon him, perhaps including their view of the canon. Probably his textual studies, especially his disillusionment with the Septuagint and his use of the Hebrew, sharpened his opinion about the canon but were not the origin of it.

Jerome began his new Latin Bible about A.D. 390. In the prologue to the first books translated, Samuel and Kings, and intended as a preface to the whole, he wrote as follows:

'This prologue to the Scriptures may serve as a kind of helmeted preface for all the books that we have rendered from Hebrew into Latin in order that we [all] may know that whatever is outside these is to be set apart among the apocrypha. Accordingly, [the book of] Wisdom, commonly ascribed to Solomon, and the book of Jesus son of Sirach and Judith and Tobit and the Shepherd are not in the canon.'

Apart from the restriction of the Old Testament canon to the Hebrew Bible, the prologue is noteworthy in other respects.

1. It lists the books of the Old Testament, often with the Hebrew names followed by the Latin, in the masoretic sequence of the Law (5), the Prophets (8) and the Hagiographa (9).[99]

2. It not only shows an acquaintance with a Hebrew canon of twenty-two books but also explains the origin of the masoretic canon of twenty-

---

[99] Jerome, *Prol. in Libr. Regum*: Genesis, Exodus, Leviticus, Numbers, Deuteronomy; Joshua, Judges-Ruth, Kindgoms (1, 2), Kingdoms (3, 4), Isaiah, Jeremiah, Ezekiel, Twelve [Minor Prophets]; Job, David: Psalms, Solomon: Proverbs, Ecclesiastes, Song of Songs; Daniel, Chronicles (1, 2), Ezra, Esther. 'Ezra' = Ezra-Nehemiah, as the list in his letter to Paulinus shows (see note 100).

four books: some *(nonnulli)* Jews placed Ruth and Lamentations among the Hagiographa, counted them separately and thus obtained a canon corresponding to 'the twenty-four elders of the Apocalpyse of John' (cf. Rev. 4:4).[100] The problem of the two different enumerations of the Old Testament books thus appears to be resolved.

3. The reference to the *helmeted preface,* incorporated into the later title of the prologue, *Prologus Galeatus,* apparently anticipates opposition both to a translation from the Hebrew (rather than from the Septuagint) and to the exclusion from the canon of Septuagint additions. Such opposition was not long in coming, especially from the African church.[101]

4. The classification 'apocrypha' for non-biblical books used in the church agrees with the terminology of Epiphanius, whom Jerome had known for a decade or more. It also accords with the general attitude of the Greek church although the term 'ecclesiastical' was more often preferred.

Like other Christian writers, Jerome introduces apocryphal and canonical citations with similar formulas.[102] But he distinguishes the two kinds of books, in terms reminiscent of Origen and Rufinus, with respect to their authority:

'As the church reads the books of Tobit and Judith and the Maccabees but does not receive them among the canonical scriptures, so also it reads these two volumes [of Ben Sira and Wisdom] for the edification of the people [but] not as authority for the confirmation of doctrine.'[103]

This would perhaps not have been opposed in principle even by Augustine. But Jerome was single-minded and he did not temporize. He never tired of reminding his readers that the Septuagint additions were not part

---

[100] A slightly different enumeration is given in a second, annotated catalogue found in Jerome's *Epistulae* 53, 8: Genesis, Exodus, Leviticus, Numbers, Deuteronomy, Job, Joshua, Judges, Ruth, Samuel, Kings (1, 2), Twelve Prophets:..., Isaiah, Jeremiah, Ezekiel, Daniel, David, Solomon, Esther, Chronicles (1, 2), Ezra-Nehemiah 'in a single book'. The order follows the general sequence of the Hebrew Bible but without the precise sequence of divisions of the masoretic text.

[101] Even from Augustine (*Letters* 82, 35), who was sympathetic to Jerome's intentions. As Swete (note 26, 264–277) rightly observes, the issue was more than translation: Much patristic exegesis had been built upon the Septuagint renderings.

[102] E.g. Jerome, *Against the Pelagians* 1, 33 (Sir 3:21); *Letters* 58, 1 (Wis 4:9, 'Solomon says'); 75, 2 (Wis 4:11–14, 'as it is written in the book of Wisdom') 66, 5 (Sir 3:30, 'it is written'); 77, 4 (Bar 5:5, cited as a prophet); *Against Jovianus* 2, 3 (Sir 27:5, 'in another place it is written').

[103] Jerome, *Prol. in Libr. Sal.*:... 'Non ad auctoritatem ecclesiasticorum dogmatum confirmandam' (cf. Fischer, note 41, II, 957).

of the canon. Apart from a hasty version of Tobit and Judith, made at the request of friends, and perhaps the additions to Daniel and Esther he declined even to make a translation of books not in the Hebrew canon. He applied the principle in such thoroughgoing fashion probably because he wished to make 'the distinction between the Hebrew canon and the apocrypha as clear in the Latin as it was in the Greek churches.'[104]

Conclusion

To determine the Old Testament of the early church, the above presentation has given priority to explicit canonical affirmations and has interpreted the usage of the writers in the light of them. The opposite approach would infer the canon of the writer from the books that he cites or from the contents of the Septuagint codex that he uses. This not only is a questionable method but also sometimes involves the patristic writer in self-contradictions since he would affirm one canon in his catalogue and reflect another in his citations.

If the approach taken in this essay is correct, early Christianity, as it is represented by its writers, received as its Old Testament a collection of twenty-two or, in the later masoretic count, twenty-four books.[105] At the same time many writers quoted authoritatively and occasionally as 'Scripture' documents that they elsewhere explicitly excluded from their canonical catalogues; furthermore, they used a Septuagint that differed in content from their professed canon. How are these discrepancies to be explained?

As we have seen, formulas such as 'Scripture says' or 'it is written' may introduce both express citations of canonical writings and 'rewritten'

---

[104] Westcott (note 19), 182.

[105] On the priority of the twenty-two book arrangement cf. Zahn (note 19), II, 336 ff.; G. Hölscher, *Kanonisch und Apokryph*, Leipzig 1905, 25–28; Audet (note 70), 145; P. Katz, 'The Old Testament Canon...," *ZNTW* 47 (1956), 199–203. The numerical variation was originally of no consequence for the content of the canon since, as Jerome informs us, it reflects only the arrangement and not the content of the Hebrew Bible. Similarly, Epiphanius, *Panarion* 8, 6. Curiously, Beckwith (note 11), 256–262, thinks that an earlier 24-book enumeration was literally lessened (by merging) to 22 books in order to conform the number of canonical books to the number of letters in the Hebrew alphabet. The earliest reference to a 22-book enumeration appears to be in the first or second century B.C.: Jubilees 2:23 (cf. R.H. Charles, *The Book of Jubilees*, London 1902, xxxix–xl, 17 f.; Beckwith [note 11], 235–240).

interpretive renderings of these texts.[106] Equally, they may introduce citations of non-canonical documents that are regarded as correct commentary (midrash) on canonical books[107] or as authoritative in some way.[108] Even when they are employed in their technical reference to holy or religious writing, they sometimes have a broader connotation than canonical or covenantal writing.[109] Ordinarily, then, introductory formulas do not in themselves constitute evidence for the canonical authority of the book cited.

The Septuagint originally referred to a Greek version of the Pentateuch translated in Alexandria in the third century B.C. and, according to legend, the inspired work of seventy Jewish elders. However, the same name and origin came to be ascribed to the Greek version of the rest of the Hebrew canonical books that by 132 B.C. also existed on Greek scrolls,[110] sometimes with a quite different text-form from the masoretic Bible.[111] Later the name was applied to certain other Jewish religious writings that originated or were translated in Greek.

When the Septuagint was put into codex form, apparently sometime after the mid-second century A.D., it became even more a *corpus mixtum*. In some manuscripts it included two partially overlapping translations of parts of Chronicles and Ezra-Nehemiah (i.e. I Esdras and II Esdras) as well as a collection of excerpts from the Old Testament, the Apocrypha and Luke 1–2 (i.e. the Odes). Furthermore, it placed Jewish apocrypha not only among the Old Testament books but also, in one codex, at the end of the New Testament (the Psalms of Solomon). No two Septuagint codices contain the same apocrypha, and no uniform Septuagint 'Bible' was ever the subject of discussion in the patristic church. In view of these

---

[106] E.g. I Cor 2:9; II Cor 6:16–18; see note 16.

[107] E.g. Jude 14f.; cf. E.E. Ellis, *Prophecy and Hermeneutic*, Tübingen and Grand Rapids 1978, 225. See notes 53, 73.

[108] E.g. Josh 10:13; II Sam 1:18; Eph 5:14; Jas 4:5. See note 53.

[109] For example, the usage of Gregory, Cyril, Jerome and Augustine noted above, which hardly sprang forth full-grown in the fourth century. For earlier examples cf. Jas 4:5; Jn 7:38 and probably Barn 16:5 since I Enoch was not in any Septuagint manuscript and, according to Origen, did not circulate in the churches as a 'divine' writing. Beckwith (note 11, 69–79, 387 ff.) seems to put too much weight on introductory formulas as an invariable indicator of a reference to canonical authority.

[110] Ben Sira, prologue.

[111] For example, in Daniel and Esther, which contain considerable additional matter not in the Hebrew text. On the origin of the Septuagint cf. Swete (note 26), 1–28 and Jellicoe (note 47), 29–73.

facts the Septuagint codices appear to have been originally intended more as service books than as a defined and normative canon of scripture.[112]

There is no evidence that elements of Diaspora or Palestinian Judaism had an expanded Septuagint canon distinct from the twenty-two book Hebrew canon, and the historical probabilities weigh heavily against such a supposition. There is also no evidence that the ante-Nicene church received or adopted a Septuagint canon although it did apparently consider the Septuagint to be inspired and its text-forms to be superior to those of the masoretic Bible.[113] Nevertheless, unknowledgeable persons tended to give equal authority to all books used in the church, books that varied from time to time and place to place and that included both apocryphal and other, sometimes heretical books. They were probably confirmed in this attitude by the inclusion of various writings used in church within one or a few codices and tended to equate the resulting volumes with the canonical Bible.

In the face of this situation the fourth century church was compelled to define more clearly the Old Testament canon of the church. The bishops and other writers of the Greek church and, one must assume, the council of Laodicea affirmed on the basis of testimony reaching back to Josephus (A. D. 96) that the twenty-two books of the Hebrew canon and, thus, of the apostles constituted the church's Old Testament. On the other hand

---

[112] The codex gradually replaced the scroll in the early centuries of the Christian era. No codices were found at Qumran (pre-A.D. 70), or Pompeii (pre-A.D. 79). Jerome († 420) is said to have been the first scholar to have a library consisting entirely of codices. Cf. T. Birt, *Das Antike Buchwesen*, Aalen 1959 (1882), 115; C.H. Roberts-T.C. Skeat, *The Birth of the Codex*, London ²1987, 24–29, 61: '[It] is impossible to believe that the Christian adoption of the codex can have taken place any later than *circ.* A. D. 100 (it may, of course, have been earlier) …;' U. E. Paoli, *Rome, its People, Life and Customs*, London 1983 (1940), 177 f., who dates the first reference to the codex form to A. D. 84: Martial, *Epigrams* 1, 2, 2 f. *(libellis)*.

[113] Alexandrian Judaism remained a loyal daughter of Jerusalem even though cultural differences had developed (cf. L. H. Feldman, 'The Orthodoxy of the Jews in Hellenistic Egypt,' *Jewish Social Studies* 22 [1960], 215–237; P. Borgen, 'Philo of Alexandria,' *Compendia* II, 2 [1984], 257 ff.). According to Philo, its major spokesman in the first century, it sent tribute *(De Spec. Leg.* I, 78) and pilgrims (in Eusebius, *Praep. Evang.* 8, 14, 64; cf. Acts 2:10) to Jerusalem. Philo, moreover, does not even quote the apocryphal books, much less hint at a separate Alexandrian canon of Scripture. Also, Josephus could hardly have spoken as he did in his work, *Against Apion*, an Alexandrian opponent of Judaism, had he been aware of a disagreement in Judaism about the canon. On the status of the apocryphal books in Hellenistic Judaism, see Beckwith (note 24), 81–84. For a critique of the theory of an Alexandrian canon see Beckwith (note 11), 382–386.

Augustine and the councils of Carthage affirmed as canonical, on the basis of current usage and of citations by the Fathers, an additional number of Jewish apocryphal writings. Even if the North African churches had the theological right to define their canon, the churches of the East, and Jerome as he sharpens and mediates their convictions, had the stronger historical claim to represent the Old Testament canon of Jesus and his apostles. For although the apostolic church left no canonical lists, in all likelihood it agreed with the mainstream of Judaism in this regard. Not without significance for the question is the fact that no explicit quotation from the Septuagintal apocrypha appears in the New Testament, in Philo or in the literature from Qumran.

In its conception of the Old Testament the messianic community of Jesus differed from the mainstream of Judaism not in the content of its Bible but in the interpretive key that it used to open the Bible. Since this key was molded in part by theological conceptions implicit in the process of canonization, it is necessary to consider more closely this aspect of the subject.

The Canon as a Hermeneutical Process

Introduction

The evidence offered in the preceding section demonstrates, I believe, that in the first Christian century (Philo, Josephus) and even two centuries earlier (Ben Sira, Qumran) Judaism possessed a defined and identifiable canon, twenty-two books arranged in three (or four) divisions and regarded as an inspired and normative authority for the community. As the church's librarian it preserved and passed on these sacred writings to the Christian community.

How the canon of Judaism developed the form and content in which the apostolic church received and used it requires a further word. First of all, the criteria used in Judaism to set apart the canon from other religious literature are not unimportant for the early church's conception of 'Scripture'. Also, there are scholarly disagreements that need to be evaluated. Finally, the growth of the Old Testament canon involves an interpretive process that continues in the biblical interpretation of Jesus and of his apostles and prophets.

The Tripartite Division of the Old Testament

The Failure of the Three-Stage Canonization Theory

The theory that the three divisions of the Hebrew Old Testament represented three successive acts or stages of canonization was increasingly attractive to nineteenth-century scholars.[114] In its most popular form it postulated the canonization of the Law at the time of Ezra and Nehemiah (Neh 8–10; c.? 400 B.C.), the Prophets about 200 B.C. and the Hagiographa by the rabbinic academy of Jamnia (Yabne) c. A.D. 90.[115] In spite of reservations[116] and opposition[117] it rapidly gained and continues to have a widespread acceptance.[118]

---

[114] E.g. Westcott (note 19), 297–301: 'At the return [from the Exile] a collection of the Prophets was probably made by Ezra and added to the sacred Law. Afterwards the collection of the Hagiographa was... completed during the period of Persian supremacy' (297). For criticisms of the nineteenth-century consensus cf. B.S. Childs, *Introduction to the Old Testament as Scripture*, Philadelphia ³1982, 52ff.

[115] H. Graetz (*Kohelet*, Leipzig 1871, 147–173) apparently was the first to attribute to Jamnia the role of 'closing' the canon: Both the Law and the Prophets were established by the assembly of Nehemiah since the departure of the Samaritans was occasioned in part by the introduction of readings from the Prophets; the majority of the Hagiographa were confirmed by a rabbinic assembly in c. A.D. 65 (cf. *M. Yadayim 4:6; Shabbat 1:4*) and the final two books, Ecclesiastes and Song of Songs, by the school at Jamnia. However, Graetz, who was followed by S. Zeitlin, offered only a makeshift reconstruction designed to accommodate his first century A.D. dating of Ecclesiastes and the Maccabean dating of other Hagiographa (12f., 148). Cf. Beckwith (note 24), 58–61. Cf. S. Zeitlin in *PAAJR* 3 (1930–31), 121–158.

[116] Cf. W.R. Smith, *The Old Testament in the Jewish Church*, London ²1892: The work of Graetz is 'a model of confused reasoning' (169). But 'the third collection [of Hagiographa] was formed after the second had been closed' by a sifting process not easily explained (179).

[117] E.g. W.J. Beecher, 'The Alleged Triple Canon of the Old Testament,' *JBL* 15 (1896), 118–128; W.H. Green, *General Introduction to the Old Testament: the Canon*, London 1899, 19–118, who makes some telling points and shows a commendable caution: 'We have no positive evidence when or by whom the sacred books were collected and arranged' (111). But he offers little evidence for his own hypothesis that the second division of the canon grew with each prophet adding his book until Malachi completed the collection.

[118] Wildeboer (note 42), 144; F. Buhl, *Canon and Text of the Old Testament*, Edinburgh 1892, 9–12, 25ff.; Ryle (note 25), 105, 119: The Torah received its final recognition by

The theory was not unrelated to earlier Roman Catholic hypotheses that, consequent upon the decision of the Council of Trent,[119] sought to show that the Apocrypha had canonical status in first-century Judaism.[120] And it was later adapted to this end.[121] Its popular reception, however, may be largely attributed to the Maccabean (c. 150 B.C.) and later dating of certain of the Hagiographa by many scholars of the day. Such dating was incompatible with the older tradition that ascribed the formation of the canon to Ezra and 'the men of the great synagogue' (c. 400–200 B.C.),[122] and it produced a pressing need for a new explanation.

The three-stage theory was thought to fill this need, but on several counts it has proved to be unsatisfactory.

1. It was based not on concrete historical evidence but on inferences, none of which were necessary and some of which were clearly mistaken. Specifically to be faulted was its estimate of the evidence of Josephus, Ben Sira and the academy of Jamnia (Yabne).

2. For certain books it presupposed a late dating that, especially since the discovery of the Qumran library, can no longer be entertained.

---

the fifth century BC and the Prophets by 200 BC; for the Writings AD 100 marks an official confirmation that 'had long before been decided by popular use' (183). Cf. O. Kaiser, *Introduction to the Old Testament*, Oxford 1975, 405–413; L. M. McDonald, *The Formation of the Christian Biblical Canon*, Nashville 1988, 48–66; P. Schäfer, 'Die Sogenannte Synode von Jabne,' *Judaica* 31 (1975), 54–64, 116–24, 122; H. Gese, *Vom Sinai zum Zion*, München 1974, 13f., 16f. (= *ZTK* 67 [1970], 419f., 422f.).

[119] The fourth session (8 April 1546) declared certain apocrypha to be canonical, *viz.* the additions to Esther and Daniel, Ben Sira, Wisdom, Tobit, Judith, I and II Maccabees. The North African councils were influential but were not followed precisely. For example, they accepted I Esdras (= III Esdras) and apparently rejected II Maccabees. Cf. H. P. Rüger in *Wissenschaft und Kirche*, ed. K. Aland, Bielefeld 1989, 336–345.

[120] G. Genebrard, *Chronographia*, Lugdensi 1572, II, 190 (cited in J. Cosin, *A Scholastic History of the Canon*, London 1684, 14): The Hebrew canon was received at the time of Ezra, certain Apocrypha at the translation of the Septuagint (c. 250 B.C.) and I and II Maccabees in the first century A.D. Similar was the Roman Catholic scholar, F. C. Movers, *Loci Quidam Historiae Canonis, Veteris Testamenti Illustrati*, Breslau 1842, 20–22: Books peculiar to the Septuagint were at first canonical also in Palestine but were excluded in the second century A.D. in deference to the rabbinic opinion that inspiration ceased with Malachi (*T. Sota* 13:2). Graetz (note 115) cites Movers' work.

[121] E. g. by Sundberg (note 42), 108, 126, 129.

[122] Cf. Ryle (note 25), 261–283; Graetz (note 115). Simon the Just, the last member of the great synagogue according to rabbinic tradition (*M. Abot* 1:2f.), is identified by some with the son of Onias I (c. 300 B.C.) and by others with the son of Onias II (c. 200 B.C.). See note 151.

1. The testimony of Josephus in c. A.D. 96 to a universal, clearly defined and long settled canon[123] contradicts any theory of an undetermined canon in first-century Judaism. And it cannot easily be set aside. As Thackeray has pointed out, Josephus was writing a closely reasoned polemic against *inter alia* the work of an erudite Alexandrian grammarian,[124] and he could not afford to indulge in careless misstatements that could be thrown back at him. Also, he wrote as a representative of his people and did not transmit only the views peculiar to his own (Pharisaic) religious party or to the Pharisaic-rabbinic traditions:[125]

(1) His canon follows a substantially different arrangement from the rabbis.

(2) He reflects anti-Pharisaic traits elsewhere,[126] and his writings found no apparent acceptance among the rabbis and eventually had to be preserved by the Christians.

Similar to Josephus, and two centuries earlier, the book of Ben Sira also speaks of a tripartite canon of 'the law and the prophets and the rest of the books'. According to the three-stage theory this statement indicates that the law and the prophets were completed collections and 'the rest' or 'the other' books were a less defined miscellany. Apparently the only reason for this odd conclusion is the variable terminology used for the third division. It is scarcely acceptable since even in the first century A.D. the terminology for all three divisions was still flexible: the Psalms could be called 'the law' (John 15:25), 'the law' could be designated 'the writings' (γραφαί, Matt 22:29; cf. Rom 4:3) and 'the law and the prophets' described variously as 'Moses and the prophets' or simply as 'the prophets' (Luke 24:27; Acts 13:27). The statement in Ben Sira mentions each of the three divisions with the same degree of preciseness and, to be meaningful to the

---

[123] J. Barr (*Holy Scripture*, Philadelphia 1983, 49–74, 51), viewing 'canonization' as explicit acts of choosing and listing some books and excluding others, concludes that early Judaism had no 'canon'. He seems to confuse the concept with a particular terminology and process. For a criticism of Barr cf. W.D. Davies, 'Reflections about... the Old Testament in the New...,' *JQR* 74 (1983–84), 123n, 127n.

[124] H. St. John Thackeray, *Josephus the Man and the Historian*, New York 1929, 122f.

[125] *Pace* R. Meyer, '... Hintergrund der Kanontheorie des Josephus,' *Josephus Studien*, ed. O. Betz, Göttingen 1974, 285–299, 298.

[126] E.g. Josephus, *Works*, 9 vols., ed. H. St. J. Thackeray, London 1926–1965, IV, viii: In the proem to the *Antiquities* Josephus alludes to the legitimacy of paraphrasing the Scriptures. In this 'the author is doubtless controverting the views of the contemporary rabbinical schools.' Cf. S. Mason, *Josephus and the Pharisees*, Leiden 1991, 372–375.

reader, it must refer to definite, identifiable books. It could be interpreted otherwise only if one were already convinced that the tripartite canon could not have existed as a subsistent entity at that time. The same applies to the epistle from Qumran (c. 150 B.C.).

The rabbinic academy of Jamnia affirmed, after discussion, that the Song of Songs and Ecclesiastes 'defiled the hands', that is, were canonical.[127] Such pronouncements were not peculiar to Jamnia, resolved nothing and continued into the following centuries.[128] Misunderstanding the proceeding at Jamnia as an act of canonization and associating it with other Talmudic discussions addressing quite different questions, advocates of the three-stage theory concluded that the third division of the canon was officially 'closed' at this time. Most likely the questions at Jamnia about the Song of Songs and Ecclesiastes had no more to do with the canonization of the Old Testament than the questions of Luther about the letter of James had to do with the canonization of the New Testament. Insofar as they were not discussions of theoretical possibilities, they apparently expressed only a reaffirmation of books long received and now disputed by some.

2. All twenty-two books of the Hebrew Bible with the exception of Esther were contained in the Qumran library. These books must therefore be dated before c. A.D. 68 when the community was destroyed, and probably before the accession of Jonathan as high priest in 152 B.C., when, apparently, the community separated from the mainstream of Judaism.[129] For books after that time, if written by the other sects, would

---

[127] *M. Eduyot* 5:3; *T. Eduyot* 2:7; *M. Yadayim* 3:5. Cf. J. P. Lewis, 'What Do We Mean by Jabneh?' *JBR* 32 (1964), 125–132; R.C. Newman, 'The Council of Jamnia and the Old Testament Canon,' *WTJ* 38 (1976), 319–349: 'The rabbis seem to be testing a *status quo* which has existed beyond memory' (349). My assessment regarding Jamnia (and this chapter as a whole) was drafted on a sabbatical leave at Tübingen, 1975–76, before I knew of the work of Leiman (note 10), Childs (note 114, 53) and Beckwith (note 11, 276f.). Thus, it represents a conclusion independent of but very similar to theirs.

[128] Jerome, *Comm. in Eccl.* 12:13f. (c. A.D. 390); cf. *B. T. Megillah* 7a (R. Meir, c. A.D. 150). Cf. Childs (note 114), 53.

[129] Cf. Beckwith (note 24), 76–81. Cf. Leiman (note 35), 23–36 (= I.H. Eybers in *Die Ou-Testamentiese Werksgemeenskap in Suid-Afrika*, Stellenbosch 1962) for a discussion of the canon of the Qumran sect. The rabbinic discussions about Esther (*B. T. Megillah* 7a) and its absence from Quman, from New Testament citations and from the canon of Melito and some of the later Fathers (notes 32, 65, 66) suggest that there may have been widespread doubt about its canonicity.

not likely have found acceptance at Qumran or, if produced by the Qumran sect, would not have been received by the rest of Judaism. Moreover, the textual history of the manuscripts,[130] the dates of specific scripts and other considerations led W. F. Albright to conclude that, with the exception of Ecclesiastes and Daniel, all of the Old Testament books were written before the end of the Persian period, that is, before 330 B. C.[131]

What of Ecclesiastes and Daniel? In the light of Qumran and of other evidence Ecclesiastes cannot have been composed later than the third century B.C. and it may be considerably earlier.[132] Even the book of Daniel, which in its present form has for the past century usually been assigned to the Maccabean period, *viz.* 165 B.C., must almost certainly have originated before that time.[133] Six manuscript fragments of Daniel reflecting different textual families, one in a script from the second century B.C., were found at Qumran.[134] There is also a quotation from Daniel

---

[130] Leiman (note 35), 334–348 (= F. M. Cross, *IEJ* 16, 1966, 81–95). The Qumran texts disclose no lists of canonical books. But see above, note 31. Whether the sect received as inspired or canonical any books rejected by mainstream Judaism is a moot point. It probably gave some such status to apocryphal Psalms attributed to David and to the writings of its (prophetic) Teacher and of its other *maskilim*. But its use of other apocrypha and pseudepigrapha should not, on the analogy of Josephus, the rabbis and the Fathers, be regarded as implying canonicity.

[131] W. F. Albright, *Recent Discoveries in Bible Lands*, New York 1955, 129; cf. F. M. Cross, *The Ancient Library of Qumran*, Garden City NY ²1961, 165 (¹1958, 121 f.): Qumran supports a dating of the latest canonical Psalms from the Persian period and a *terminus ad quem* for Ecclesiastes in the third century B. C.; H. G. M. Williamson, *Israel in the Book of Chronicles*, Cambridge 1977, 83–86: The evidence points to the Persian period, i. e. pre-330 B. C., for the date of Chronicles.

[132] Cross (note 131).

[133] For other evidence cf. the form of the Aramaic in Dan 2:4b–7:28, which on balance favours a third-century B.C. or earlier date (W.F. Albright, 'The Date and Personality of the Chronicler,' *JBL* 40 [1921], 104–124; K.A. Kitchen, 'The Aramaic of Daniel,' *Notes on Some Problems in the Book of Daniel*, ed. D.J. Wiseman, London 1965, 76, 79.). Cf. H.N. Bate, *The Sibylline Oracles: Books III-V*, London 1918, 64 f.: The whole passage (c. 150 B.C.) is partly based on Dan 7–9 (65n.). Cf. I Macc 1:54; 2:60 with Daniel 11:31; 6:22. Josephus, *Ant.* 11, 337, relates a story that Alexander the Great was shown the prophecy of Daniel (8:21) predicting his conquest. Since Josephus (cf. *c. Apion.* 1, 183–195) used the historian Hecataeus of Abdera (c. 300 B.C.), who wrote a book on the relationship of the Jews to Alexander, he presumably found the story there. While he may have elaborated it and perhaps supplied the (obvious) name Daniel, there are no historical reasons to dismiss it as a fiction. Otherwise: V. Tcherikover, *Hellenistic Civilization and the Jews*, New York 1975, 42–46.

[134] Cf. Cross (note 131), 43, 164n; A. A. DiLella-L. F. Hartman, *The Book of Daniel*, Garden City NY 1978, 72f.

12:10; 11:32, introduced by the formula, 'As it is written in the book of Daniel the prophet' (4QFlor 2:3). As was shown above, introductory formulas are no guarantee of a canonical citation. However, this formula is identical with an earlier one introducing a citation of Isaiah (4QFlor 1:15), identifies Daniel as one book (and not a cycle of traditions) and accords with an older division of the Hebrew canon in which Daniel was placed among the Prophets.

Customarily today it is supposed that Daniel, originally among the Writings *(Ketubim)*, was only later placed among the Prophets *(Nebiim)*. But the historical evidence, on balance, does not support this view of the matter. The first century witnesses place Daniel among the Prophets. Matthew (24:15) reflects this perspective by its designation of Daniel as 'the prophet.' Josephus (note 25) and the *Bryennios list* (note 70), which J. P. Audet and Peter Katz on rather firm grounds date to the late first or early second century, clearly do so.[135] Giving the same evidence are the lists of Melito and Origen, which illustrate the canon used by certain Palestinian Jews and/or Jewish Christians in the second and early third centuries.

Of the early evidence only *B. T. Baba Batra* 14b counts Daniel among the Writings. It probably dates from before the end of the second century but, although it may represent an older tradition, it must be judged secondary to the earlier-witnessed and more widely attested order. Qumran, with its reference to 'Daniel the prophet' (4QFlor 2:3), lends further weight to this judgement. Given the deep influence of Daniel on the Qumran sect and its known and undisputed canonical standing throughout first-century Judaism, it is altogether likely that at the time the Qumran community became distinct from mainstream Judaism the book was received among them in the canonical collection known in Ben Sira as 'the prophets.'[136]

---

[135] Audet (note 70), 145; Katz (note 105), 196. Otherwise: Beckwith (note 11), 188, who thinks that the Bryennios list cannot be Jewish 'since it mixes the Prophets and Hagiographa indiscriminately.' But see H. M. Orlinsky, 'Prolegomenon' to Ginsburg (note 36), xix (= Leiman [note 35], 852): '[It] may well be that the Christian, essentially fourfold division of the Bible ... [is] actually Jewish in origin'.

[136] The absence of Daniel in Ben Sira's (48–50) annotations on famous men is no more significant for his canon than is the absence of Ezra or the presence of Enoch. It can also hardly indicate that Ben Sira classified Daniel among the Writings rather than the Prophets since David and Nehemiah, both of whose works were among the Writings, are included.

A Maccabean origin of the Daniel narratives (Dan 1–6) has increasingly given way to the view that they were formed and in use well before the Maccabean period.[137] For a number of reasons the Maccabean origin of the visions (Dan 7–12) is also open to doubt.

(1) It is intrinsically improbable that visions composed as *vaticinia ex eventu* in c. 165 B.C. could, within a few decades and without a trace of opposition, be widely and authoritatively received as the revealed word of a sixth century prophet.

(2) The theory of the specifically Maccabean origin of Daniel apparently arose less from historical considerations than from the philosophical, i.e. confessional assumption that this kind of explicit predictive prophecy was impossible.[138]

(3) The theory does not take into account the 'contemporizing' alterations characteristic of the periodic rewriting of biblical books.

To whatever degree the language of Dan 7–12 reflects an origin in the second century B.C., it is best explained as a contemporization of an earlier prophecy:[139]

(1) The recopying of many Old Testament books was a necessity after the widespread destruction of the Scriptures by Antiochus Epiphanes in

---

[137] For example, M. Hengel, *Judaism and Hellenism* 2 vols., London [2]1974, I, 113, 29f. ('current... in the third century B.C.'). A. Jepsen, 'Bemerkungen zum Danielbuch,' *VT* 11 (1961) 386–391: Apparently there was 'a collection of Daniel narratives and visions already in the time of Alexander' (?chapters 4, 5, 6, 10, 12) supplemented by chapters 2, 7, 8; in the Maccabean period, perhaps, chapters 1, 3 and 4 were added and 7 and 8 elaborated. For an instructive discussion of the date of Daniel cf. J.G. Baldwin, *Daniel*, Leicester UK 1978, 13–74.

[138] Apparently first made by Porphyry († 303). Cf. Jerome, *Commentary on Daniel*, ed. G.L. Archer, Grand Rapids 1958 (A.D. 407), 15 (Prologue): Porphyry alleged that 'whatever [pseudo-Daniel] spoke of up to the time of Antiochus [Epiphanes] contained authentic history whereas anything that he may have conjectured beyond that point was false, inasmuch as he would not have foreknown the future.'

[139] Cf. C.H.H. Wright, *Daniel and his Prophecies*, London 1906: '... in the Maccabean period there was a wholesale destruction of the sacred books... In re-editing in that period the book of Daniel, it may have been a matter of importance that its language would to some extent approximate to that of the common people' (xix). Dan 11 'is a Hebrew translation of a lost Aramaic original, combined with an exposition... portions [of which], as in the Targums of a later age, are embedded in the chapter' (242). See note 141. Cf. M. Noth, *Gesammelte Studien*, München 1969, 11–28, 25: Dan 7, which is to be dated from the time of Alexander [c. 330 B.C.], was later interpolated and supplemented. Otherwise: G.L. Archer, 'The Hebrew of Daniel Compared with ... Qumran,' *The Law and the Prophets*, ed. J.H. Skilton, Nutley NJ 1974, 470–481.

c. 169 B.C.[140] and such activity, like scribal transmission generally, inevitably included some alterations and also incorporated in greater or lesser degree an 'up-dating' of orthography and terminology along with other explanatory elaboration (midrash).

(2) Such elaboration appears earlier in manuscript-transmission and in the translation (as in the Septuagint), revision (as in Esther and Jeremiah) and rewriting (as in Chronicles) of biblical books.[141]

(3) Both the Qumran library and the New Testament make evident that such elaboration was not precluded by the fact that the texts were regarded as canonical scripture and that

(4) on the above analogies it would very likely have been employed in the transmission of the book of Daniel.

The Canon and the Cult

With the failure of the three-stage canonization theory, at least in its traditional form, the origin and meaning of the tripartite division of the Hebrew Bible remain very open questions.[142] The following suggestions may, it is hoped, contribute to a more satisfactory answer. Arrangements other than the tripartite were, of course, known in Judaism. The Septuagint preserves a fourfold division – Pentateuch, Historical Writings, Poetic

---

[140] Cf. I Macc 1:56f.; II Macc 2:14f.; Josephus, *c. Apion.* 1, 35f.; M. H. Segal, 'The Promulgation of the Authoritative Text...,' *JBL* 72 (1953), 39–45; Cross (note 35), 91. Whether such activity created a standard text (Segal) or one of its forerunners (cf. Cross) need not be discussed here. Beckwith (note 11), 80–86, 153 argues with some cogency that the standard for canonicity was whether a book was laid up in the Temple and that Judas Maccabaeus was instrumental in regathering the Temple Scriptures after the liberation of Jerusalem in 165 B.C. (cf. II Macc 2:14), but he is less convincing in his view that Judas also classified and ordered the sacred books in the arrangement later found in *B. T. Baba Batra* 14b.

[141] Cf. S. Talmon in *Qumran and the... Biblical Text*, ed. F. M. Cross, Cambridge MA 1975, 327–381. On the orthographic modernization of transmitted texts cf. Kitchen (note 133), 60–65; E. Y. Kutscher in *Current Trends in Linguistics* 6 vols. ed. T. A. Sebaeck, The Hague 1963–, VI (1970), 399–403.

[142] F. F. Bruce (*The Canon of Scripture*, Downers Grove IL 1988, 9) rightly describes recent developments as 'the collapse of the century-old consensus.' For attempts to reconstruct the history of the reception of the Old Testament canon cf. Childs (note 114), 54–57, passim; D. N. Freedman, 'The Law and the Prophets,' *Congress Volume 1962* (*SVT* 9), ed. G. W. Anderson et al., Leiden 1963, 250–265: The Law and Former Prophets (Genesis-II Kings) were published as one literary unit by 550 B.C. and supplemented by the Latter Prophets (Isaiah, Jeremiah, Ezekiel, Twelve) before 450 B.C.

(Wisdom) Literature, Prophets – that is probably pre-Christian,[143] and other sources indicate that a tripartite pattern was not a fixed or necessary conception.[144] The later masoretic Bible in a number of ancient manuscripts shifts to a fourfold division: Pentateuch, Megillot, Prophets, Hagiographa.[145] However, the tripartite scheme, attested by Ben Sira, Josephus and the rabbinic tradition and perhaps by Qumran, the New Testament and Philo, was apparently the prevailing usage in first century Judaism. It seems to have arisen from the role of Scripture in the cultus, if the synagogue readings and the activity and traditional picture of Ezra are accurate guides in the matter.

At least from the first century and probably much earlier the Law and the Prophets were read in the synagogue every sabbath on a systematic basis;[146] the Hagiographa, on the other hand, were used only on special occasions or, in the case of the Psalms, for different parts of the service. Certain rabbis rearranged the masoretic Bible into four divisions 'for liturgical or ritual purposes',[147] and others, who at an earlier time transferred two of the Megillot (Ruth, Lamentations) and the book of Daniel from the Prophets to the Hagiographa, may have been motivated by similar considerations.[148] That is, if Ruth, Lamentations and Daniel were excluded from the cycle of weekly readings or were designated for reading

---

[143] So, Orlinsky (note 135). Cf. Swete (note 26), 217 ff. It may possibly be reflected by Qumran and Philo (see notes 29, 31).

[144] 'The Law and Prophets,' often used for the whole of Scripture (e.g. in Matt 5:17; 7:12), expresses a twofold division. Cf. II Macc 2:13 (c. 100 B.C.): Nehemiah 'collected the books about the kings [= ?Samuel-Kings] and the Prophets, the works of David and the letters of Kings concerning sacred offerings [= ?Ezra 6–7]'. Although probably traditional idiom, such passages show that the divisions of Scripture were not always perceived within a tripartite framework.

[145] Cf. Ryle (note 25), 292. The five Megillot together with the Pentateuch also were sometimes transmitted separately.

[146] Acts 13:15, 27; 15:21; Luke 4:16; cf. Josephus, *c. Apion.* 2, 175; Philo, *De Somn.* II, 127; *M. Megillah* 3:4. Cf. C. Perrot, *La lecture de la Bible dans la synagogue*, Hildesheim 1973; idem, 'The Reading of the Bible in the Ancient Synagogue,' *Compendia* II, 1 (1988), 137–159.

[147] Ginsburg (note 36), 3.

[148] This was first suggested to me in a lecture of A. A. MacRae, who apparently was following his teacher, R. D. Wilson, *Studies in the Book of Daniel: Second Series*, New York 1938, 59 ff., 64. Cf. also R. D. Wilson, 'The Book of Daniel and the Canon,' *PTR* 13 (1915), 404 f., 408 = *Studies*, 59 f., 64. Anti-apocalyptic tendencies in post-70 rabbinic Judaism could have occasioned the transfer of Daniel to the Hagiographa and, consequently, its removal from the Haftara readings.

only on special occasions, this would on the above analogy have resulted in their transferral to the Hagiographa.

Jewish tradition associates Ezra the priest both with the establishment of the public reading of Scripture and with the ordering of the canon.[149] If it in part represents a later idealized picture, it supports nonetheless an early and close connection between the canon and the cultic usage.[150] It also supports the supposition that between the time of Ezra (c. 400 B.C.) and of the epistle from Qumran (c. 150 B.C.) and prologue of Ben Sira (c. 132 B.C.), when the tripartite canon is first attested, priestly circles or another body or bodies related to them[151] classified the biblical books to accord with their use in worship. When the use varied, these circles apparently reclassified the affected book within the canonical divisions, a relatively simple procedure before the advent of the codex. They thereby maintained the relationship established by Ezra between the canonical structure and the hermeneutical context.

The Growth of the Old Testament

Typological Correspondence

The Old Testament displays a hermeneutical progression in which, on the one hand, sacred accounts of God's acts in the past provided models for later accounts of his present and future activity and, on the other hand, the received sacred literature was from time to time conformed to its con-

---

[149] Re the canon cf. IV Ezra 14:38–48; *B. T. Baba Batra* 15a; *B. T. Sanhedrin* 21b-22a; Ezra 7:6. Re public reading cf. Neh 8–10; *B. T. Baba Kamma* 82a; Perrot, 'Reading' (note 146), 155f.; I. Elbogen, *Der jüdische Gottesdienst in seiner geschichtlichen Entwicklung*, Hildesheim 1967 (1913), 157f. On the problem of dating Ezra's ministry cf. R.W. Klein, 'Ezra and Nehemiah in Recent Studies,' *Magnalia Dei* (note 15), 370ff.; S. Talmon, 'Ezra and Nehemiah,' *IDBS*, 317–328; J.S. Wright, *The Date of Ezra's Coming to Jerusalem*, London 1958.

[150] Cf. G. Östborn, *Cult and Canon*, Uppsala 1950, 15ff., 96f.

[151] A. Kuenen, 'Over de mannen der Groote Synagoge,' 1876 = GT: *Gesammelte Abhandlungen*, Freiburg 1894, 125–160, showed that most rabbinic references to a 'great synagogue' between Ezra and Simon the Just are late and confused. But his conclusion (149) that they are based on a fiction created out of Neh 8–10 is doubtful. *M. Abot* 1:1f. and, perhaps, *B. T. Baba Batra* 15a probably preserve traditions of the role (though not the name) of some such body or bodies in the reception and transmission of the canon. See note 122; cf. W. Bacher, 'Synagogue, The Great,' *JE* XI, 640–643.

temporary or future application and fulfilment. The first aspect of the process is evident in the way in which the prophets 'placed the new historical acts of God... in exactly the same category as the old basic events of the canonical history':[152] a new creation,[153] a new Exodus,[154] a new covenant,[155] a new Davidic kingdom,[156] a new Zion or temple.[157] It also is present in those Psalms (e.g. 8, 68, 106, 136) in which the appeal or praise for God's present and future help is keyed to his past acts of redemption. It represents a typological correspondence that is not a mere cyclical repetition but rather a progression in which the new surpasses the old. The process appears to embody a canonical principle as well. That is, inspired prophetic writings are received as normative for the faith and worship of the community as they are recognized to be valid contemporary expressions of and abiding supplements to the ancient election and convenantal traditions. As we hope to show in chapter three below, the early Christians' understanding of the Old Testament and of its actualization in their own time and community stands within the same perspective.[158]

Rewriting

The hermeneutical process has a second aspect, also to be found later in the New Testament, that likewise involves a contemporization of God's ancient word and work. However, it is carried out in a different way, by a

---

[152] G. von Rad, *Old Testament Theology*, 2 vols., London 1975 (1957), II, 113, cf. 112–19, 272; cf. L. Goppelt, 'τύπος,' *TDNT* 8 (1972), 254.

[153] Isa 11:6–9; 51:3; 65:17; 66:22; Ezek 36:35; 47:7–12; cf. Dan 7:13f. with Ps 8:4ff. and Gen 1:26 ('dominion'); Ellis (note 107), 167.

[154] Jer 16:14f.; Isa 11:15f.; 43:16–21; 48:20f.; 51:9ff.; cf. Ezek 36:8 with 47:13.

[155] Hos 2:18 (20); Jer 31:31f.; Isa 54:10.

[156] Hos 3:5; Amos 9:11; Mic 5:2 (1); Isa 11:1; Ezek 37:24; cf. II Sam 7:6–16; Ps 2:7; Ellis (note 107), 199f.

[157] Isa 2:2ff.; 54:11f.; Ezek 40–48; Amos 9:11. See below, 141–157.

[158] Professor B.S. Childs (note 114, 659–671) rightly underscores the importance of the substantive unity and continuity of the Christian Bible with the Hebrew Scriptures. While Professor J.A. Sanders (*From Sacred Story to Sacred Text*, Philadelphia 1987, 166–172) raises a justifiable question about Childs' identification of the canonical text-form of the Old Testament with the masoretic text, his own view that 'the canonical process... continues today' (172) is doubtful. It seems to confuse two related but discrete matters, (1) the recognition of the biblical canon as the written locus of the church's inspired and authoritative Word of God and (2) the continuing task of translation, interpretation and application of that Word.

rewriting of the ancient accounts. The process takes several forms: (1) It appears in Deuteronomy (a 'second law') as a reworking and reapplication of Exodus traditions and in Chronicles as a reinterpretation of (mainly) Samuel-Kings. The same procedure is carried further in the non-canonical I Esdras, a Greek rewriting of parts of Chronicles and Ezra-Nehemiah.[159] (2) A kind of rewriting also occurs within a book's own manuscript transmission. This has been suggested above in the case of Daniel. On a broader scale it appears to be supported by the textual history of other biblical books in both their 'creative' and 'recensional' stages.[160] That is, the kind of interpretive alteration usually associated with later scribal activity was in all likelihood made from time to time from the inception of a book. The work was 'reproduced' (with variations) by circles who, even as they transmitted it, contributed to its final canonical form. Among other things the alterations involved a reordering and contemporizing of the text, as is evident in the Septuagint and may be inferred at least in some cases for the Hebrew text underlying the Septuagint.[161] (3) Finally, the older writings were likewise brought into the

---

[159] Cf. the examples in S. R. Driver, *Deuteronomy*, Edinburgh 1960 (³1902), viii–ix; xxxvii–xxxix; T. Willi, *Die Chronik als Auslegung*, Göttingen 1972, 48–198; B. S. Childs, 'Midrash and the Old Testament,' *Understanding the Sacred Text*, ed. J. Reumann, Valley Forge PA 1972, 53 ff. and the literature cited; P. R. Ackroyd, 'The Chronicler as Exegete,' *JSOT* 2 (1977), 2–32.

[160] Cf. Talmon (note 141): 'It appears that the extant text types must be viewed as the remains of a yet more variegated transmission of the Bible text in the preceding centuries' (325). An 'undetermined percentage of these *variae lectiones* [in biblical manuscripts at Qumran] derive from the ongoing literary processes of an intra-biblical nature...' (380). Cf. D. W. Gooding, 'A Recent Popularization of Professor F. M. Cross' Theories...,' *TB* 26 (1975), 130 f.; R. P. Gordon, '[III Kgdm 12:24]: History or Midrash,' *VT* 25 (1975), 368–393. Admittedly, this view of the matter complicates the problem of dating Old Testament books since some internal evidence may reflect the time of a 'revision' and not of the origin of the work.

[161] E.g. Isa 9:11 (LXX: Greeks; MT: Philistines). Cf. D. W. Gooding, *Relics of Ancient Exegesis*, Cambridge 1976; idem, '... Translation-revision in 3 Reigns IX 10–X 33,' *VT* 19 (1969), 448–463; idem, 'Problems of Text and Midrash...,' *Textus* 7 (1969), 1–29: The Septuagint III Kingdoms 'is quite obviously a commentary on I Kings' (28). Further cf. J. A. Sanders, *Canon and Community*, Philadelphia 1984, 22 f., 30 ff., whose views are both similar to and critiqued by Childs (note 114), 56 f., 171 ff., 367–70, 434 ff. Neither Sanders nor Childs gives sufficient attention to the specific (prophetic disciple-circle) context for the creative rewriting and up-dating of received prophetic books. To my mind a recognized inspired status of the traditioning circles best explains how the 'community,' who are the recipients not the makers of books, could accept the rewritten material on a par and in continuity with the prophetic *Vorlage*. Cf. J. Blenkinsopp, *Prophecy and Canon*, Notre Dame IN 1977, 134–137; J. V. M.

present by the exposition and application of the later canonical writers. For example, Ezek 16 is an allegory built upon themes drawn from earlier books and Ps 132 apparently a 'midrashic reflection' on II Sam 7.[162]

The hermeneutical process seen to be unfolding within the Old Testament continued beyond the canonical boundaries. In some circles, for example, Jeremiah, Daniel and Esther were supplemented with material not received as canonical by messianic (i.e. Christian) and rabbinic Judaism and their predecessors. The book of Jubilees provided a rewriting of Genesis, I Esdras of Chronicles-Ezra; and in a somewhat different way Qumran's *Temple Scroll* reworked and supplemented parts of the Pentateuch, and Ben Sira, along the lines of Proverbs, extended further the reunderstanding of the Law in terms of Wisdom. Yet none were received as canonical. And, of course, at some point literary alterations and supplements in the manuscript-transmission were no longer regarded as part and parcel of a canonical book's essential form but as departures from it.

The Limits of the Canon

What caused the hermeneutical process characteristic of the canonical progression to cease providing the valid form and continuation of the canon? Our sources provide no clear answer, but they do permit certain inferences to be drawn. They do not speak of a 'closing' of the canon, which is apparently a modern conception, but rather of a time after which no subsequent writings were placed on a par with canonical books. Josephus marks this time at the death of Artaxerxes; the rabbis refer to the same general period or, alternatively, to the time of Ben Sira. More significantly, however, both sources also associate the cessation of the growth of the canon with the cessation of a particular kind of prophetic inspiration or succession.[163] That is, the chronological limits of the canon were inextricably combined with convictions about the activity of the prophetic Spirit in the community as well as in the individual writing.

Sturdy, 'The Authorship, of the "Prose Sermons" of Jeremiah,' *Prophecy*, ed. J.A. Emerton, Berlin 1980, 143–149f.; R.P. Carroll, 'Canonical Criticism,' *ET* 92 (1980–81), 73–78; S.Foul, 'The Canonical Approach of Brevard Childs,' *ET* 96 (1984–85), 173–176.

[162] Cf. R. Bloch, 'Midrash', *DBS* 5 (1957), 1271, 1274. For a somewhat different re-use of biblical traditions cf. G.W.E. Nickelsburg, *Resurrection, Immortality… in Intertestamental Judaism*, Cambridge MA 1972, 82–92.

[163] Cf. *B. T. Sanhedrin* 11a (= *T. Sota* 13:2); *Seder Olam Rabba* 30; cf. Leiman (note 10), 66.

The communities of Qumran and of Jesus, in which prophetic manifestations continued to be quite evident,[164] do not agree with the judgement of Josephus and rabbinic Judaism. In their respective ways they continued a canonical progression that resulted *inter alia* in a supplement to the twenty-two book canon received in pre-Maccabean Judaism. They did so not by an undefined 'openness' with regard to the canon but by the recognition of the prophetic inspiration and normative authority of certain of their own books. Although it is difficult to document explicitly, Qumran adherents very probably gave such recognition to the works of their Teacher. The Christian community clearly did so for certain of its writings, not only the New Testament as it was finally defined but also, from a very early time, individual books and traditions.

Conclusion

The community of Jesus, then, did not differ from other groups in Judaism in the Old Testament canon that it received, but it continued a hermeneutical process that inevitably brought into being a further supplement to the ancient canon. That hermeneutical process also brought about a radically new perception of the Old Testament itself. But this must be considered in chapter three below.

---

[164] I Thess 2:13; II Thess 2:15; Rom 16:26; Eph 3:3–5; Col 4:16; Acts 15:28f.; II Pet 3:15f. On prophetic manifestations at Qumran and in the New Testament cf. Ellis (note 107), 45–62. Cf. also Y. Yadin, *The Temple Scroll*, 3 vols., Jerusalem 1983, I, 73–82; 390ff., where *inter alia* Yahweh passages in the third person in the Old Testament are shifted to the first person. This suggests a prophetic consciousness on the part of the author and, in Yadin's words, 'the belief that the author... construed the Pentateuchal laws correctly' (390). Otherwise: B. Z. Wacholder, *The Dawn of Qumran*, Cincinnati OH 1983, 4, 30f., 229, who supposes that the Scroll presents a new and superior Torah to replace the Mosaic Torah.

II

Old Testament Quotations in the New: A Brief History of the Research

Introduction

Quotations appear in the New Testament from many sources, including non-canonical Jewish writings,[1] Christian and classical sources.[2] But they are overwhelmingly quotations from the Old Testament, which occur some 250 times[3] or, if allusions are included, over 2500 times.[4] Many passages are cited more than once, giving a somewhat smaller total number of cited Old Testament texts.[5] On the other hand some citations may merge two or more passages but be counted as one. According to H. B. Swete specific quotations total about 160 references, largely from the Pentateuch (51), Isaiah (38) and the Psalms (40) and, following Swete and L. Venard, they may be classified as follows: Synoptic Gospels 46 (46), John 12 (14), Acts 23 (24), Paul 78 (88), Hebrews 28 (30).[6] No explicit Old Testament citations occur in Philippians, Colossians, 1 and 2 Thessalonians, Titus, Philemon, 1–3 John, Jude and Revelation. Other General Epistles contain very few.[7] Of the many allusions only a small

---

[1] For example, I Enoch 1:9 in Jude 14f. Cf. E. Nestle-K. Aland, *Novum Testamentum Graece*, Stuttgart [26]1979, 775.

[2] For example, Acts 15:23–29; I Cor 15:33. Cf. Nestle-Aland (note 1), 769–775.

[3] Cf. Nestle-Aland (note 1), [25]1960, 658–671.

[4] Nestle-Aland (note 1), 739–769.

[5] Cf. H. B. Swete, *An Introduction to the Old Testament in Greek*, Cambridge 1914, 386.

[6] Swete (note 5); L. Venard, 'Citations de l'ancient Testament dans le Nouveau Testament,' *DBS* II (1934), 24–28. The numbers in parentheses represent Venard's count.

[7] The quotations are listed, with columnar comparisons with the Septuagint and with the Masoretic Text, by G. L. Archer and G. Chirichigno (*Old Testament Quotations in the New Testament*, Chicago 1983), W. Dittmar (*Vetus Testamentum in Novo*, 2 vols., Göttingen 1903), C. H. Toy (*Quotations in the New Testament*, New York 1884) and D. M. Turpie (*The Old Testament in the New*, London 1868). Although textually dated (except Archer) and in some ways flawed, these studies remain useable tools.

Other books provide New Testament and Septuagint parallels of quotations in Paul (Ellis, Koch) and Acts (Clarke); for John, Freed offers comparisons of the Septuagint, the Masoretic Text, Targums and Qumran Texts. Cf. E. E. Ellis, *Paul's Use of the Old Testament*, Grand Rapids [5]1991 (1957); D. A. Koch, *Die Schrift als Zeuge des Evangeliums:... zum Verständnis der Schrift bei Paulus*, Tübingen 1986; W. K. L. Clarke, 'The Use of the Old Testament in Acts,' *The Beginnings of Christianity*, edd. F. J. F. Jackson and K. Lake, 5 vols., London 1921–1933, II, 66–105; E. D. Freed, *Old Testament Quotations in the Gospel of John*, Leiden 1965.

number give an express reference to an Old Testament text. Some of these references are found in one Gospel but are lacking in the parallel passage of another Gospel;[8] others are introduced by a copyist.[9]

Such is the phenomenon of Old Testament quotations in the New. It has attracted the attention and spurred the investigation of Christian writers from the early church until the present day. The state of the art in contemporary New Testament studies will be considered at length in the following chapter. It can be best appreciated, I believe, if one has some understanding of the history of the research of the subject. To that prior question we now turn our attention.

A Sketch of the History of the Research

From the Second through the Nineteenth Century

The Patristic Church

In the early centuries Christian authors, for example, those in the theological schools of Antioch and Alexandria, raised questions about the applications of the Old Testament in the New.[10] In Gaul Irenaeus addressed the matter of the textual background of the citations and found it in the Septuagint, which he regarded as inspired.[11] Jerome of Bethlehem, who rejected its inspiration, saw the matter differently:

'Wherever the Seventy agree with the Hebrew, the Apostles took their quotations from that translation. But where [the two] disagree, they set down in Greek what they had found in the Hebrew.'[12]

Augustine of Hippo, who recognized the inspired if secondary character of the Septuagint, reconciled its differences with the Hebrew text in a hermeneutical fashion:

---

[8] Cf. Matt 21:4f. with Mark 11:3; Luke 19:31.

[9] Cf. Luke 9:54 in the NKJV and in the RSV.

[10] Cf. F.W. Farrar, *History of Interpretation*, London 1886, 218; R.M. Grant and D. Tracy, *A Short History of the Interpretation of the Bible. Revised Edition.* London 1984, 63–72.

[11] Irenaeus, *Adv. Haer.* 3, 21, 3.

[12] Jerome, *Apologia contra Rufinum* 2, 34.

'[The Septuagint at Jonah 3:4 is] not saying something against the sense [of the Hebrew], but... in another signification... It is as if the Septuagint intended to stir the reader to look further into the matter than mere history.'[13]

In a similar fashion Irenaeus regarded the Septuagint reading παρθένος ('virgin') in Isa 7:14 as a 'just interpretation of what had been truly prophesied.'[14]

These examples may serve to show that the problems of the text and of the application, ever the two crucial issues for New Testament quotations, were brought together very early.[15] After the Reformation both received renewed and intensive investigation.

The Sixteenth through the Eighteenth Centuries

Studies in the sixteenth and seventeenth centuries were mainly concerned with publishing the biblical data. In 1550 Robert Stephanus gave an abbreviated list of quotations in his edition of the Greek New Testament (Paris [3]1550) and, forty years later, Johannes Drusius (van der Driesche) set out in a four-column arrangement the Old Testament (Hebrew, Latin) and the New Testament (Latin, Greek) parallels with critical notes on variant readings.[16] In the following century Ludwig Cappellus and Jakob Alting (on Matt 1–12) pursued similar tasks and discussed textual variations that posed significant problems.[17]

William Whiston, taking a new departure in the early eighteenth century, sought to justify the textual form of New Testament quotations by arguing that they were identical with Old Testament Greek and Hebrew texts of the first century but that the Jews, because of their opposition to Christianity, soon altered their manuscripts and produced the present textual discrepancies.[18] In support of his thesis he pointed to the different biblical texts displayed by Philo, the Samaritan Pentateuch and Josephus, who probably had official texts from the temple in

---

[13] Augustine, *De Civ. Dei* 18, 42–44.

[14] Irenaeus, *Adv. Haer.* 3, 21, 4.

[15] Cf. also B. Smalley, *The Bible in the Middle Ages*, Oxford [2]1952, 101, 138, 165, 350 ff., who, however, is more concerned with biblical interpretation in general.

[16] J. Drusius, *Parallela Sacra*, Franeker 1588, reprinted in *Tractatium Bibliocorum Volumen Prius...*, London 1660, VIII, 1266–1326.

[17] L. Cappellus, *Critica Sacra*, Paris 1650, 53–67; J. Alting, *Operum Tome II, Appendix*, Amsterdam 1685.

[18] W. Whiston, *An Essay Toward Restoring the True Text of the Old Testament*, London 1722, 220–280.

Jerusalem.[19] Seven years later, wondering 'why so pernicious a book has escaped so long without an answer,' M. Marcus, a Jewish Christian, translated J. G. Carpzov's reply. In Carpzov's view textual variations from the Hebrew in New Testament citations were an interpretation or elaboration:

'[They were] sometimes the application of a testimony to the present purpose, which might be properly made by changing the words of the prophecy a little; sometimes a synonymous expression wanted to be unfolded and explained.'[20]

Whiston's remarks on several diverse first-century textual traditions, in addition to the Septuagint and the masoretic texts, and Carpzov's conclusion that texts may have been altered for hermeneutical purposes or contemporary applications, were important for subsequent research. These two observations influenced, respectively, the later eighteenth-century authors, Thomas Randolph and Henry Owen. Randolph allowed that some quotations may have been taken from 'other translations or paraphrases.' Owen argued,

'[The New Testament writers generally followed the Septuagint but] might assume the liberty of altering some words the better to express the sense of the original... For it is the *sense* and *meaning* and not the *words* of it that is truly and properly Scripture.'[21]

In 1713 G. Surenhusius published perhaps the most significant contribution of the period.[22] Besides extensively discussing the issues of the textual variants and the applications of quotations, he examined the introductory formulas and the practices of combining quotations and of citing seriatim from the Law, the Prophets and the Writings. In all of these matters he demonstrated widespread agreements of method with the rabbinic writings. His more comprehensive approach continued in the works of J. G. Major and of Henry Owen.[23]

A. A. Sykes addressed the problems of typology and the meaning of the formula ἵνα πληρωθῇ ('that it might be fulfilled'), concluding that typology represents 'only an analogy of things of a general likeness.' He rejected any 'double completion' of prophecy and regarded many 'fulfilments' in

---

[19] Josephus, *Vita* 75; cf. Whiston (note 18), 414–421.

[20] J. G. Carpzov, *A Defense of the Hebrew Bible*, London 1729, 111. So also, J. Major, *De dictorum Veteris Testamenti in Novo allegatione*, London 1729.

[21] H. Owen, *Modes of Quotation Used by the Evangelical Writers*, London 1789, 10; T. Randolph, *The Prophecies and Other Texts Cited in the New Testament*, London 1782, 26f.

[22] G. Surenhusius, ספר המשוה *sive* βίβλος καταλλαγῆς, Amsterdam 1713.

[23] Cf. Major (note 20); Owen (note 21).

the Gospels and Acts as 'an accommodation of Scriptural language to a present occasion.'[24] With better insight Thomas Sherlock tied the twofold sense of Old Testament prophecies to the two covenants (Gal 3:17).[25]

The Nineteenth Century

The issue of prophecy continued to be important during the nineteenth century. In a brief review of German research F. A. G. Tholuck stated the exegetical problem:[26] To establish the propriety of the New Testament usage, one must show either that the New Testament application of the text was the original sense or that there was a double sense, a ὑπόνοια. He granted, however, that πληροῦν ('to fulfill') in Matt 2:15 might mean only 'to illustrate;' that unidentifiable quotations, for example, Matt 2:23, might refer to the general sense of Scripture and that variations of sense[27] might represent a generalizing application. In such matters he was in agreement with Leonard Woods who, in turn, was following the eighteenth-century author, A. A. Sykes.[28] These writers were offering expedients, however, that were generally found to be inadequate.

Also writing at mid-century, Patrick Fairbairn turned again to typological exegesis and contended that it was not necessarily based on a double sense:

'The Scripture fulfilled [for example, in Matthew 2:15 or John 19:36] was prophetical simply because the circumstance it recorded was typical.'[29]

Fairbairn was anticipated in these views by A. T. Hartmann and was generally followed by a number of scholars.[30] The distinction he drew

---

[24] A. A. Sykes, *An Essay Upon the Truth of the Christian Religion*, London 1725, 194, 211, 249.

[25] T. Sherlock, *The Use and Intent of Prophecy in the Several Ages of the World*, London 1728, 127–172 (reprint: New York 1978).

[26] August Tholuck, *Ueber die Citate des Alten Testaments im Neuen...*, Gotha ³1849, 1–66, 4f.; ET: 'The Citations of the Old Testament in the New,' *Bib Sac* 11 (1854), 568–616, 569.

[27] Compare, for example, II Cor 6:17f. with Isa 52:11 and II Sam 7:14; Heb 12:6 with Prov 3:11f.

[28] Sykes (note 24); L. Woods, *Objections to the Inspiration of the Evangelists and Apostles*, London 1824.

[29] P. Fairbairn, *Typology of Scripture*, 2 vols. in 1, Grand Rapids 1953 (1847), I, 110.

[30] For example, F. Gardiner, *The Old Testament and the New Testament in their Mutual Relations*, London 1887, 262–273; F. Johnson, *Quotations of the New Testament from the Old*, London 1896, 186–198. Cf. A. T. Hartmann, *Die enge Verbindung des Alten Testaments mit dem Neuen Testament*, Hamburg 1831, 731–768.

between a purely predictive and a typological understanding of prophecy (without denying the reality of either) was in the twentieth century to be sharpened.

Nineteenth-century scholars continued to address the textual problem. H.B. Swete, followed by F.H. Woods, demonstrated that the Septuagint was the principal source of New Testament quotations,[31] but they did not thereby resolve the problem of the textual differences. Other scholars, as William Whiston had earlier, sought to locate the origin of the variants in a first-century text no longer extant. Some supposed that it lay in an Aramaic 'people's Bible,'[32] others in oral targums.[33] Edwin Hatch considered their source to be in 'manuals... of extracts from the Old Testament.'[34] Also like Whiston, he suspected that some discrepancies were the alterations of Jewish scribes who wanted to avoid Christian interpretations. Franklin Johnson, however, justified the variants as the product of literary license. In Greco-Roman literature he found parallels for the New Testament practice of (1) exegetical paraphrase, (2) pointer quotations 'designed to bring to mind the longer passages,' (3) summary and combined (i.e. merged) quotations and (4) a typological or double reference (not double sense) of a text. With this evidence in hand he concluded that such practices were the legitimate tools of any writer in antiquity.[35]

The Twentieth Century: 1900–1950

In the later nineteenth century attention had been given to a book by book analysis of quotations in the New Testament (Clemen) or a portion of it, particularly Matthew (Massebieau), the four Gospels (Haupt) and Paul's letters (Kautzsch).[36] This continued in the first half of the twentieth

---

[31] Swete (note 5), 381–405, 392; F.H. Woods, 'Quotations,' *HDB* 4 (1902), 184–188, 186f.

[32] Eduard Böhl, *Forschungen nach einer Volksbibel*, Wien 1873.

[33] Toy (note 7).

[34] E. Hatch, *Essays in Biblical Greek*, Oxford 1889, 136f., 203–214.

[35] Johnson (note 30), 64, passim; similarly, J. Scott, *Principles of New Testament Quotations*, Edinburgh 1875.

[36] A. Clemen, *Der Gebrauch des Alten Testaments in den neutestamentlichen Schriften*, Gütersloh 1895; E. Massebieau, *Examen des citations de l'Ancien Testament dans l'Evangile selon Saint Matthieu*, Paris 1885; E. Haupt, *Die alttestamentlichen Citate in den vier Evangelien erördert*, Colberg 1871; E. Kautzsch, *De veteris testamenti locis a Paulo Apostolo allegatis*, Leipzig 1869.

century with works on the Pauline Epistles (Michel), on Acts (Cerfaux, Clarke), on Hebrews (Harder, van der Ploeg)[37] and on Revelation,[38] as well as on Jesus' use of the Old Testament (Kähler, Oepke, T.W. Manson) and on the use of certain biblical texts by the early church (H.W. Wolff).[39] The two continual issues were given renewed emphasis: the origin of textual variations and the interpretation of Old Testament prophecies.

The 'Testimony Book' and Targumic Translations

The investigation of textual differences continued in traditional patterns (Atkinson)[40] and also introduced two new topics, the hypothesis of a 'testimony book' (Harris)[41] and the argument that Greek (as well as Aramaic) targums were the literary form of the earliest Bible translations (Kahle).[42]

A 'testimony book' was inferred from the following considerations.

---

[37] O. Michel, *Paulus und seine Bibel*, Darmstadt [2]1972 (1929); L. Cerfaux, 'Citations scriptuaires et tradition textuelle dans le livre des Actes,' *Aux sources de la tradition chrétienne*, ed. O. Cullmann et al., Neuchatel 1950, 43–51; Clarke (note 7); G. Harder, 'Die Septuagintazitate des Hebraerbriefs,' *Theologia Viatorum*, ed. M. Albertz et al., München 1939, 33–52; J. van der Ploeg, 'L'exégèse de l'ancien testament dans l'épitre aux Hébreux,' *RB* 54 (1947), 187–228. For other literature on Hebrews cf. M. Barth, 'The Old Testament in Hebrews: An Essay on Biblical Hermeneutics,' *Current Issues in New Testament Interpretation*, ed. W. Klassen, New York 1962, 264f.

[38] H.B. Swete, 'Use of the Old Testament and Other Literature,' *The Apocalypse of St. John*, London [3]1909, cxl–clviii.

[39] M. Kähler, *Jesus und das Alte Testament*, Neukirchen 1965 (1907); A. Oepke, *Jesus und das Alte Testament*, Leipzig 1938; T.W. Manson, 'The Old Testament in the Teaching of Jesus,' *BJRL* 34 (1952), 312–332; H.W. Wolff, *Jesaja 53 im Urchristentum*, Giessen 1984 ([3]1952).

[40] B.F.C. Atkinson, 'The Textual Background of the Use of the Old Testament by the New,' *JTVI* 79 (1947), 39–70; cf. K.J. Thomas, 'The Old Testament Citations in Hebrews,' *NTS* 11 (1964–65), 303–325; G. Howard, 'Hebrews and the Old Testament Quotations,' *NT* 10 (1968), 208–216. The bearing of textual variations on biblical authority also has continued in discussion; cf. M. Silva, 'The New Testament Use of the Old Testament,' *Scripture and Truth*, ed. D.A. Carson, Grand Rapids 1983, 147–165 and the literature cited.

[41] J.R. Harris, *Testimonies*, 2 vols., Cambridge 1916, 1920; cf. N.J. Hommes, *Het Testimoniaboek*, Amsterdam 1935. Cf. Ellis (note 7), 98–107: 'The "Testimony Book" Hypothesis.'

[42] P. Kahle, *The Cairo Geniza*, Oxford [2]1959 (1947); cf. Ellis (note 7) 16–20: 'The Problem of the Septuagint.' For criticisms see note 50.

1. Some recurring New Testament and patristic quotations agree with one another in contrast to any extant Old Testament text.

2. At times they represent a combination of the same Old Testament passages, supporting the same argument and grouped around some common key-word such as 'stone' (1 Peter 2:6–8).

3. Since these quotations occur in documents that are very likely independent of each other, for example, Romans 9:25, 33 and 1 Peter 2:6–10, they are most likely derived from a common source.

Building upon these data and upon the suggestion above of Edwin Hatch, Rendel Harris concluded that the source of such citations was a precanonical Christian collection of Old Testament texts, that is, a 'testimony book,' consisting of anti-Jewish polemic.[43] While his thesis was criticized,[44] it received striking support from the presence of testimonies among the Dead Sea Scrolls discovered in 1947 and succeeding years.[45] If there was no 'testimony book,' there were probably written collections of testimony texts used in common by Christians for polemic and for the proclamation of messianic claims for Jesus. What was the source and rationale for the peculiar and common textual variants in these collections?

Aramaic targums, interpretive and sometimes contemporizing paraphrases, appear to have been the earliest translations of the Hebrew Old Testament. They were rendered orally in the synagogue services[46] and some, at least, were in written form by the first century B. C.[47] According to some scholars targums developed from simple translation and paraphrase to a more developed and standardized form and sometimes had more extensive midrashic, i. e. commentary-type elaboration in their earlier than in their later recensions.[48] Did perhaps Greek translations of the Old Testament arise in the same way?

---

[43] Harris (note 41); Hatch (note 34).

[44] Cf. T.W. Manson, 'The Argument from Prophecy,' *JTS* 46 (1945) 129–136; C.H. Dodd, *According to the Scriptures*, London 1952, 26: '[The] evidence... is not sufficient to prove so formidable a literary enterprise at so early a date.'

[45] 4QTest; 4QFlor.

[46] *M. Megillah* 4:4. Cf. Martin McNamara, *Targum and Testament*, Grand Rapids 1972, 48 ff.

[47] The Targum of Job found at Qumran is dated to c. 100 B.C. Cf. McNamara (note 45), 63, 182–189; J.A. Fitzmyer, *A Wandering Aramean*, Missoula MT 1979, 161–182, 165 ff.

[48] For example, A. Díez Macho, 'The Recently Discovered Palestinian Targum,'

In a radical revision of established opinion Paul Kahle argued that different textual traditions found in the Greek Old Testament, i.e. the Septuagint, also did not derive from an archetype but originated instead from a number of written Greek targums used in the synagogues of the Diaspora.[49] He concluded that the later Septuagint was an imperfect unity imposed upon an original diversity.

His view has been disputed,[50] but it remains probable that at least some Greek Old Testament textual traditions had a targumic basis. If so, the phenomena of textual variation and theological application, the two core problems of quotations of the Old Testament in the New, were from the earliest pre-Christian times aspects of one 'targumizing' process. Both Greek and Aramaic textual variations, then, represented not only scribal errors or different text-types but sometimes, more significantly, deliberate interpretations with a theological design.[51] The interpretive aspect was elaborated in the Qumran biblical commentaries, i.e. midrashim (see below). Thus, the relationship of midrash and targum and its bearing on the nature of New Testament quotations, including the testimony texts, became important questions that the subsequent research could not avoid.[52]

Typological Exegesis

'[The] Scripture is not a text-book teaching conceptual truths but rather a document of an historical process...'[53] Taking this salvation-history

---

Congress Volume 1959 (SVT 7), ed. G.W. Anderson et al., Leiden 1960, 222–246, 237, 244. Cf. Kahle (note 42), 197.

[49] Kahle (note 42), 236, 247.

[50] Cf., for example, E. Ulrich, 'Horizons of Old Testament Textual Research...,' *CBQ* 46 (1984), 619–624; S. Jellicoe, *The Septuagint and Modern Study*, Oxford 1968, 59–63; F.M. Cross, *The Ancient Library of Qumran*, Garden City NY [2]1961, 169–181; P. Katz, *Philo's Bible*, Cambridge 1950, 95ff. But see S. Talmon, 'The Textual Study of the Bible...,' *Qumran and the History of the Biblical Text*, edd. F.M. Cross and S. Talmon, Cambridge MA 1975, 325 (for his comment see above, 48).

[51] For the same phenomenon in the rewriting of the transmitted Hebrew Old Testament see Chapter 1 above, 47–50.

[52] Cf. E.E. Ellis, *Prophecy and Hermeneutic in Early Christianity (WUNT* 18), Tübingen 1978, 188–197.

[53] J.C.K. von Hofmann, *Interpreting the Bible*, Minneapolis 1972 (1880), 204. One may ask whether this way of stating the matter is not a false dichotomy, but von Hofmann was responding to the heirs of J.P. Gabler for whom 'truth' existed only in the non-historical realm of 'universal ideas.' J.P. Gabler, 'On the Proper Distinction Between Biblical and Dogmatic Theology' (1787), in *Kleiner theologische Schriften*, Ulm

principle of J.C.K. von Hofmann, Leonhard Goppelt sought to establish the definitive marks of typological exegesis:

1. In contrast to allegorical exegesis, with its indifference to the historical and literal sense of the text, typology regards historicity and the literal sense as the foundation on which the meaning of the text rests. While allegorical exegesis views the words and concepts of the Old Testament as metaphors hiding a deeper meaning (ὑπόνοια), the typological approach treats them 'as a true, though merely provisional redemptive history...' (202).[54]

2. In contrast to the history-of-religions school, which interpreted the New Testament from parallels adduced from various religions, typological exegesis seeks to understand the New Testament situations through a particular history, the salvation-history of Israel as presented in the Old Testament. Thus the New Testament writers viewed their own time as a midline segment in the continuing historical unfolding of God's purpose that began in the Old Testament. From those events they discovered the meaning of the contemporary time of salvation, which was their primary interest. Similarly, they regarded present events of redemption as typological prophecies of the future development and consummation of salvation-history.[55]

3. In contrast to haggadic midrash (see below), typology is not a systematic hermeneutical method but a 'spiritual approach' and perspective. Like the haggada of the rabbis, it brings the text into the present, but it does so, not by symbolic and homiletic explanations, but by appropriating the prophetic and representational character of Old Testament persons, events and institutions.[56]

4. As the predominant method of New Testament biblical interpretation, typology appears not only in Old Testament citations but also in the Christian community's total representation of itself and of its mission. Each typology is constituted by two characteristics, historical correspond-

---

1831, 179–198, 192; ET in *SJT* 33 (1980), 134–144. Cf. E. E. Ellis, 'Historical-Literary Criticism – After Two Hundred Years,' *Proceedings of [a Debate] on Biblical Inerrancy*, edd. M. Ashcraft et al., Nashville 1987, 411–421, 411; idem, *The Making of the New Testament Documents*, forthcoming.

[54] L. Goppelt, *TYPOS: The Typological Interpretation of the Old Testament in the New*, Grand Rapids 1982 (1939), 12, 17f., 201–205; GT: 13, 18f., 243–249.

[55] Goppelt (note 54), 195ff., 200, 205; GT: 236ff., 242, 248f.; cf. von Hofmann (note 53), 169–180, 223–236.

[56] Goppelt (note 54), 30f., 152, 198, 201f.; GT: 33, 183, 239, 243f.

ence and escalation or 'heightening' *(Steigerung)*, by which the divinely ordered prefigurement finds a complement in the subsequent and greater event.[57]

In a masterful essay Rudolf Bultmann identified the origin of typology in a cyclical-repetition view of history (cf. Barn 6:13) and distinguished it from the salvation-history, promise-fulfilment foundation of Old Testament prophecy.[58] While the two were already combined in Judaism, Bultmann argued that some New Testament typology, for example, Adam/Christ (Rom 5:14) was not a heightening of salvation-history but cyclical-repetitions, parallels and contrasts between the primal time and the end time. He therefore rejected Goppelt's conclusion that salvation-history is constitutive for New Testament typology. However, against Bultmann, it must be said that the recapitulation element in New Testament typology is never mere repetition and is always combined with a change of key in which some aspects of the type are not carried over and some are intensified (see below). Exegetically Goppelt made the better case and provided an important frame of reference for the subsequent interpretation of many New Testament quotations.

The Twentieth Century: 1950–1990

Since the middle of the twentieth century writers have continued to treat the subject of Old Testament quotations in the New Testament as a whole,[59] in the teachings of Jesus[60] and in the respective books, for

---

[57] Goppelt (note 54), 198f., 202. Cf. W.G. Kümmel, 'Heilsgeschichte im Neuen Testament?' *Heilsgeschehen und Geschichte*, 2 vols., Marburg 1965, 1978, II, 157–176.

[58] R. Bultmann, *Exegetica*, Tübingen 1967, 369–380 = *TLZ* 75 (1950), 205–212.

[59] E. g. D. A. Carson, ed., *Scripture Citing Scripture*, Cambridge 1988, 1–21 (I. H. Marshall); A. T. Hanson, *The Living Utterances of God: The New Testament Exegesis of the Old*, London 1983; R. Longenecker, *Biblical Exegesis in the Apostolic Period*, Grand Rapids 1975; H. M. Shires, *Finding the Old Testament in the New*, Philadelphia 1974; J. A. Fitzmyer, 'The Use of Explicit Old Testament Quotations in the Qumran Literature and in the New Testament,' *Essays on the Semitic Background of the New Testament*, Missoula 1974, 3–58; M. P. Miller, 'Targum, Midrash and the Use of the Old Testament in the New Testament,' *JSJ* 2 (1971) 29–82 (with a survey of previous research); M. Black, 'The Theological Appropriation of the Old Testament by the New Testament,' *SJT* 39 (1986), 1–17.

[60] E. g. O. Betz and W. Grimm, *Jesus und das Danielbuch*, 2 vols., Frankfurt 1985; W. Grimm, *Die Verkündigung Jesu und Deuterojesaja*, Frankfurt 1981; R. T. France, *Jesus and the Old Testament*, London 1971; Manson (note 39).

example, the Gospels,[61] the Pauline Epistles,[62] Matthew,[63] Mark,[64] Luke,[65] John,[66] Acts,[67] Romans,[68] I Corinthians,[69] II Corinthians,[70]

[61] E.g. J.A. Sanders, '... Psalm 118 and [Jesus' entrance] to Jerusalem,' *Early Jewish and Christian Exegesis*, ed. C.A. Evans, Atlanta 1987, 179–190; D.J. Moo, *The Old Testament in the Gospel Passion Narratives*, Sheffield UK 1983; J.H. Reumann, 'Psalm 22 at the Cross,' *Int* 28 (1974), 39–58; H. Gese, 'Psalm 22 und das Neue Testament,' *Vom Sinai zum Zion*, München 1974, 180–201; J.W. Doeve, *Jewish Hermeneutics in the Synoptic Gospels and Acts*, Assen 1954.

[62] E.g. R.B. Hays, *Echoes of Scripture in the Letters of Paul*, New Haven 1989; Carson (note 59), 265–291 (D.M. Smith); Koch (note 7) and the literature cited; A.T. Hanson, *Studies in Paul's Technique and Theology*, London 1974; Ellis (note 7); Michel (note 37); idem, 'Zum Thema: Paulus und seine Bibel,' *WW* 2 (1972), 114–126; P. Vielhauer, 'Paulus und das Alte Testament,' *Studien zur Geschichte und Theologie der Reformation*, ed. L. Abramowski, Neukirchen 1969, 33–62.

[63] E.g. Carson (note 59) 205–219 (G.N. Stanton); P. Sigal, *The Halakah of Jesus of Nazareth According to the Gospel of Matthew*, Lanham MD 1986; G.M.S. Prabhu, *The Formula Quotations in the Infancy Narrative of Matthew*, Rome 1976; L. Hartman, 'Scriptural Exegesis in the Gospel of St. Matthew...,' *L'Evangile selon Matthieu*, ed. M. Didier, Gembloux 1972, 131–152. R.H. Gundry, *The Use of the Old Testament in St. Matthew's Gospel*, Leiden 1967; K. Stendahl, *The School of St. Matthew and its Use of the Old Testament*, Lund 1969 (1954).

[64] E.g. Carson (note 59), 220–230 (M.D. Hooker); H.C. Kee, 'The Function of Scriptural Quotations and Allusions in Mark 11–16,' *Jesus und Paulus*, edd. E.E. Ellis and E. Grässer, Göttingen 1975, 165–188; A. Suhl, *Die Funktion der alttestamentlichen Zitate und Anspielungen im Markusevangelium*, Gütersloh 1965.

[65] E.g. Carson (note 59), 231–244 (C.K. Barrett); D.L. Bock, *Proclamation from Prophecy*, Sheffield 1987; M. Rese, *Alttestamentliche Motive in der Christologie des Lukas*, Gütersloh 1969; T. Holtz, ... *[A]lttestamentlichen Zitate bei Lukas*, Berlin 1968.

[66] E.g. Carson (note 59), 245–264 (Carson); C.A. Evans, '... The Use of the Old Testament in the Fourth Gospel,' in Evans (note 61), 221–236; A.T. Hanson, *The New Testament Interpretation of Scripture*, London 1980, 97–109 [Jn 1:14–18], 110–121, 157–176; G. Reim, *Studien zum alttestamentlichen Hintergrund des Johannesevangeliums*, Cambridge 1974.

[67] E.g. Carson (note 59), 231–244 (C.K. Barrett); F.F. Bruce 'Paul's Use of the Old Testament in Acts,' *Tradition and Interpretation in the New Testament*, ed. G.F. Hawthorne with O. Betz, Grand Rapids and Tübingen 1987, 71–79; J. Jervell, '... Zum lukanischen Verständnis des Alten Testamentes,' *Die Mitten des Neuen Testaments*, ed. U. Luz, Göttingen 1983, 79–96; M. Rese, 'Die Funktion der alttestamentlichen Zitate...,' *Les Actes des Apôtres*, ed. J. Kremer, Gembloux 1978, 61–79.

[68] E.g. H. Hübner, *Gottes Ich und Israel. Zum Schriftgebrauch des Paulus in Römer 9–11*, Göttingen 1984; W.R. Stegner, 'Rom 9:6–29 – A Midrash,' *JSNT* 22 (1984), 37–52; R. Vicent, 'Derash homiletico en Romanos 9–11,' *Sales* 42 (1980), 751–788; R. Scroggs, 'Paul as Rhetorician: Two Homilies in Romans [1–4; 9–11],' *Jews, Greeks and Christians*, ed. R. Hamerton-Kelly, Leiden 1976, 271–298; Ellis, 'Exegetical Patterns in 1 Corinthians and Romans' (note 52), 213–220.

[69] E.g. O. Betz, 'Der gekreuzigte Christus,... (Der alttestamentliche Hintergrund von 1. Korinther 1–2),' in Hawthorne (note 67), 195–215; E.E. Ellis, 'Traditions in 1

Galatians,[71] Hebrews,[72] James,[73] I Peter,[74] II Peter,[75] I–III John,[76] Jude[77] and Revelation.[78] They have also investigated the use of particular Old Testament books or passages in the New Testament.[79]

In recent decades three topics have attracted special interest: the relationship of New Testament quotations to midrash, including the exegesis at Qumran, the use of testimonies and the significance of typology. Each topic addresses the two perennial problems of biblical citations: their textual nature and their exegetical application. And each has pointed the way to a solution of them by revealing that in many instances the two issues are really one: the textual question itself becomes a hermeneutical question.

Corinthians,' *NTS* 32 (1986), 490f. on I Cor 2:6–16; 10:1–13; W. A. Meeks, '… Midrash and Paraenesis in 1 Corinthians 10.1–22,' *JSNT* 16 (1982), 64–78.

[70] E. g. on II Cor 3:7–18: W.J. Dumbrell in *God Who is Rich in Mercy*, ed. P. T. O'Brien, Homebush West, Australia 1986, 179–194; E. Richard in *RB* 88 (1981), 340–367; see J. A. Hickling in *NTS* 21 (1975), 380–395; S. Schultz in *ZNTW* 49 (1958), 1–30.

[71] E. g. C. K. Barrett, 'The Allegory of Abraham, Sarah and Hagar…,' *Essays on Paul*, London 1982, 154–170; F. Pastor, 'Alegoria o tipología en Gal. 4, 21–31,' *Est Bib* 34 (1975), 113–119; P. Borgen, *Bread from Heaven*, Leiden 1965, 48–51 (on Gal 3:6–29).

[72] E. g. Carson (note 59), 292–302 (A. T. Hanson); J. Swetnam, *Jesus and Isaac:… Hebrews in the Light of the Aqedah*, Rome 1981; J. C. McCullough, 'The Old Testament Quotations in Hebrews,' *NTS* 26 (1980), 363–379; G. Hughes, *Hebrews and Hermeneutics*, Cambridge 1979, 47–66; H. J. B. Combrink, '… Old Testament Citations in… Hebrews,' *Neot* 5 (1971), 22–36; F. Schröger, *Der Verfasser des Hebräerbriefes als Schriftausleger*, Regensburg 1968; Howard (note 40); Thomas (note 40); M. Barth, 'The Old Testament in Hebrews,' *Current Issues in New Testament Interpretation*, ed. W. Klassen, New York 1962, 53–78; S. J. Kistemacher, *The Psalm Citations in the Epistle to the Hebrews*, Amsterdam 1961.

[73] E. g. Carson (note 59), 303–317 (R. Bauckham).

[74] E. g. W. L. Schutter, *Hermeneutic and Composition in I Peter*, Tübingen 1989; Bauckham (note 73); N. Hillyer, '"Rock-Stone" Imagery in I Peter,' *TB* 22 (1971), 58–81.

[75] E. g. E. E. Ellis, *The Making of the New Testament Documents*, forthcoming; Bauckham (note 73).

[76] E. g. Carson (note 59), 245–264 (Carson).

[77] E. g. Ellis (note 52), 221–236; Bauckham (note 73).

[78] E. g. Carson (note 59), 318–336 (G. K. Beale). Cf. R. H. Charles, *The Revelation of St. John*, 2 vols., Edinburgh 1920, I, lxv–lxxxii.

[79] E. g. D. Juel, *Messianic Exegesis*, Philadelphia 1988 (on II Sam 7; Psalms; Isa 42; 53 and Dan 7); S. Kim, '… Zechariah in the Self-Identification of Jesus,' in Hawthorne (note 67), 134–148; Betz (note 60); Grimm (note 60); L. C. Allen, 'Psalm 45:7–8 (6–7) in Old and New Testament Settings,' *Christ the Lord*, ed. H. H. Rowden, Leicester 1982, 220–242; Sanders (note 61); Reumann (note 61); Gese (note 61);

New Testament Quotations and Midrash

As an earlier scholar noted,[80] Old Testament writers utilized the language of prior Scriptures in their citations and allusions.[81] They also employed successively the same themes, for example, Israel as the unfaithful wife, as the unproductive vine and as the rescued flock. Sometimes they updated or reapplied earlier biblical phraseology[82] or ideas[83] to a current situation.[84]

According to Renée Bloch, who followed up these insights, two traits, reference to Scripture and updating or contemporization, were the very soul of the midrashic procedure.[85] Such contemporizing and interpretive glossing occurred not only in the employment of prior Scriptures by Old Testament (and later) writers but also in successive redactions of the Hebrew text, in the Greek Septuagint and in the Aramaic Targums. Thus, in Isa 9:12 (9:11 LXX) 'Aramaeans and Philistines' became in the Septuagint the contemporary 'Syrians and Greeks.' In Exod 4:24–26 'Lord' became in the Septuagint and Targum Onkelos 'angel of the Lord,' and 'the blood' was given an explicit sacrificial merit. The contemporizing exegetical changes in these translations warranted calling both the Septuagint and the Targum a 'rewriting of the Bible.'[86]

Such *'implicit midrash,'* that is, interpretive paraphrase of the Old Testament text, was distinguished from 'explicit midrash,'[87] that is, a biblical quotation plus commentary on it. It occurred not only in paraphrastic renderings of the Old Testament but also when an explicit midrash was disassembled in transmission, leaving only the commentary. For exam-

---

D.M. Hay, *Glory at the Right Hand: Ps 110 in Early Christianity*, Nashville 1973; Wolff (note 39).

[80] A. Robert, 'Littéraires (Genres),' *DBS* V (1957), 411–421.

[81] Pss 78; 105–106. Cf. Hos 12; Mal 2:10–17.

[82] Cf. Jer 32:18 with Exod 20:5f.; Dan 11:30 with Num 24:24.

[83] Cf. Jer 7:21f. with Am 5:25ff.

[84] Cf. Jer 48:45 with Num 21:28. The earlier accounts were apparently regarded by the later writers, even in the days of Hosea (cf. 12:3ff., 12f.), as canonical in the sense of a divine and normative authority. Whether their canonical status had been recognized by a specific communal action is another question. See above, 39f., 46–50.

[85] R. Bloch, 'Midrash,' *Approaches to Ancient Judaism*, ed. W.S. Green, Missoula MT 1978, 29–50, 32f. = *DBS* V (1957), 1263–1281, 1266. Cf. Doeve (note 61), 116.

[86] So, G. Vermes, *Scripture and Tradition in Judaism*, Leiden 1961, 179; cf. idem, 'Bible and Midrash,' *The Cambridge History of the Bible*, 3 vols., ed. P.R. Ackroyd, Cambridge 1963–70, I (1970), 199–231. He elaborated Bloch's thesis.

[87] By M. Gertner, 'Midrashim in the New Testament,' *JSS* 7 (1962), 267–292. He termed it 'covert' midrash. See below, 91–100.

ple, such is the case in Lk 15:3–6 where the parable seems to be the residual 'commentary' of an earlier explicit midrash.[88] In a number of investigations implicit midrash was found to be present in many New Testament passages,[89] including the Infancy Narratives,[90] the Temptation,[91] Mk 5[92] and 13;[93] II Cor 3.[94]

Although the question is disputed,[95] *explicit midrash* has also been identified in the New Testament. In the well-argued thesis of Peter Borgen, such a pattern was demonstrated in Jn 6:31–58 where the quotation of an initial Old Testament text (31) is followed by exposition and a subordinate quotation (45) and is concluded with an allusion to the initial text (58).[96] It was confirmed elsewhere in the New Testament and in Philo,[97] and it corresponded in considerable measure to a pattern that had been identified in the rabbinic writings as a 'proem midrash.'[98]

At about the same time a second midrash-pattern used in the later rabbinic writings, the *yelammedenu rabbenu* ('let our master teach us'), was also discerned in the New Testament by J. W. Bowker.[99] Following these breakthroughs, both patterns were detected in various New Testament

---

[88] I. e. on Ezek 34:11. Further, Mk 4:1–22 on Jer 4:3; Jn 10 on Ezek 34. Cf. Ellis (note 52), 162; Gertner (note 87).

[89] Cf. Bloch (note 85), 48f. (= 1279f.). Earlier, cf. G. Klein, 'Zur Erläuterung der Evangelien aus Talmud und Midrasch,' *ZNTW* 5 (1904), 144–153.

[90] E. g. Lk 1:76–79 on Num 6:24ff. Cf. Gertner (note 87), 268–271. S. Farris (*The Hymns of Luke's Infancy Narrative*, Sheffield UK 1985), like many others, recognizes the Old Testament 'background' of the hymns (e. g. 120f.) but rejects the designation 'midrash.' Somewhat differently: R. E. Brown, *The Birth of the Messiah*, Garden City NY 1977, 557–562.

[91] B. Gerhardsson, *The Testing of God's Son*, Lund 1966, 11ff., passim.

[92] Mk 5:1–20 on Isa 65:1–5. Cf. H. Sahlin, 'Die Perikope vom gerasenischen Besessenen...,' *ST* 18 (1964), 159–164.

[93] Mk 13 on Dan 7–9, 11–12. Cf. L. Hartmann, *Prophecy Interpreted*, Lund 1966.

[94] E. g. II Cor 3:16. Cf. Doeve (note 61), 98f.

[95] A. J. Saldarini, 'Judaism and the New Testament,' *The New Testament and its Modern Interpreters*, ed. E. J. Epp, Philadelphia 1989, 34–42, 44. He is also generally doubtful about the presence of implicit midrash in the New Testament.

[96] Borgen (note 71), 33–43, 51–54.

[97] Rom 4:1–22; Gal 3:6–29; Philo, *Leg Alleg.* III, 162–168. Cf. Borgen (note 71), 46–51.

[98] S. Maybaum, *Die ältesten Phasen in der Entwicklung der jüdischen Predigt*, Berlin 1901, 14–17.

[99] J. W. Bowker, 'Speeches in Acts: A Study in Proem and Yelammedenu Form,' *NTS* 14 (1967–68), 96–111. Cf. Ellis (note 52), 198ff.

passages.[100] While in the New Testament they exhibited many differences in detail from the rabbinic forms,[101] they had substantive correspondences that could not be coincidental and that pointed to a common root in first-century Jewish practice.

Using the above approach, midrash was defined not only in terms of form, that is, a cited text plus a commentary, but also in terms of content and procedure, that is, the reapplication of biblical language (e.g. Lk 1–2) or the contemporizing redaction of a biblical text (e.g. some parts of the Septuagint).[102] This broad definition was challenged by some scholars.[103] As a literary genre, they argued, 'midrash' of either an explicit or an implicit sort should be used only of writings that have a textually manifest intention to illumine a cited text. It should not be used for reapplications of biblical language or for contemporizing redactions.[104] However, in ancient Judaism the term designated an activity as well as a literary genre,[105] and the broader definition seems to accord best with the historical usage.[106]

Exegesis at Qumran and in the New Testament

Since 1947 the relationship of biblical exegesis in the Dead Sea Scrolls to citations in the New Testament has been given extensive treatment.[107] Of special interest has been an exegetical practice known as 'pesher' mid-

---

[100] Ellis (note 52), 154–159, 213–220, 247–253, passim. Cf. V. P. Branick, 'Source and Redaction Analysis of 1 Corinthians 1–3,' *JBL* 101 (1982), 251–269.

[101] See chapter 3 below, 97.

[102] Cf. E. Tov, 'The Septuagint,' *Compendia* II, 1 (1988), 173–178. Cf. also W. H. Brownlee, 'The Background of Biblical Interpretation at Qumran,' *Qumran*, ed. M. Delcor, Leuven 1978, 183–193.

[103] E.g. A. G. Wright in *CBQ* 28 (1966), 105–138, 417–457 (= *The Literary Genre Midrash*, New York 1967). Cf. R. Le Déaut, 'Apropos a Definition of Midrash,' *Int* 25 (1971) 259–282 (= *Bib* 50, 1969, 395–413).

[104] Wright (note 103), 451 f., *contra* Vermes (note 86).

[105] As Wright admitted (note 103), 456. Cf. Ben Sira 51:23; CD 20:6; 4QFlor 1:14; W. Bacher, *Die exegetische Terminologie der jüdischen Traditionsliteratur*, 2 vols. in 1, Darmstadt 1965 (1905), I, 103.

[106] Further on the problem cf. Ellis (note 52), 188–192. The restricted definition apparently reflected less a historical distinction than a current and practical interest.

[107] Brownlee (note 102); Ellis (note 52), 151–162, passim; O. Betz, *Offenbarung und Schriftforschung in der Qumransekte*, Tübingen 1960; Fitzmyer (note 59); F. F. Bruce, *Biblical Exegesis in the Qumran Texts*, Grand Rapids 1959. Cf. J. Schmitt, 'Qumrân et la Première Génération judéo-chrétienne,' in Delcor (note 102), 385–402.

rash, so named because the explanation of an Old Testament text is often preceded by the phrase, 'the interpretation' (פשר) or 'its interpretation (פשרו) concerns.' It may also use the equivalent formula, 'this is' (הוא = LXX, οὗτος [ἐστίν]).[108] 'Midrash pesher' has been defined in several ways. (1) By some it was understood to include all of the peculiarities of Qumran theology and hermeneutics and was thus, by definition, not to be found in the New Testament.[109] (2) It was also understood to be the interpretation of dreams and visions since it was used at Qumran for the interpretation of Scripture where dreams and visions were involved, particularly of Daniel (Elliger) and of other Old Testament prophets, who also received their revelations in this way (Silberman).[110] However, such a qualified definition became unsupportable when it was observed that the pesher formula was also used for interpreting words of Moses to whom God spoke not in dreams but 'mouth to mouth' (Ellis).[111] More appropriately, pesher was identified in a general way as 'prophetic' midrash (Neusner).[112]

Pesher midrash should probably be defined not in terms of structure or of a specific subject matter but, more usefully, in terms of method and of a prophetic perspective focused on the 'last' = 'eschatological' time. It reflects a situation in which a charismatic exegete gives the Old Testament text an interpretive shaping, *ad hoc* or with reference to selected textual traditions, so that present events may be more clearly presented as the 'eschatological' fulfilment of the Old Testament Scriptures.[113] In this frame of reference pesher-type midrash, sometimes using the same formula (in Greek) found at Qumran, e.g. οὗτος ἐστίν, was identified in

---

[108] E.g. 1QpHab 3:2; 4QFlor 1:2f., 11f., 14; LXX Isa 9:14f. Cf. Ellis (note 52), 160, 203f.; M. Fishbane, '... Interpretation of Mikra at Qumran,' *Compendia* II, 1 (1988), 373.

[109] J.J. Collins, 'Prophecy and Fulfilment in the Qumran Scrolls,' *JETS* 30 (1987), 257–278, 277.

[110] Dan 2; 4; 5; 7:16. K. Elliger, *Studien zum Habakkuk-Kommentar vom Toten Meer*, Tübingen 1953, 156–164; L.H. Silberman, 'Unriddling the Riddle,' *RQ* 3 (1961–62), 323–364, followed by D. Patte, *Early Jewish Hermeneutic in Palestine*, Missoula MT 1975, 301. Further, cf. G.J. Brooke, *Exegesis at Qumran*, Sheffield UK 1985, 149–156.

[111] Cf. 1Q22 Moses 1:3f. ([ור] פש) with Num 12:6ff.; Ellis (note 52), 189 n.

[112] J. Neusner, *What is Midrash*, Philadelphia 1987, xi, 7f., 31–40: 'Midrash as prophecy' is seen in the Dead Sea Scrolls and in the School of Matthew where there is 'a reading of... ancient Scripture in light of an available scheme of concrete events' (40). Cf. Fishbane (note 108), 373ff. Otherwise: Maurya P. Horgan, *Pesharim*, Washington DC 1979, 249–259.

[113] Cf. W.H. Brownlee, *The Midrash Pesher of Habakkuk*, Missoula MT 1979, 25–32.

various New Testament writings including Matthew,[114] Mark,[115] John,[116] Acts, the Pauline letters and Jude.[117]

Unlike the rabbis, Qumran and the New Testament writers have a common eschatological perspective in which the end of the age is impending and their own time is 'the last generation,' to which the Old Testament prophecies referred.[118] Thus, in their pesher exegesis they couple certain midrashic procedures to a prophetic perspective of eschatological fulfilment.[119]

The Use of Testimony-Texts

In the last half of the twentieth century the testimony-book hypothesis, advanced earlier by J. R. Harris, continued in the discussion with two questions in the forefront: Were collections of Old Testament testimonies made for the instruction of converts or for apologetic use in evangelizing or refuting Jews? Were they extracted from prior explicit midrashim or were they original proof-texts later incorporated into the midrashic expositions?

Since the same testimonia were employed with reference to Messiah's resurrection, to his suffering and to his origins,[120] they were thought to have been used successively in that sequence by a developing Christian apologetic that first focused on Messiah's resurrection and only later on his suffering and then on his origins.[121] However, the texts addressed issues that in some cases were already in discussion in Jesus' earthly ministry and, indeed, in pre-Christian Judaism.[122] As such examples show, they were not first employed theologically at Jesus' resurrection but were, with appropriate changes, only given a new application at that time.

---

[114] Stendahl (note 63) 183–202. Otherwise: Moo (note 61), 388–392.

[115] Kee (note 64), 179–182.

[116] E. D. Freed, *Old Testament Quotations in the Gospel of John*, Leiden 1965, 129f.

[117] Ellis (note 52), 159ff., 173–181, 189f., 201–204, 225.

[118] 1QpHab 2:7; 7:1–13; CD 1:12; Mt 4:14–17; Lk 16:16; Acts 2:16f.; 3:24; Rom 15:4; I Cor 10:11; I Jn 2:18.

[119] Cf. P. Grelot, 'The Formation of the Old Testament,' *Introduction to the Old Testament*, edd. A. Robert-A. Feuillet, New York 1968, 596f.; B. Lindars, *New Testament Apologetic*, London 1961, 15–28; Betz (note 107), 79, 169; Wright (note 103), 422.

[120] E. g. Ps 2:7 in Acts 13:33 (resurrection) and in Mk 1:11 (baptism); Ps 110:1 in Acts 2:34 (resurrection), in Mk 12:36 (origins) and in Heb 1:13 (origins).

[121] Lindars (note 119), 251–259.

[122] E. g. Am 9:11 in CD 7:16f., 4QFlor 1:12f. and Acts 15:16; Deut 18:18 in 4QTest 7f. and Acts 3:20ff.; II Sam 7:14 in 4QFlor 1:10, Heb 1:5 and II Cor 6:18.

The Christian apologetic use of the Old Testament, therefore, must have been many-faceted from the beginning and its development hardly subject to a chronological reconstruction by stages.[123]

The view that the testimony-texts were primarily an apologetic device used against Jews, as had earlier been supposed,[124] continued to find support in the interpretation of certain patristic citations in Barnabas[125] and in Irenaeus.[126] However, in a treatise of Cyprian they appear to be more instructive than directly apologetic[127] and, for this purpose, are arranged in a thematic order.[128]

In the opinion of a number of earlier writers the independent testimony quotations preceded their later use in explicit New Testament midrashim.[129] Against this, J. W. Doeve contended that, in fact, the testimony texts could have no force standing alone and must have been derived from their prior use in a biblical exposition:

'Words lifted from their scriptural context can never be a *testimonium* to the Jewish mind.'[130]

Especially for Gentile Christians unschooled in midrashic techniques, leading (and subordinate) quotations in explicit midrashim were probably often extracted from the expository pattern to create testimonia. The testimonia sometimes had already received interpretive alterations in the exposition, alterations that remained in their testimony form, for exam-

---

[123] As Lindars (note 119), 29, admitted.

[124] Harris (note 41).

[125] Barn 6:2–4 (Isa 28:16), passim. Cf. L. W. Barnard, 'The Use of Testimonies in... Barnabas,' *Studies in the Apostolic Fathers and their Background,* Oxford 1966, 109–135, 116 f.; J. Danielou, *Études d'exégèse Judéo-Chrétienne: Les Testimonia,* Paris 1966, 99–107 (on Barn 12:1); P. Prigent, *L'épître de Barnabé I–XVI et ses sources,* Paris 1961, 29–83 (anti-cultic polemic).

[126] E. g. Irenaeus, *Adv. Haer.* 4, 17, 1–5 (Ps 50:19 + ? Apcl. Adam). Cf. A. Benoît, 'Irénée Adversus haereses IV, 17, 1–5 et les Testimonia,' *Studia Patristica IV, 2 (TU* 79), ed. F. L. Cross, Berlin 1961, 20–27.

[127] In spite of the title, *To Quirinus: Testimonies Against the Jews (ANF* 5, 507–557).

[128] E. g. *To Quirinus* (note 127), II, 16, 28 ff.: Christ the Stone, the King, the Judge, the Exalted One. Cf. J. P. Audet, 'L'hypothèse des Testimonia,' *RB* 70 (1963), 382–396, 404 f.

[129] E. g. Harris (note 41), II, 16 f., 21–28, on Rom 4:9–11; L. Cerfaux, 'Vestiges d'un florilège dans I Cor., i, 18–iii, 24?' *RHE* 27 (1931), 521–534, 525 ff. Cf. R. Hodgson, 'The Testimony Hypothesis,' *JBL* 98 (1979), 362 f.

[130] Doeve (note 61), 116. See below, 100, for the fuller quotation. In rabbinic usage also, for the priority of the midrashic form to the topically arranged Mishnah cf. D. W. Halivni, *Midrash, Mishnah and Gemara,* Cambridge MA 1986, 34 f., 37, 91.

ple, in Mark 1:2f., although the method and rationale on which the text was altered were no longer apparent.

This view of the matter may serve at times to define the hypothesis of C. H. Dodd that, before testimonia collections were formed, citations from Old Testament 'text-plots' had already been contextually interpreted and sometimes textually altered.[131] In any case testimonia were being collected and used in first-century Judaism and in earliest Christianity even if not on the scale envisioned by J. R. Harris.[132] Where they were derived from Christian explicit midrash, they must have been virtually immediate complements to it and must have continued a midrash-to-testimony process already in use in Judaism. In the patristic period Christian testimonia developed a greater variety of themes and applications.

Typology and Its Alternatives

As was now recognized, a historical and eschatological dimension set New Testament typology apart from the philosophical framework of Philonic allegory.[133] It found parallels in the Dead Sea Scrolls,[134] and it also determined 'the fuller sense' given the Old Testament by the New.[135]

However, for understanding the New Testament interpretation of certain Old Testament texts, alternatives to typology have been suggested. They are existentialist explanations,[136] 'the real presence of the pre-existent Jesus' in the Old Testament[137] and 'the fuller meaning' or *sensus*

---

[131] Dodd (note 44), 57–60, 108f.; Ellis (note 7), 106f.

[132] See above, notes 41, 45, 88, 120, 122.

[133] Cf. D. L. Baker, *Two Testaments: One Bible*, Leicester UK 1976, 245–270, 259; G. W. H. Lampe and K. J. Woolcombe, *Essays on Typology*, London 1957, 26–30, 50–60; for Paul, Ellis (note 7), 126–135; somewhat differently, Koch (note 7), 202–220; for Hebrews, C. K. Barrett, 'The Eschatology of the Epistle to the Hebrews,' *The Background of the New Testament and its Eschatology*, ed. W. D. Davies, Cambridge 1956, 388–393; Barth (note 72), 65–71; G. B. Caird, 'The Exegetical Method of Hebrews,' *CJT* 5 (1959), 44–51; S. G. Sowers, *The Hermeneutics of Philo and Hebrews*, Richmond 1965, 92–97, 139f.

[134] CD 4:10f. Cf. Test. of Levi 15:1f.; 17:8f.; Test. of Jud. 23:5; B. Gärtner, 'The Habakkuk Commentary (DSH) and the Gospel of Matthew,' *ST* 8 (1954), 1–24, 8.

[135] So, P. Grelot, 'The Catholic Interpretation of Sacred Scriptures,' *Interpreting the Scriptures*, ed. A. Robert, New York 1969, 171–211; C. Smits, *Oud-testamentische Citaten in het Nieuwe Testament*, 4 vols., 'Hertogenbosch 1952–63, IV, 658–677.

[136] Cf. H. Braun, 'Das Alte Testament im Neuen Testament,' *ZTK* 59 (1962), 16–31, 30f.; Suhl (note 64). See Appendix II below, 141–148.

[137] A. T. Hanson, *Jesus Christ in the Old Testament*, London 1965, 6f.

plenior hidden in the Old Testament text but revealed only in the light of further revelation.[138]

Sensus plenior, which has been pursued largely by Roman Catholic scholars, 'deals on the abstract values of language and the typical [i.e. typological] sense with concrete realities of person, thing and event.'[139] For example, the 'fuller meaning' of the language of Gen 1:26; 3:22; Isa 6:3 is the Trinity; of Gen 1:2, the Holy Spirit; of Pss 8, 69, 98, the Messiah; of Song of Songs, Christ and the church.

In its location of the fuller meaning in the language, *sensus plenior* is reminiscent of word-play in rabbinic exegesis,[140] and it apparently has affinities with the ὑπόνοια or 'double sense' of nineteenth-century hermeneutics and with 'the new hermeneutic' of some Protestant theologians.[141] In criticism, it has been characterized as a verbal approach that 'may have implications for abstract semantics or for depth psychology, [but] it can hardly shed any light on the art of communication.'[142] Whether *sensus plenior* shades off into a new form of allegorical interpretation[143] depends on the criteria established for defining it.[144] All in all, it is doubtful that *sensus plenior* provides an acceptable hermeneutical tool to explain the New Testament's interpretation of Scripture.

---

[138] Cf. D.S. Oss, 'Canon as Context: The Function of *Sensus Plenior* in Evangelical Hermeneutics,' *GTJ* 9 (1988), 105–127; D. J. Moo, 'Sensus Plenior,' *Hermeneutics, Authority and Canon*, ed. D. A. Carson, Grand Rapids 1986, 301–315; Baker (note 133), 263–266; W.S. LaSor, '*Sensus Plenior* and Biblical Interpretation,' *Scripture, Tradition and Interpretation*, ed. W.W. Gasque, Grand Rapids 1978, 260–277; R. E. Brown, *The Sensus Plenior of Sacred Scripture*, Baltimore 1955.

[139] R. E. Brown, 'The *Sensus Plenior* in the Last Ten Years,' *CBQ* 25 (1963), 262–285, 269; idem (note 138), 149.

[140] This appears a few times in the New Testament, e.g., Mt 2:23.

[141] Cf. J.M. Robinson, 'Scripture and Theological Method,' *CBQ* 27 (1965), 6–27, 18f.

[142] B. Vawter, 'The Fuller Sense: Some Considerations,' *CBQ* 26 (1964), 85–96, 89.

[143] So, J.L. McKenzie, 'Problems of Hermeneutics in Roman Catholic Exegesis,' *JBL* 77 (1958), 197–204, 202f.

[144] Cf. Brown (note 139), 274ff.; J. Schmid, 'Die alttestamentliche Citate bei Paulus und die Theorie vom Sensus plenior,' *BZ* 3 (1959), 161–173, 164, 173.

Conclusion

From the patristic church until the present day the research on Old Testament quotations in the New reveals a continuing concern about (1) their textual nature and (2) their hermeneutical application. It has resolved the textual problem, in part, by demonstrating that the New Testament writers were dependent on a specific antecedent text-form – the Septuagint, a targum or the Hebrew – or that they intended only to summarize or to allude to the Old Testament passage. However, in recent decades the research has shown that, in part, the textual question is itself a hermeneutical question and that textual variations are sometimes deliberate alterations, a kind of implicit midrash adapting the text more clearly to its present application.

With these and other insights of previous studies in hand, we may now proceed to a contemporary analysis of biblical interpretation in the New Testament church.

III

Biblical Interpretation in the
New Testament Church

Introduction

In its interpretation of Scripture the community of Jesus is rooted in and remains in continuity with the larger community of religious Judaism. It follows exegetical methods very similar to other groups and is distinguished primarily in the emphasis given to some procedures and in the boldness with which they are applied. In its general conceptual frame of reference it is closest to apocalyptic Judaism and thus, in some respects, to the Qumran community, but here also it is not without affinities with the Pharisaic-rabbinic and Sadducean parties. Jesus and his apostles and prophets, as they are represented by the New Testament, make their unique contribution to first-century Jewish exposition by their thoroughgoing *reinterpretation of the biblical writings to the person, ministry, death and resurrection of Jesus the Messiah.*

This messianic interpretation of Scripture could be understood as a break with Judaism since it involves a new covenant of God (Luke 22:20; Heb 8:8-13) that depicts Israel's preceding institutions and Scriptures as an old covenant, i.e. Old Testament, now superceded. However, Jesus and his apostles and prophets present the new covenant as a 'fulfilment' that was prophesied by the Old Testament (Jer 31:31) and that remains in a typological relationship to it (I Cor 10:1-11). In this way the messianic hermeneutic continues, admittedly in a highly climactic manner, earlier prophetic interpretations of Israel's Scriptures in terms of the current acts of God within the nation. And it is employed not only in matters of specific interest to the Christian community, but also in issues of general importance for contemporary Judaism: the Kingdom of God, the Messiah, the role of ritual and the place of the temple, the way to righteousness and to eternal life.

Jesus* and the New Testament writers give a prominent place to the Old Testament in the formulation of their teachings. Like other Jewish groups, they concentrate their biblical quotations on certain portions of the Scriptures, especially the Pentateuch, Isaiah, and the Psalms; and they employ them more in some New Testament books than in others. In

---

* On Jesus and the Old Testament see Appendix I below, 123-138.

all likelihood this reflects the writers' selected themes, traditions, and interests, and not their limited acquaintance with[1] or regard for the Old Testament.[2]

In their textual form the citations accord with the audience addressed and the argument pursued. They frequently follow the Septuagint, both because this Greek version was used in Palestine and in the Diaspora and, at times, because the Septuagint rendering fit the writer's viewpoint.[3] For the same reasons some citations, on occasion against the Septuagint, agree with the Hebrew text (Matt 2:15) or with the targum (cf. Eph 4:8). *Ad hoc* renderings usually serve an interpretive interest.[4]

The Bible was the touchstone not only of the New Testament writers' religious teachings but also of their total life and culture. As might be expected, it was used occasionally for an analogy or an illustration or for an expressive idiom.[5] But even in this literary usage it continued to carry theological implications. Similarly, as will be shown below, biblical citations containing widespread variations from the Old Testament textforms were more often intentional alterations than unintentional lapses.

---

[1] But see T. Holtz, ... *Untersuchungen über die alttestamentlichen Zitate bei Lukas*, Berlin 1968, 169f.; G. Reim, ... *Studien zum alttestamentlichen Hintergrund des Johannesevangeliums*, Cambridge 1974, 94f., who think that the Evangelists had only a limited access to Old Testament books. On Jesus' use of selected portions of Scripture cf. R. T. France, *Jesus and the Old Testament*, London 1971, 172–226; W. Grimm, *Die Verkündigung Jesu und Deuterojesaja*, Frankfurt 1981; W. Grimm und O. Betz, *Jesus und das Danielbuch*, 2 vols., Frankfurt 1985.

[2] *Pace* A. von Harnack, 'Das Alte Testament in den paulinischen Briefen,' *Sitzungsberichte der Preussischen Akademie der Wissenschaften*, Berlin 1928, 124–141 (= *Kleine Schriften zur alten Kirche*, 2 vols., Leipzig 1980, II, 823–841), who thinks that Paul used the Old Testament only as a matter of convenience. Cf. E. E. Ellis, *Paul's Use of the Old Testament*, Grand Rapids [5]1991, 30–33; L. Goppelt, *TYPOS: The Typological Interpretation of the Old Testament in the New*, Grand Rapids 1982 ([2]1964), 2ff.; GT: 2ff.

[3] E.g. in Gen. 12:3; 18:18 the Hebrew may be passive or reflexive ('bless themselves'); the Septuagint is passive and accords with Paul's understanding of the verses (Gal 3:8). On the use of the LXX cf. H. B. Swete, *An Introduction to the Old Testament in Greek*, Cambridge 1900, 381–405; Ellis, *Paul's Use* (note 2), 11–20.

[4] Cf. E. E. Ellis, *Prophecy and Hermeneutic in Early Christianity*, Tübingen 1978, 173–187.

[5] I Cor 15:32; Heb 12:14f. (expressive idiom); Rom 10:6–8; Jas 5:11 (illustration); Rom 2:24; Jas 5:17f. (analogy).

Exegetical Methods

General Form and Usage

In many respects New Testament citations of Scripture display methods that are common to all literary quotations: paraphrase, combined citations, alterations in sense and reference.[6] Even when they have special affinity with wider Jewish practice, they often reflect adapted forms of the common usage of the Greco-Roman world.[7] However, some citations display features that, although not unique, do set forth distinctively Christian conceptions. These features include certain introductory formulas, merged citations and *testimonia*.

Introductory Formulas

Introductory formulas often serve to specify the authority of a citation and, for the most part, they are formulas widely used in Judaism.[8] They also may point to the particular context within the Christian movement in which a citation was originally employed. For example, the formula 'have

---

[6] For comparisons with secular literature cf. F. Johnson, *The Quotations of the New Testament from the Old*, London 1896. For comparisons with Judaism cf. Ellis, *Paul's Use* (note 2), 45 ff.; R. Le Déaut, 'Traditions targumiques dans le corpus paulinien?' *Bib* 42 (1961), 28–48.

[7] Re Hillel's rules cf. D. Daube, 'Rabbinic Methods of Interpretation and Hellenistic Rhetoric,' *HUCA* 22 (1949), 239–264; R. Kasher, 'The Interpretation of Scripture in Rabbinic Literature,' *Compendia* II, 1 (1988), 584–585. Certain aspects of the *yelammedenu* midrash, e. g. the dialogic structure, also may have their background in Hellenistic rhetoric, e. g. Socratic interrogation or the diatribe style; cf. D. Daube, *The New Testament and Rabbinic Judaism*, London 1956, 151–157, 161; R. Bultmann, *Der Stil der paulinischen Predigt und die kynische-stoische Diatribe*, Göttingen 1984 (1910) 67, 73 f. More generally, D. Daube, 'Alexandrian Methods of Interpretation and the Rabbis,' *Festschrift Hans Lewald*, ed. M. Gerwig et al., Vaduz 1978 (1953), 27–44: '[The] whole Rabbinic system of exegesis initiated by Hillel about 30 B. C. E. and elaborated by the following generations was essentially Hellenistic...' (44).

[8] For parallels with formulas in Philo, rabbinic literature and especially at Qumran, e. g. 'as it is written,' 'Moses says,' 'God said,' 'Scripture says,' cf. H. E. Ryle, *Philo and Holy Scripture*, London 1895, xlv; B. M. Metzger, 'The Formulas Introducing Quotations of Scripture...,' *JBL* 70 (1951), 297–307; Ellis, *Paul's Use* (note 2), 48 f.; J. A. Fitzmyer, 'The Use of Explicit Old Testament Quotations in Qumran Literature and in the New Testament,' *NTS* 7 (1960–61), 299–305.

you not read', found in the NT only on the lips of Jesus, usually occurs in debates between Jesus and his religious opposition:

Have you not read this Scripture: 'The stone that the builders rejected, this one has become the head of the corner.'[9]

Two other formulas, 'in order that it might be fulfilled' (ἵνα πληρωθῇ) and 'says the Lord' (λέγει κύριος), apparently were utilized, respectively, by prophetic circles of the Hebraist and of the Hellenist missions. And both introduce quotations whose creatively altered text-forms adapt them to an eschatological, messianic interpretation.[10]

As a formula introducing a biblical citation, ἵνα πληρωθῇ appears only in the Gospels of Matthew and John which are, respectively, the products of the Jacobean and of the Johannine missions.[11] Along with other 'fulfilment' formulas, it is favoured by the Hebraist missioners to underscore their perception of salvation history as it is consummated in Jesus:

---

[9] Mark 12:10. Cf. Matt 12:3, 5; 19:4; 21:16, 42; 22:31. Cf. Luke 10:26. It may imply that the opponent has read but has not understood the passage cited (cf. Daube, *New Testament* [note 7], 433). Cf. Justin, *Dial.* 11, 3; 29, 2; 113, 1. On the connection between the Pharisaic opponents of Jesus and the rabbinic circles of Mishnah and Talmud, a question that is highly debatable, cf. J. W. Bowker, *Jesus and the Pharisees*, Cambridge 1973; I. M. Gafni, 'The Historical Background', *Compendia* II, 3, i (1987), 7–8; U. Luz, 'Jesus und die Pharisäer,' *Judaica* 38 (1982), 229–246; E. P. Sanders, *Paul and Palestinian Judaism*, Philadelphia ²1983, 60–62; P. Sigal, *The Halakah of Jesus of Nazareth According to the Gospel of Matthew*, Lanham MD 1986, 157ff.: Jesus is not in controversy with the predecessors of the scholars of Jamnia, the proto-rabbis, but with separatist extremists, i. e., the Pharisees of the New Testament.

[10] Cf. Ellis (note 4), 182–187; E. D. Freed, *Old Testament Quotations in the Gospel of John*, Leiden 1965, 129; R. H. Gundry, *The Use of the Old Testament in St. Matthew's Gospel*, Leiden 1967, 89–122; K. Stendahl, *The School of St. Matthew*, Lund ²1969 (1954), 97–120. Of quotations employing these formulas only Matt 2:15 has a text-form in agreement with the masoretic text; only John 12:38 and 19:24 agree with the Septuagint. On the two-fold mission of the Jewish-Christian church cf. Ellis (note 4), 101–128, 246: In New Testament usage (e.g., Acts 6:1) it appears that Hebraists designated those Jews with a strict, ritualistic viewpoint; and Hellenists those with a freer attitude toward the Jewish Law and cultus (Ellis [note 4], 116–128). It is usually supposed that the terms reflect only a difference in language, Hebrew/Aramaic speakers and Greek speakers, but as Schmithals and Ellis have shown, this view cannot explain the New Testament or wider usage. Cf. W. Schmithals, *Paul and James*, London 1965, 16–27 (GT: 9–19).

[11] Matt 1:22; 2:15; 4:14; 12:17; 21:4; cf. 2:23; 8:17; 13:35; John 12:38; 13:18; 15:25 (17:12); 19:24, 36. The formula introduces words of Jesus in John 18:9, 32. It apparently does not occur at Qumran or in rabbinic writings. But see Fitzmyer (note 8), 303. In the early patristic writings the phrase occurs once (Ignatius, *Ad Smyr.* 1:1) but with a different connotation.

This happened in order to fulfil the word through the prophet saying, 'Say to the daughter of Zion: Behold your king is coming to you...'[12]

The λέγει κύριος formula, as an addition to the Old Testament text, appears only in a quotation attributed to Stephen and in the Pauline letters:

For it is written, 'Vengeance is mine,
says the Lord, I will repay.'[13]

Elsewhere the phrase is substituted where the Old Testament has φήσι κύριος.[14] The formula is characteristic of Old Testament prophetic proclamation and it, or its equivalent, occasionally appears in the oracles of Christian prophets.[15] For these and other reasons[16] it is probable that the idiom reflects the activity of the prophets, especially those within the Hellenist mission.

The more commonly used formulas, no less than those discussed above, also locate the 'Word of God' character of Scripture in the proper interpretation and application of its teaching. Thus, a messianically interpreted summary of biblical passages can be introduced with the formula 'God said' (II Cor 6:16) and those persons who have a wrong understanding of the Old Testament are regarded as 'not knowing the Scriptures' (γραφάς, Matt 22:29) or as 'making void the Word of God' (Mark 7:13 = Matt 15:6). What 'is written', i.e. of divine authority, is not the biblical text in the abstract but the text in its meaningfulness for the current situation. The introductory formulas show, in the words of B.B. Warfield, that 'Scripture is thought of as the living voice of God speaking in all its parts directly to the reader.'[17] However, to this statement one should add, 'to

---

[12] Matt 21:4f. The verb is also used occasionally in the literature of the Hellenist mission as a formula (e.g. Gal 5:14) or otherwise (e.g. Mark 14:49), but not in the same way. The traditional piece in Acts 1:16 is not an exception although Peter may be later associated with the Hellenist mission (cf. I Cor 3:22; Gal 2:12; I Pet 1:1).

[13] Rom 12:19. Also, Acts 7:49; Rom 14:11; I Cor 14:21; II Cor 6:17, 18 (Heb 10:30A). Cf. Acts 2:17; 7:7 ('says God', 'God said'). At Isa 66:1f. (= Acts 7:49) and II Sam 7:14, 8 (= II Cor 6:18) the formula does appear in the immediate context. In Acts 15:16f. it reproduces the Old Testament text. On a few occasions in patristic writings it also occurs within a citation as an addition to the biblical text. Cf. Barn. 3:1; 6:8, 14; 9:1; Justin, *Dial.* 136, 2.

[14] Heb 8:8–10; 10:16.

[15] Rev 1:8; cf. 2:1, 8, 12, 18; 3:1, 7; Luke 11:49; Acts 21:11.

[16] Detailed in Ellis (note 4), 186.

[17] B.B. Warfield, *The Inspiration and Authority of the Bible*, Philadelphia 1948, 148; cf. R. Bloch, 'Midrash', *DBS* V (1957), 1266 (ET: *Aproaches to Ancient Judaism*, ed. W.S.

the reader who has ears to hear' (cf. Matt 11:15). The formulas, then, reveal not only a method of citation but also something of the theological convictions of the New Testament writers.

Exegetical Terminology

Other exegetical terminology is also associated with the use of the Old Testament in the New, a small part peculiar to the New Testament writers and the rest the common property of Jewish exposition. Four examples may be noted: the formula, 'faithful is the Word;' the Qumran-like formula, 'this is;' the adversative, 'but;' and the terms, 'hear' and 'learn.'

1. One idiom that apparently occurs only in the New Testament is the formula 'faithful is the word' (πιστὸς ὁ λόγος).[18] Found in the Pastoral letters, it appears to be a favourite idiom of Paul and/or his amanuensis or co-workers at a later stage of his mission. Broadly speaking, it is used to refer to a traditioned teaching-piece of prophets or inspired teachers.[19] But it is also used in connection with their exposition of the Old Testament. For example, in I Tim 3:1a the formula appears to conclude the preceding interpretation of Gen 3 that forbids a wife 'to practice teaching' or 'to have authority' over her husband (I Tim 2:11–15). In Titus 1:9, 14 'the faithful word' is contrasted to the false biblical interpretations of Paul's opponents, and in Titus 3:5f., 8 it appears to refer to a Pentecostal interpretation of Joel 3:1:

When the goodness and loving kindness of God our Saviour appeared..., he saved us by the washing of regeneration and renewal of the Holy Spirit, which he poured out upon us... Faithful is the Word.

A more explicit connection with prophecy occurs in a similar formula in Rev 22:6:

Green, Missoula MT 1978, 33): Scripture 'always concerns a living word addressed personally to the people of God and to each of its members...' Cf. Matt 4:4–10; Acts 15:15; Rom 15:4.

[18] E.g. I Tim 1:15; 4:9; II Tim 2:11; cf. I Cor 1:9; II Thess 3:3; see G.W. Knight, *The Faithful Sayings in the Pastoral Epistles*, Kampen 1968; E.E. Ellis, 'Traditions in the Pastoral Epistles,' *Early Jewish and Christian Exegesis*, ed. C.A. Evans, Decatur GA 1987, 239–242. The idiom apparently does not occur elsewhere although similar phrases appear in II Clem 11:6 (citing Heb 10:23) and Ignatius, *Tral.* 13:3 and in the Qumran *Book of Mysteries* (see note 20).

[19] Cf. I Tim 4:1 ('the Spirit says') with 4:6 ('by the words of the faith'). See also Rev 19:9; 21:5; Ellis (note 18).

Faithful are these words and true (οὗτοι οἱ λόγοι πιστοὶ καὶ ἀληθινοί), seeing that (καί) the Lord God of the spirits of the prophets sent his angel to show his servants what things must shortly come to pass.

The Qumran *Book of Mysteries*, which uses a similar expression with reference to a prophecy, probably represents the Jewish apocalyptic antecedent of the New Testament idiom:[20]

Certain is the word to come to pass (נכון הדבר לבוא) and true (אמת) the oracle.

2. More common is the exegetical usage of such terms as 'this is' (οὗτός ἐστιν), 'but' (ἀλλά, δέ), 'learn' (μανθάνειν), 'hear' (ἀκούειν). In the Greek Old Testament οὗτός ἐστιν translates terms that introduce the explanation of divine revelation through a divine oracle (Isa 9:14f.), parable (Ezek 5:5), vision (Zech 1:10, 19; 5:3, 6), dream (Dan 4:24, [21]) and strange writing (Dan 5:25f.). For example,

The Lord will cut off from Israel head and tail:
The elder and the honoured man, this is (הוא) the head,
And the prophet who teaches lies, this is (הוא) the tail.
Isa 9:14f.

Again I lifted up my eyes and saw... a flying scroll...
And [the angel] said to me, 'This is (זאת) the curse...'
Zech 5:1,3

And this (דנה) is the writing..., 'Mene, mene, tekel, ufarsin,
This is the interpretation (דנה פשר)...
Dan 5:25f.

In Daniel and at Qumran these terms are used in a similar way in conjunction with or as an equivalent of *pesher* (פשר):[21]

'Because of bloodshed in the city and violence in the land...' (Hab 2:17).
It's interpretation (פשרו): 'The *city*', that is (היא) Jerusalem...
1QpHab 12:6f.; cf. 12:3ff.

---

[20] 1Q27 1:8. According to I. Rabinowitz ('The Authorship... of an Unknown Work,' *JBL* 71 [1952], 29), this work concerns 'the fulfilment of the words of Israel's Prophets.' It has another significant parallel with the Pauline literature in the phrase 'mysteries of iniquity' (1Q27 1:2 רזי פשע). Cf. II Thess 2:7; D. Dimant, 'Qumran Sectarian Literature,' *Compendia* II, 2(1984), 536 n. 256.

[21] Cf. also 4QpIsa[b] 2:6f., 10; 4QpNah 1:11. The Qumran usage is not restricted to revelations through dreams or visions, as some scholars have supposed, for it is used in the explanation of 'Words of Moses' (1Q22 1:3f.) to whom God spoke not in vision but 'mouth to mouth' (Num 12:6–8). For the use of these exegetical formulas in rabbinic writings cf. L. H. Silberman, 'Unriddling the Riddle,' *RQ* 3 (1961–62), 326–330;

They come to strike and plunder the cities of the land. For this is (הוא) that which is said:

> To seize habitations not their own (Hab 1:6)...
> Its interpretation (פשר) concerns the Kittim...
>
> 1QpHab 3:1–4

The books of the law, they are (הם) the tabernacle of the King, as he said: 'I will raise up the tabernacle of David that is fallen' (Amos 9:11).

CD 7:15f.

'I will be to him a father and he will be to me a son' (II Sam 7:14). This is (הואה) the branch of David... As it is written, 'I will raise up the tabernacle of David that is fallen' (Amos 9:11). This is (היאה) the fallen tabernacle of David who will arise to save Israel. Exposition (מדרש) of: 'Blessed is the man who does not walk in the counsel of the ungodly' (Ps 1:1). The interpretation (פשר) concerns the backsliders from the way...

> 4QFlor 1:11–14

In the New Testament οὗτος (ἐστίν) is also employed with the same eschatological orientation and exegetical framework that is found at Qumran. This formula is an equivalent of the Qumran *pesher* and may introduce either an explanation following cited biblical texts or a biblical citation used to explain the described event:[22]

'In Isaac shall your seed be called' (Gen 21:12).
That is (τοῦτ' ἔστιν), not the children of the flesh... but the children of the promise... For this is (οὗτος) the word of promise, 'About this season I will return and Sarah will have a son' (Gen 18:10).

Rom 9:7–9

But this is (τοῦτό ἐστιν) that which was spoken by the prophet Joel 'And it shall be in the last days, says God...' (Joel 3:1).

Acts 2:16f.

3. The use of the adversative 'but' (ἀλλά, δέ) in the exposition of Scripture also displays a Jewish ancestry. In the New Testament (1) it may follow a biblical citation or allusion in order to correct, qualify or underscore a

---

J. Bonsirven, *Exégèse rabbinique et exégèse paulinienne*, Paris 1939, 42–46; in Gnosticism cf. *Pistis Sophia* 65–67 (131–147); Hippolytus, *Refutatio* 6, 14 (9).

[22] Cf. also John 6:31f., 50; Rom 10:6–8; Heb 7:5; I Pet 1:25 and, introducing the citation, Matt 3:3; 11:10; Acts 4:11.

particular understanding of it,[23] or (2) it may introduce a citation to correct, qualify or underscore a preceding statement[24] or citation:[25]

You have heard (ἠκούσατε) that it was said...,
'You shall not kill' (Exod 20:13)...
But (δέ) I say to you that everyone who is angry...
Matt 5:21f.

I know whom I have chosen.
But (ἀλλά) that the scriptures might be fulfilled:
'He who ate my bread lifted his heel against me' (Ps 41:10).
John 13:18

The usage represents an exegetical technique, a dialectial procedure by which apparent contradictions are resolved and the meaning of Scripture is drawn out or more precisely specified. A similar contrast between Scripture and Scripture or Scripture and commentary is observable in rabbinic exposition even though an adversative conjunction may not be used:[26]

'And if he smite out his bondsman's tooth' (Exod 21:27). I might understand (אני שומע) this to mean... milk tooth.
But it also says (תלמוד לומר), 'Eye' (Exod 21:26)...
Just as the eye... the tooth must be such as cannot grow back...
Mekilta Nezikin 9 on Exod 21:26f.

When Scripture says, 'And David... wept as he went up' (II Sam 15:30), one might suppose [he lamented].
But... he was composing a Psalm, as it is said,
'A Psalm of David, when he fled from Absalom' (Ps 3:1).
Midrash Tehillim 119, 26 on Ps 119:75.

---

[23] Cf. also Matt 19:8; Mark 11:17; 14:28f.; Luke 20:37f.; John 6:31f.; Rom 10:15f.; I Cor 2:10 A, 16; 15:45f.; Gal 4:22f.; Heb 10:37ff.; 12:26f.

[24] Cf. also Acts 2:15f.; Rom 9:7; 15:21; I Cor 2:8f.; 10:4f.; Gal 4:30; 3:12; Heb 2:16; II Pet 3:12f.

[25] Cf. Acts 7:47f.; Rom 8:37; 10:18f.; 11:2ff.; 12:20; Jude 8ff.

[26] Cf. *Mekilta*, 3 vols., ed. J. Z. Lauterbach, Philadelphia 1976, I, 63; III, 72; *Midrash on Psalms*, 2 vols., ed. W. G. Braude, New Haven 1959, II, 267; *The Mishnah*, ed. H. Danby, Oxford 1933, 191f. Whether the New Testament usage is, like the rabbinic, concerned with resolving apparent contradictions in Scripture is less certain to me. But see N. A. Dahl, *Studies in Paul*, Minneapolis 1977, 159–177 (GT: *ST* 25, 1971, 1–19).

All shofars are valid save of that of a cow, since it is a horn.
But are not (והלא) all shofars called... 'horn'? For it is written,
'When they... blast with the ram's horn' (Josh 6:5)...
'When Moses held up his hand, Israel prevailed' (Exod 17:11).
But (וכי) could the hands of Moses promote the battle?...

M. Rosh Hashanah 3:2,8

4. The terms 'hear' (ἀχούειν) and 'learn' (μανθάνειν), appear occasionally in the NT with reference to 'understanding' Scripture:

Go learn what it means,
'I will have mercy and not sacrifice' (Hos 6:6).[27]

Matt 9:13

... Then 'all the tribes of the land will lament' (cf. Zech 12:12)
And 'shall see the Son of man coming on the clouds of heaven'... (Dan 7:13)
And his elect... 'from one end of heaven to the other' (Deut 30:4).
From the fig tree learn the mystery (παραβολή)...[28]

Matt 24:30ff.

In Matt 21:33 the words, 'Hear another mystery' (παραβολή), like the apparently equivalent phrase, 'Learn the mystery' (Matt 24:32), refer to an exposition of Scripture.[29] Also, a biblical exposition may be opened with the words, 'Hear the law', or concluded with the expression, 'He who has ears, let him hear'.[30]

---

[27] Cf. also Matt 11:27, 29: 'No one knows the Father except the Son and anyone to whom the Son chooses to reveal him... Take my yoke upon you and learn from me.' The 'yoke' implies a 'law of Christ' that, when followed, brings a knowledge of God. Specifically, it is a knowledge of 'the mysteries of the kingdom of the heavens' (Matt 13:11 parr) that, along the lines of the book of Daniel, Jesus unveils *exempli gratia* in his exposition of Scripture. Cf. Sirach 51:23, 26; *M. Abot* 3:5; *M. Berakot* 2:2; W. D. Davies, *The Setting of the Sermon on the Mount*, Cambridge 1964, 94, 214; L. Cerfaux, 'La connaisance des secrets du Royaume...,' *NTS* 2 (1955–56), 244f.

[28] That is, the παραβολή apparently is not only the story of the fig tree (Luke 21:29) but also the 'mystery' (רז) in the Scriptures that Jesus has 'interpreted' (פשר). Cf. 1QpHab 7:1–8; Ellis (note 4), 160ff. For this meaning of παραβολή cf. Jeremias, *The Parables of Jesus*, New York ⁶1963, 16; E. Schweizer, *Das Evangelium nach Markus*, Göttingen 1967, 51 (ET 92f.). Cf. Matt 13:35 = Ps 78:2; Mark 4:11f.; 7:17f. (cf. ἀσύνετοι); Heb 9:9; John 10:6; 16:25, 29. On the expository, i.e. midrashic origin of Matt 24 = Mark 13 see below, note 99. Unlike those of I Enoch (e.g. 1:2f.; 37:5; 43:4), Jesus' parables of the kingdom are drawn mostly from daily life (but cf. Matt 25:31–46; Luke 16:19D). However, like the parables of I Enoch and other apocalyptic literature (IV Ezra 4:12–22; 7:3–14; 8:41) and unlike those of the rabbis, his are not merely illustrations but are truly 'mysteries,' i.e. a hidden eschatological word of revelation, clothed in the form of a story. But see M. Gilbert, 'Wisdom Literature,' *Compendia* II, 2 (1984), 319f.

[29] I.e. Matt 21:33–46. See below, 98, 117.

[30] I.e. Gal 4:21–5:1; Matt 11:7–15. Cf. Rev 1:3; 13:9. See above, 84f.

In rabbinic literature the terms 'learn' (לִמֵּד) and 'hear' (שָׁמַע) are similarly employed in formulas coupling biblical texts to commentary upon them.[31]

Behold we have thus learned [from the preceding exposition]
that work is forbidden during the intervening days of the festival.
Mekilta Pisha 9 on Exod 12:16

'She shall go out for nothing'. I might understand (שָׁמַע) 'for nothing' to mean without a bill of divorce.
Mekilta Nezikin 3 on Exod 21:11

Hillel's Rules of Interpretation

Seven exegetical rules were, according to later rabbinic tradition, expounded by the great teacher Hillel († c. A.D. 10). They represent general hermeneutical principles of inference, analogy and context that were probably in use before that time.[32] They may be derived, as D. Daube argues, from rules of Hellenistic rhetoric current in Alexandria in the first century B.C.[33] As attributed to Hillel, they went as follows:

1. An inference drawn from a minor premise to a major and vice versa (*Kal wa-homer* = 'light and heavy').
2. An inference drawn from analogy of expressions, that is, from similar words and phrases elsewhere (*Gezera Shawa* = 'an equivalent regulation').
3. A general principle established on the basis of a teaching contained in one verse (*Binyan 'ab mi-katub 'ehad* = 'constructing a leading rule from one passage').
4. A general principle established on the basis of a teaching contained in two verses (*Binyan 'ab mi-shenei ketubim* = 'constructing a leading rule from two passages').

---

[31] Further, cf. (H.L. Strack and) P. Billerbeck, *Kommentar zum Neuen Testament*, 4 vols., München 1922–1928, I, 499 (on Mt 9:13), 604 (on Mt 11:15); W. Bacher, *Die Exegetische Terminologie der jüdischen Traditionsliteratur*, 2 vols. in 1, Darmstadt 1965 (1909), I, 75, 94f., 189; II, 220. R. Le Déaut, 'La tradition juive ancienne et l'exégèse chrétienne primitive,' *RHPR* 51 (1971), 37.

[32] E.g. Prov 11:31; cf. I Pet 4:17f. On Hillel see *T. Sanhedrin* 7:11; *Abot de R. Nathan* 37, 10 (Neusner). Cf. H. Danby, *Tractate Sanhedrin: Mishna and Tosephta*, London 1919, 76f.; *The Minor Tractates of the Talmud*, 2 vols., ed. A. Cohen, London 1971, I, 185. The rules were expanded, with a few innovations, from 7 to 13 by R. Ishmael († c. A.D. 135). See Kasher (note 7), 585f.

[33] Daube, 'Rabbinic' (note 7), 239–264; cf. R. Hamerton-Kelly, '... Philo's Allegorical Commentary...,' *Jews, Greeks and Christians*, ed. R. Hamerton-Kelly, Leiden 1976, 46–53.

5. An inference drawn from a general principle in the text to a specific example and vice versa (*Kelal u-ferat* = 'general and particular').

6. An inference drawn from an analogous passage elsewhere (*Kayotse' bo mi-makom 'aher* = 'something similar in another passage').

7. An interpretation of a word or passage from its context (*Dabar halamed me-'inyano* = 'explanation from the context').

For example, a negligent man whose animal kills someone is liable to death, but he may be delivered by the payment of money (Exod 21:29f.); *a fortiori (rule 1)* a man who maims another, a non-capital case, may also compensate by the payment of money and not literally 'eye for eye' (Exod 21:24). It is true that Scripture says, 'If a man maims his neighbour..., so shall it be done to him' (Lev 24:19); but this *general principle* cannot include more than the following specific example, 'eye for eye' (Lev 24:20), which allows monetary compensation *(rule 5).*[34] A master must free a slave whose eye or tooth he has knocked out (Exod 21:26f.); these two examples establish the general principle *(rule 4)* that a slave must be freed for such an injury to any important, visible and irreplaceable member of his body.[35]

Daily sacrifice 'in its due season' is offered on the sabbath (Num 28:2, 10); by a *Gezera Shawa* analogy *(rule 2)* the Passover sacrifice (Num 9:2) should also be offered on the sabbath since the same expression, 'due season', is used.[36] One might understand 'Honour your father and your mother' (Exod 20:12) to signify that the father should be given precedence since he is mentioned first; but in a similar passage 'mother' precedes 'father' (Lev 19:3) and, by analogy *(rule 6)*, shows that both are to be honoured equally.[37] The commandment, 'you shall not steal,' refers to stealing a man and not money; for in the context *(rule 7)* the prohibitions against murder and adultery concern capital crimes and so must this one.[38]

---

[34] *Mekilta, Nezikin* 8 on Exod 21:24.

[35] *Mekilta, Nezikin* 9 on Exod 21:27. Or one might regard Exod 21:26f. as one passage and take this to be an application of rule three.

[36] *T. Pesahim* 4:1f.; *P. T. Pesahim* 6:1 (33a); *B. T. Pesahim* 66a.

[37] *Mekilta, Pisha* 1 on Exod 12:1.

[38] *Mekilta, Bahodesh* 8 on Exod 20:15; cf. *B. T. Sanhedrin 86a.* For other examples in rabbinic literature cf. Bacher (note 31), I, 9ff., 13–16, 75f., 80ff., 172ff.; Bonsirven (note 21), 77–113; J. W. Doeve, *Jewish Hermeneutics in the Synoptic Gospels and Acts*, Assen 1954, 52–90; Ellis, *Paul's Use* (note 2), 41f.; M. Mielziner, *Introduction to the Talmud*, New York 1968 (1925), 130–187; H. L. Strack, *Introduction to the Talmud and Midrash*, New York 1959 (1920), 93ff., 285–289.

The use of a number of these principles may be observed in the New Testament:[39]

Rule 1: Inference *a fortiori.*
If [one sheep] should fall into a pit on the sabbath, [who] will not... lift it out (cf. Exod 23:5)? Of how much more value is a man than a sheep (Matt 12:11f.). If God so clothes the grass... that is alive today and tomorrow is cast into the oven (Gen 1:11f.), how much more will he clothe you... (Luke 12:28). If the covenant at Sinai came with glory (Exod 34:30), how much more does the new covenant (Jer 31:31ff.) abound in glory (II Cor 3:7–11). If in the old covenant the blood of animals could effect a ceremonial, external cleansing (Lev 16; Num 19), how much more shall the blood of (the sacrificed) Messiah cleanse our conscience (Heb 9:13f.).[40]

Rule 2: Inference from similar words.
David, who received the kingdom from God, was blameless when he and those with him violated the Law in eating the showbread (I Sam 21:6; cf. 15:28); the Son of Man, who also received a kingdom from God (Dan 7:13f.), is equally blameless when those with him violate the sabbath law in similar circumstances (Luke 6:1–5).[41] The righteousness 'reckoned' to Abraham (Gen 15:6) may be explained in terms of forgiveness of sins in Ps 32:1f. since the word 'reckoned' is also employed there (Rom 4:3, 7). Gen 14:17–20 may be interpreted in the light of Ps 110:4 where alone in the Old Testament the name 'Melchizedek' again appears (Heb 7:1–28). Gen 15:5f. may be interpreted by Gen 22:9–19 and Isa 41:8 since the texts contain a common reference to Abraham's seed (Jas 2:21ff.).

Rule 3: General principle from one verse.
God is not the God of the dead, and yet in Exod 3:14f. he affirmed a continuing covenant relationship with dead Abraham. Therefore, he must intend to raise Abraham out of death, and from this conclusion one may infer the resurrection of all the dead who have a similar convenantal relationship (Mark 12:26 parr). Cf. Jas 5:16ff.

Rule 4: General principle from two verses.
The uncircumcised Abraham (Gen 15:6) and the circumcised David (Ps 32:1f.) establish the general principle that the righteousness of God is graciously given to

---

[39] Cf. Doeve (note 38), 91–118; B. Gerhardsson, 'The Hermeneutic Program in Mt 22:37-40,' in Hamerton-Kelly (note 33), 129–150; J. Jeremias, 'Paulus als Hillelit,' *Neotestamentica et Semitica,* edd. E. E. Ellis and M. Wilcox, Edinburgh 1969, 92ff. For a critique of H. Hübner's ('Gal 3, 10...,' *KD* 19, 1973, 222–229) view that Paul was, contra Jeremias, a Shammaite cf. Sanders (note 9), 138n. Further cf. D. Cohn-Sherbok, 'Paul and Rabbinic Exegesis,' *SJT* 35 (1982), 117–132. See below, 130ff.

[40] See further Luke 6:3–5; Rom 5:15, 17; 11:24; 11:12; I Cor 6:2f.; 9:9; Heb 2:2ff.; 10:28f.; 12:24f.

[41] The grounds on which this analogy can be drawn are considered by Doeve (note 38), 165. It is elaborated below, 131.

the circumised Jew and to the uncircumcised Gentile apart from works (Rom 4:1–25). From the commands to unmuzzle the working ox (Deut 25:4) and to give the temple priests a share of the sacrifices (Deut 18:1–8) one may infer the general right of ministers of the gospel to a living (I Cor 9:9, 13). The examples of Abraham (Gen 22:9–19) and Rahab (Josh 2:1–16) establish the general principle that genuine faith is manifested by works (Jas 2:22–26).

Rule 5: Inference from a general principle.
'The [particular] commandments, "you shall not commit adultery,... commit murder,... steal,... covet" (Exod 20:13–17; cf. Lev 18:20; 19:11) and any other commandment are summed up in this [general] sentence, "You shall love your neighbour as yourself" (Lev 19:18) ... Therefore, love is the fulfilling of the law' (Rom 13:9f.). That is, the particular commandments are apparently regarded as illustrative examples of the general.[42]

Rule 6: Inference from an analogous passage.
The prophecy in Gen 12:3 that all nations shall be blessed in Abraham may, in the light of the analogous passage in Gen 22:18, be understood of Abraham's offspring and thus of Messiah (Gal 3:8, 16). One might understand the 'rest' promised to God's people to have been fulfilled by Joshua (Num 14:21–30; Josh 1:13–15; 22:4), but the analogous and much later passage in Ps 95:7–11 shows that the prophecy is still outstanding (Heb 4:7–9). The covenant at Sinai (Exod 19:5f.; Lev 26:9–12) is shown to be inadequate and temporary by a subsequent and similar passage (Jer 31:31–34) in which God speaks of a new covenant (Heb 8:7–13).

Rule 7: Interpretation from the context.
Indissoluble marriage was established at creation (Gen 1:27, 2:24), a context that takes priority over later (Deut 24:1) provisions for divorce (Matt 19:4–8). That righteousness was reckoned to Abraham (Gen 15:6) before he was circumcised (Gen 17:10f.) enables him to be the father of both Jewish and (uncircumcised) Gentile believers (Rom 4:10f.). Equally, because the covenant promise was established with Abraham (Gen 22:18) 430 years before the Mosaic Law (Exod 12:40), it has validity independent of that law (Gal 3:17). That God rested after the completion of the present creation, i. e. on the seventh or sabbath day (Gen 2:2), implies that those who enter God's future sabbath rest (Ps 95:7–11) will do so only when their and his present work is completed, i. e. at the resurrection (Heb 4:9f.; cf. 11:13–16, 35–40).

Some of the above New Testament passages are clearer than others, and since no 'rules' are mentioned, one cannot prove that the writer or the speaker cited by him had a specific exegetical rule consciously in mind.

---

[42] Cf. Daube, *New Testament* (note 7), 63–66.

Nevertheless, a number of these texts almost certainly reflect the use of an exegetical principle or combination of principles. As a whole the examples show that the principles attributed to Hillel were also used by the messianic Judaism represented by Jesus and the New Testament writers. Certain of the principles, especially the association of biblical texts containing similar ideas (rule 6) or common words and phrases (rule 2), are important for the formation of larger commentary patterns in the New Testament. They are also evident in other techniques such as a string (חרז) of quotations[43] and merged or composite quotations[44] that often have appended to one text a snippet from another.[45] The latter practice appears to be infrequent in other Jewish literature.

Midrash

The Hebrew verb *darash* (דרש) and its substantive form *midrash* (מדרש) were used in pre-Christian Judaism for the interpretation of Scripture[46] or for commentary on Scripture.[47] For example, the 'house of midrash' in Ben Sira 51:23 refers to the place of instruction in the Law of God.[48] Similarly, at Qumran 'midrash' can mean the 'study' of Torah.[49] This study, i.e. interpretation of Scripture, was an established practice in first-

---

[43] E.g. Rom 11:8–10; 15:9–12; I Cor 3:19f.; Heb 1:5–13; I Pet 2:7f. Some of these combine citations from the Law, the Prophets and the Writings. In the Talmud cf. *B. T. Berakot* 6a. Cf. W. Bacher, *Die Proömien der alten jüdischen Homilie*, Farnborough 1970 (1913), 9–14; Billerbeck (note 31), III, 314; *B. T. Pesahim* 7b–8a.

[44] Rom 3:10–18; II Cor 6:16ff.; I Cor 2:9. Cf. *Mekilta, Pisha* I on Exod 12:1.

[45] Mt 21:5 (Isa 62:11 + Zech 9:9); Mk 1:2 (Mal 3:1 + Isa 40:3); Lk 4:18f. (Isa 61:1f. + 58:6); 10:27 (Deut 6:5 + Lev 19:18); Jn 12:14f. (Isa 40:9 + Zech 9:9; cf. Zeph 3:13ff.); Acts 15:16ff. (Amos 9:11f. + Isa 45:21); Rom 9:33 (Isa 8:14 + 28:16); I Cor 15:54f. (Isa 25:8 + Hos 13:14); Gal 3:8 (Gen 12:3 + 18:18); Heb 10:37f. (Isa 26:20 + Hab 2:3f.); Jas 2:23 (Gen 15:6 + Isa 41:8). Cf. Mt 12:17; 27:9; Ellis (note 4), 186.

[46] Perhaps as early as Ezra 7:10: 'Ezra had set his heart to interpret (דרש) the law of the Lord.'

[47] Perhaps as early as II Chron 13:22 ('Midrash of the prophet Iddo'); 24:27 ('Midrash on the Book of the Kings').

[48] The 'house of midrash' *(bet ha-midrash)* may already here be a technical term and certainly becomes so in later rabbinic usage. Cf. *B. T. Yoma* 35b (baraita); K. Kohler, 'Bet Ha-Midrash,' *JE*, III, 116ff.; S. Safrai, 'Education and the Study of the Torah,' *Compendia* I, 2 (1976), 960–963.

[49] 1QS 8:15, 26; CD 20:6.

century Judaism in the synagogue service[50] as well as in the academic schools.[51]

As an *interpretive activity* the midrashic procedure (1) is oriented to Scripture, (2) adapting it to the present (3) for the purpose of instructing or edifying the current reader or hearer.[52] It may take the form either of a simple clarification or of a specific application of the texts.

As a *literary expression* midrash has traditionally been identified with certain rabbinic commentaries on the Old Testament. However, in accordance with its use in Ben Sira and at Qumran, the term is now employed more broadly to designate interpretive renderings of the biblical text (= implicit midrash) and of various kinds of 'text + exposition' patterns (= explicit midrash).[53]

Implicit Midrash

Implicit midrash first appears, as has been observed above, as a process of rewriting that occurs within the Hebrew Old Testament itself. It may also involve the transposition of a biblical text to a different application. For example, the prophecy in Isa 19:19–22 transposes the words and motif of Israel's redemption *from* Egypt (Exod 1–12) to apply them to God's future redemption *of* Egypt.[54]

Implicit midrash is present also in biblical translations, that is, the Greek Septuagint and the Aramaic targums, where interpretive adaptation to a current understanding, interest, or application is interwoven into the translation process.[55] For example, in Lev 18:21 the prohibition of

---

[50] In the New Testament this is reflected, e.g. in Jesus' synagogue address at Nazareth (Lk 4:16–30) and in Paul's address at Antioch (Acts 13:16–41). Cf. Philo, *De Spec. Leg.* II, 60–64; *Hypothetica* 7, 11–13. Cf. *P. T. Megillah* 3:1 (73d): There were 480 synagogues in Jerusalem, each of which had a 'house of reading' and a 'house of learning' *(bet talmud)*.

[51] Paul's study 'at the feet of Gamaliel' (Acts 22:3) is one example. Cf. W. C. van Unnik, *Tarsus or Jerusalem*, London 1962; J. Neusner, *The Rabbinic Traditions... before 70*, 3 vols., Leiden 1971, III, 248–319.

[52] Cf. Bloch (note 17), 1263–1267. (ET: 29–34). Cf. also G. Vermes, 'Bible and Midrash,' *The Cambridge History of the Bible*, 3 vols., Cambridge 1963–70, I, 223 ff.

[53] Cf. Ellis (note 4), 188–197. See above, 66 ff.

[54] Isa 19:20 ('cry,' 'send,' 'oppressors,' cf. Exod 3:9f.), 20 ff. ('sign,' 'know,' 'sacrifice,' 'smite,' cf. MT Exod 7:27; 8:4, 18–25 = ET Exod 8:2, 8, 22–29). Cf. M. Fishbane, 'Torah and Tradition,' *Tradition and Theology in the Old Testament*, ed. D. A. Knight, Philadelphia 1977, 277.

[55] *Pace* R. Le Déaut, 'Une phénomène spontané...: le "targumisme,"' *Bib* 52 (1971),

child-sacrifice 'to the god Molech' becomes in Targum Neofiti 'to an idol.' In the Septuagint it is a simple prohibition on idolatry, i. e. to serve or worship (λατρεύειν) a ruler. In Num 24:17 a 'star' and a 'scepter' become in Targum Neofiti a 'king' and a 'redeemer,' in the Septuagint a 'star' and a 'man.' In Isa 9:11 (12) the Philistines become in the Septuagint 'the Greeks.' In Isa 52:13 'my servant' becomes in Targum Jonathan 'my servant the Messiah.'

Similarly, at Qumran rewritings of Genesis, the Genesis Apocryphon (1QGenAp) and Jubilees (1Q17, 18; etc.), may properly be designated implicit midrash. The same may be said of interpretive alterations of Old Testament texts, often based on word-play, in certain Qumran commentaries.[56]

These various forms of implicit midrash are also present in the New Testament. *Word-play* in Matt 2:23 connects Jesus' residence in Nazareth to a messianic text such as Isa 11:1 (נצר = 'branch') or Isa 49:6 (נצירי = 'preserved'?, 'branch'?, 'Nazorean'?). The *transposition* of Old Testament texts can be seen in Luke 1–2. The prophecy of Gabriel (Luke 1:30–35) is given literary expression via allusion to II Sam 7, Isa 7 and other passages. The song of Hannah (I Sam 2:1–10), supplemented by other passages, is transposed to form the Magnificat (Luke 1:46–55). Other Old Testament texts are used in the same way in the Benedictus and in the Nunc Dimittis.[57]

Events in Jesus' life that are described by the use of biblical allusions are also a form of implicit midrash. In this way the event can be clearly associated with or presented as a fulfilment of the Old Testament. Thus, the angelic annunciation to Mary is virtually a pastiche of biblical allusions.[58] Somewhat differently, the visit of the wise men and the sequel is structured upon both explicit quotations[59] and implicit allusions to Scripture.[60] The feeding of the Five Thousand is described with clear allusions

---

505–525, who distinguishes midrash proper from 'targumism,' in which the interpretive factor is spontaneous and unconditioned by hermeneutical rules and techniques.

[56] E. g. 4QTest 22 (Josh 6:26, omitting 'Jericho'); 1QpHab 8:3 (Hab 2:5, changing 'wine', היין, to 'wealth', הון). Cf. Ellis (note 4), 175ff., 190, 201f.; T. H. Lim, '... Alteration of Scripture in the Habakkuk Pesher,' *JNES* 49 (1990), 190–193.

[57] Luke 1:46–55, 68–79.

[58] Luke 1:26–38; cf. Isa 7:14, 13; Gen 16:11; Isa 9:6f.; II Sam 7:12–16; Dan 7:14.

[59] Matt 2:1–23; cf. Mic 5:1, 3 (2, 4) + II Sam 5:2; Hos 11:1; Jer 31:15; ? Isa 11:1; Jer 23:5 or Judg 13:5.

[60] Num 24:17; Exod 2:15; 4:19.

to the Exodus.[61] The raising of the widow's son highlights the people's misunderstanding of who Jesus is by plain allusions to a similar miracle by Elijah.[62] The Triumphal Entry (Mark 11:1–10) is a messianic act based upon Isa 62:11 and Zech 9:9, as the crowd recognizes and Matthew (21:4f.) and John (12:15) make explicit, and the Cleansing of the Temple and the Last Supper are presented in a similar manner.[63]

This kind of narrative midrash is in several respects different from certain rabbinic midrashim that elaborate, usually via wordplay, a biblical word or verse into a fictional story:[64]

1. While the rabbinic midrash seeks to discover some hidden element within the Old Testament text itself, the New Testament midrash with its eschatological orientation applies the text theologically to some aspect of Jesus' life and ministry.

2. While for the rabbis the text is primary, the New Testament writers give primacy to Jesus and to the surrounding messianic events, or tradition of events, and only then use Old Testament texts to explain or illuminate them. They may describe the events in biblical language and may on occasion allude to a prior fictional midrash (e.g. I Cor 10:4), but they never seem to reverse their priorities so as to make the Old Testament text the locus for creating stories about Jesus.

This holds true also for the Infancy Narratives where, even on the unlikely assumption of the writers' total loss of a salvation-history perspective, the wide-ranging mélange of citations and allusions could have coalesced only around preexisting traditions and, in any case, could not have produced the stories in the Gospels.[65] For example, only because Matthew (2:6, 23; 4:15) had a tradition that Jesus was born in Bethlehem and raised in Galilee does he use Mic 5:2(1) of Jesus' birth and Jer 23:5; Isa 11:1; 9:2f.

---

[61] Matt 14:13–21 parr; cf. Exod 16:12–15; 18:21; Deut 18:15. Further, 1QS 2:21f.; 1QSa 1:14f.; 2:1.

[62] Luke 7:11–17, 16; cf. I Kg 17:10, 23; Luke 9:19.

[63] Mk 11:1–11; Matt 21:10–17; Jn 2:17; Matt 26:20–29 parr.

[64] For examples, cf. J. Weingreen, *From Bible to Mishna*, Manchester 1976, 18 (*B. T. Sota* 36b–37a, on Psalm 68:28 [27], *etc.*); Ellis (note 4), 290–212 = *JBL* 76 (1957) 53–56 (*T. Sukka* 3:11ff., *etc.*, on Num 21:17f.).

[65] Otherwise: R. H. Gundry, *Matthew*, Grand Rapids 1982, 26–41; T. L. Brodie, '… Luke 7.11–17 as an *Imitatio* of I Kings 17.17–24,' *NTS* 32 (1986), 263; A. T. Hanson, *The Living Utterances of God*, London 1983, 76, qualifying his better judgement in *Studies in Paul's Technique and Theology*, London 1974, 207: 'We are never led to think that [the New Testament writers] are themselves inventing *Haggadah*, a narrative midrash.'

(8:23 f.) of his youth and ministry and not vice versa. The texts themselves could be applied to either eventuality.

More subtly, certain of Jesus' parables are based upon Old Testament passages; but this may be so because they are biblical expositions, excerpted from earlier explicit midrashim (see below). The Revelation of St. John represents a comprehensive adaptation of Old Testament images and motifs, using midrashic techniques, to verbalize the eschatological visions of the Seer. In I Tim 1:9f. the fifth to the ninth commands of the Decalogue are transposed to accord with a current interpretation of the violation of these commandments:

Exodus 20:12–16	*I Timothy 1:9f.*
Honour your father and your mother	Murderers of fathers and … mothers
You shall not commit murder	Manslayers
You shall not commit adultery	Immoral persons, sodomites
You shall not steal	Kidnappers
You shall not bear false witness	Liars, perjurers

Interpretive alterations within Old Testament quotations are a third and more common form of implicit midrash. They are characteristic of certain classes of New Testament citations and, as will be seen below, are frequent in quotations used within explicit midrash patterns. Sometimes they simply contemporize the citation to the current audience. For example, 'Damascus' in Amos 5:27 becomes 'Babylon' in Acts 7:43. More generally, such alterations appear to serve the writer's purpose by accenting a particular interpretation or application of the citation. They may involve either elaborate alterations of the Old Testament text[66] or the simple but significant change of one or two words, as in the following examples:

Behold, I am sending my messenger *before your face*.
Matt 11:10 (Mal 3:10)

… you shall not steal, you shall not bear false witness, you shall not *defraud*.
Mark 10:19f. (Exod 20:12–16)

The stone set at naught by *you* builders …
Acts 4:11 (Ps 118:22)

Everyone who believes on him shall not be put to shame.
Rom 10:11 (Isa 28:16)

---

[66] These are often found in merged or composite citations of several Old Testament texts, e. g. Rom 3:10–18; I Cor 2:9; II Cor 6:16ff. Cf. also the running summary of the Patriarchal and Exodus story in Acts 7. Further, E. E. Ellis, 'Quotations in the New Testament,' *ISBE*[2] IV, 23f.

In burnt offerings and sin offerings you did not *have pleasure*.   Heb 10:6 (Ps 40:6)

The textual alterations in the last two examples are designed to create verbal links within a larger exposition of Scripture, i.e. a pattern of explicit midrash.[67] We may now turn to a closer examination of that phenomenon.

Explicit Midrash

Explict midrash in the New Testament takes various forms. It may appear as a cluster of texts and commentary on a particular theme, similar to the *florilegia* found at Qumran,[68] or as a special pattern.[69] More frequently, it occurs in literary forms found in rabbinic expositions, the 'proem' and *'yelammedenu rabbenu'* ('let our master teach us') midrashim. While in the rabbinic collections these forms date from several centuries after the New Testament,[70] they were hardly borrowed from the Christians. Also, similar patterns are present in the first-century Jewish writer, Philo.[71] One may infer then, with some confidence, that their presence in the New Testament reflects a common, rather widespread Jewish usage. The rabbinic proem midrash generally had the following form:[72]

The (Pentateuchal) text for the day.
A second text, the proem or 'opening' for the discourse.

---

[67] Cf. Rom 10:12f., 16, 18; Heb 10:38.

[68] 4QFlor. Cf. Heb 1:1–14; Jude 4–23; Ellis (note 4), 221–226.

[69] E.g. John 1:1–18; Matt 4:1–11; cf. P. Borgen, 'Observations on the Targumic Character of the Prologue of John,' *NTS* 16 (1969–70), 288–295; B. Gerhardsson, *The Testing of God's Son*, Lund 1966. Perhaps Heb 1:1–2:18. Luke 4:16–30 and Mark 13:5–29 appear to reflect expository patterns that have been partly dissipated in transmission.

[70] E.g. *Pesikta Rabbati* (2 vols., ed. W.G. Braude, New Haven 1968), which apparently is a sixth or seventh century collection of the expositions of third and fourth century rabbis (I, 26). See also J.W. Bowker, *The Targums and Rabbinic Literature*, Cambridge 1969, 74–77.

[71] E.g. Philo, *De Sacrif. Abel.* 76–87: Lev 2:14 + Commentary with verbal links and supplementary texts + Concluding allusion to the opening text + Final texts (Exod 6:7; Lev 26:12).

[72] E.g. *Pesikta Rabbati* 34:1: Zech 9:9 + Isa 61:9 + Commentary, with verbal links and illustrative stories + Isa 62:2 + Final reference to Isa 61:9. Cf. Braude (note 70); further, cf. 'Lam (= Ekah) Rabbah,' *Midrash Rabbah*, 10 vols., ed. H. Freedman, London 1961, VII; *Pesikta de Rab Kahana*, ed. W.G. Braude, Philadelphia 1975; J. Mann, *The Bible as Read and Preached in the Old Synagogue*, 2 vols., Cincinnati 1940 (²1971), 1966.

Exposition, including supplementary quotations, parables and other commentary with verbal links to the initial and final texts.

A final text, usually repeating or alluding to the text for the day, and sometimes adding a concluding application.[73]

The *yelammedenu* midrash had the same general structure except for an interrogative opening in which there is posed a question or problem that the exposition serves to answer.

As might be expected, the New Testament exegetical patterns display a number of differences from those of the rabbis. They represent an earlier stage in the development of the art as well as a divergent theological orientation. In addition, they apparently have been frequently abbreviated and otherwise altered before their incorporation into the present context. Among the more notable differences are the following:

1. The New Testament midrashim do not appear to be related to a (Pentateuchal) lectionary cycle.
2. They often lack a second, proem text.
3. They use a final text that does not correspond or allude to the initial text.
4. Occasionally, they have lost their catchword connections.[74]
5. More importantly, they consistently have an eschatological orientation.

Nevertheless, the New Testament patterns show an unmistakable resemblance to rabbinic midrash that cannot be coincidental and that permits a qualified label of 'proem' and '*yelammedenu*.'

In the expositions attributed to Jesus by the Evangelists[75] the *yelammedenu* form is usually found in discussions about the halakha[76] or other

---

[73] Cf. E. Stein, 'Die homiletische Peroratio...,' *HUCA* 8–9 (1931–32), 353–371.

[74] E. g. Mt 11:7–15: Theme and initial text (7–10; Mal 3:1) + Exposition (11–13) + Final text (14; allusion to Mal 3:23 = 4:5). But note the formula οὗτός ἐστιν (10, cf. 14) and the presence in Malachi (3:2,23) of words in the Matthean exposition: ἔρχεσθαι; ἡμέρα; cf. μείζων / μεγάλη (11 f., 14).

[75] While they were somewhat altered in transmission, less so in Matthew than elsewhere apparently, these expositions belong to the bedrock of the Gospel traditions and orginate in the preresurrection mission of Jesus. Cf. Ellis (note 4), 154–159, 247–253; idem, 'Gospels Criticism,' *The Gospel and the Gospels*, ed. P. Stuhlmacher, Grand Rapids 1991, 38f. (GT: 40).

[76] Cf. on ritual defilement, Matt 15:1–9: Question and initial texts (1–4; Exod 20:12; 21:17) + Exposition/application (5–6) + Concluding text (7–9; Isa 29:13). On divorce, Mt 19:3–8: Question, answered by initial texts (3–5; Gen 1:27; 2:24) + Exposition, including a supplementary text (7–8 a; Deut 24:1) + Concluding allusion

questions[77] between Jesus and other Jewish theologians. Compare Matt 12:1–8 on what is permitted on the sabbath:[78]

1–2   – Theme and question raised by the initial texts (cf. Exod 20:10; 34:21)
3–5   – Counter question and exposition via supplementary texts (I Sam 21:7; Num 28:9; θυσία), verbally linked to the theme and the initial texts (ποιεῖν; ἐσθίειν).
6 f.   – Eschatological application via an *a fortiori* argument and a final text (Hos 6:6, θυσία).

In the teachings of Jesus given in the Gospels the proem form rarely appears. But one striking example, dealing with God's judgement on the nation's leaders for their rejection of the Messiah, occurs in Matt 21:33–46 and parallels:[79]

33   – Initial text (Isa 5:1 f.).
34–41   – Exposition via a parable, verbally linked to the initial and/or final texts (ἀμπελών, 33, 39; λίθος, 42, 44, cf. 35: Isa 5:2; cf. οἰκοδομεῖν, 33, 42).
42–44   – Concluding texts (Ps 118:22 f.; Dan 2:34 f., 44 f.) and application.

In Acts and the Epistles the proem midrash is much more frequent, the *yelammedenu* relatively less so.[80] Gal 4:21–5:1 offers an instructive example:

---

to initial texts (8 b). On the meaning of a commandment, Lk 10:25–37: Question and initial texts (25–27; Deut 6:5; Lev 19:18) + A Second text (28; Lev 18:5) + Exposition (29–36) + Concluding allusion to second text (37). Cf. Ellis (note 4), 158 f.

[77] On messianic themes e.g. Mt 21:15 f.: Theme and initial text (Ps 118:25; cf. Mt 21:9) + Objection + Counter question with concluding text (Ps 8:2). On resurrection, cf. Mt 22:23–33: Question posed by initial text and interpretation (23–28; Deut 25:5 f.) + Answer via counter interpretation and concluding texts (29–32; Exod 3:6).

[78] It is similar to the rabbinic *yelammedenu* pattern even though, like other midrashim of Jesus, it was initially an adversary context and was adapted to a teacher/ disciple context as it was summarized, learned and transmitted by Jesus' pupils. Daube (*New Testament* [note 7], 170–175) identifies the form as 'revolutionary action, protest, silencing of remonstrants.' However, the action usually involves a violation of an accepted interpretation of biblical law, the halakha, and on that basis is objected to and the objection answered. It may be, then, that this represents a biblical dispute even when express biblical references are partial or absent, perhaps having disappeared in transmission (cf. Matt 9:9–13; 12:22–30; Luke 13:10–17).

[79] Cf. Ellis (note 4), 251 f.; S. Kim, 'Jesus... the Stone...,' in Hawthorne (note 193), 135 ff., 142 ff. Another proem-like pattern, somewhat reworked, appears in John 6:31–58: Initial text (31; Exod 16:4) + Exposition with dialogue (32–44) + Supporting texts (45; Isa 54:13; Jer 31:33 f.) + Exposition and concluding reference to the initial text (58). Cf. P. Borgen, *Bread From Heaven*, Leiden 1965, 37–43.

[80] But see Ellis (note 4), 137n, 218 ff. and (for illustrations of Proem-type expositions) 155 ff. Further, Ellis (note 66), 23. Cf. Rom 4:1–25; 9:6–29; I Cor 1:18–31; 2:6–16; Gal 3:6–14; Heb 10:5–39. It may be, as J. W. Bowker ('Speeches in Acts,' *NTS* 14, 1967–68, 107 ff.) has suggested, that Acts 15:14–21 contains the remnant of a

21 f.   – Introduction and initial text (cf. Gen 21).
23–29   – A supplementary citation (27: Isa 54:1) and exposition, verbally linked to
         the initial and final text (ἐλευθέρα, 22 f., 26, 30; παιδίσκη, 22 f., 30 f.; υἱός =
         τέκνον, 22, 25, 27 f., 30 f.).
30 ff.   – Final text and application, referring to the initial text (cf. Gen. 21:10).

It is noteworthy that the initial and final texts are, in fact, implicit midrashim, the first a selective summary of Gen 21 and the last an interpolated citation shaped to underscore the key term ἐλευθέρα.[81] This kind of usage alerts one to recognize the presence of implicit (Rom 3:10–18) and explicit (Rom 4:1–25) midrashim as 'texts' in a more elaborate commentary pattern in Rom 1:17–4:25:[82]

1:17   – Initial text (Hab 2:4, δίκαιος, πίστις).
1:18–3:3 – Exposition, verbally linked to the initial and/or subsequent texts (κρίνειν,
            2:1, 3, 12, 16; δίκαιος, 2:13; πίστος, 3:3).
3:4   – Supplementary text (Ps 51:6, δικαιοῦν, κρίνειν).
3:5–9   – Exposition (δικαιοσύνη, 5; κρίνειν, 6 f.).
3:10–18   – Supplementary texts (Eccl. 7:20; Ps 14:1–3; 5:10 (9); Isa 59:7 f.; etc.; cf.
            δίκαιος, 10).
3:19–31   – Exposition (δικαιοῦν, 20, 24, 26, 28, 30; δικαιοσύνη, 21 f., 25.; δίκαιος, 26;
            πίστις 22, 25 f., 27 f., 30 f.).
4:1–25   – Final 'text'[83] (δικαιοῦν, 2, 5; δικαιοσύνη, 3, 5 f., 9, 11, 13, 22; πίστις, 5, 9,
            11 ff., 14, 16, 19 f.).

---

yelammedenu midrash on perhaps the last, decisive halakhic question that engaged the Christian community as a whole: 'Must proselytes – and by inference any believer in Jesus as Messiah – be circumcised and keep the Mosaic regulations?'

[81] Cf. also I Cor 10:1–31: Initial 'texts' (1–5; Exod 13–17; Num 14:29) + Application (6) + Supplementary text (7; Exod 32:6) + Exposition/application (8–13) + Extended application (14–30) and concluding allusion to the initial 'texts' (31). Cf. E. E. Ellis, 'Traditions in 1 Corinthians,' *NTS* 32 (1986), 490 f.; W. A. Meeks, '... Midrash and Paraenesis in 1 Corinthians 10.1–22,' *JSNT* 16 (1982) 64–78. II Peter 3:3–13 is similar: Initial 'texts' and application (3 f.; cited Christian prophecy and 5 ff.; Gen 1–6) + Supplementary text (8; Ps 90:4) + Exposition and cited *florilegium* (10) verbally linked to the texts (9–12) + Final text and applications (13: cf. Isa 65:17). Cf. also Heb 5:1–7:28: Theme and initial texts (5:1–6; Ps 2:7; 110:4) + Exposition (5:7–10 [+ Inserted exhortation (5:11–6:12)]) + Supplementary text (6:13 f.; Gen 22:16 f.) + Exposition (6:15–20) + Supplementary text (7:1 f.; Gen 14:17–20) + Exposition (7:3–27) + Concluding allusion to the initial texts (7:28). Cf. Ellis (note 4), 157.

[82] See Ellis (note 4), 217 f. Cf. also I Cor 1:18–3:20: Initial 'text' (1:18–31) + Exposition (2:1–5) + Supplementary 'text' (2:6–16) + Exposition (3:1–17) + Final texts (3:18–20; Job 5:13; Ps 94:11).

[83] Note the commentary pattern of Rom 4:1–25: Theme and initial text (1–3; Gen 15:6) + Exposition (4 ff.) + Supplementary text (7 f.; Ps 32:1 f.) + Exposition (9–16) + Supplementary text with exposition (17; Gen 17:5) + ?Supplementary text (18; Gen 15:5) + Exposition (19–21) + Concluding allusion to the initial text and application (22–25). Cf. Borgen (note 79), 47–52.

The above examples indicate the way in which explicit midrash was employed, both by Jesus and by the early Christian prophets and teachers, to establish and justify their new understanding of the Scriptures. There is some evidence that this usage represented only the first stage of a process that soon developed into an independent employment of the texts and of the expositions.

From Midrash to Testimonia

Several scholars have argued that in rabbinic literature the mishnah-form, that is, independent commentary that is topically arranged, developed in part from detaching the commentary from an earlier explicit midrash-form, that is, biblical texts + commentary.[84] Something similar seems to have occurred in the New Testament church. Explicit midrash was a means to establish a particular interpretation of Scripture while isolated proof-texts did not, apparently, have that function or that effectiveness.[85] It is likely, then, that a midrash of a given text preceded its use as an isolated 'testimony' in which a Christian understanding of the text was assumed. The use of the same texts both in midrashim and as *testimonia* supports this supposition even if the particular New Testament midrash is not the direct antecedent of the 'testimony' text. For example, midrashim in Acts 2 and Heb 5–7 and (underlying) in Mark 13 establish, respectively, that Ps 110:1 and Dan 7:13 applied to Jesus; the independent use of the verses in Mark 14:62, summarizing Jesus' response at his trial, presupposes that understanding.[86]

---

[84] Cf. J. Z. Lauterbach, 'Midrash and Mishna,' *JQR* 5 (1914–15), 503–527, 509, 513; 6 (1915–16), 23–95, 303–323 (= *Rabbinic Essays*, Cincinnatti 1951, 163–256); D. W. Halivni, *Midrash, Mishnah and Gemara*, Cambridge MA 1986, 18–37, 93–104. Otherwise: S. Safrai, 'Halakha,' *Compendia* II, 3, i (1987), 148, 153–55. For a similar process in the targums cf. P. Kahle, *The Cairo Geniza*, London 1947, 125 f.; Oxford ²1959, 202.

[85] Cf. Doeve (note 38), 116: 'Words lifted from their scriptural context can never be a testimonium to the Jewish mind. The word becomes a testimonium... after one has brought out its meaning with the aid of other parts of scripture.'

[86] On Mk 13 and Heb 5–7 see notes 99 and 81. Cf. Acts 2:14–36: Theme and initial text (14–21; Joel 2:28–32 = 3:1–5) + Exposition (22–24) + Supplementary text (25–28; Ps 16:8–11) + Exposition (29–34) + Final text and application (34 ff.; Ps 110:1). See Ellis (note 4), 199–205. Cf. also Heb 2:6–9 with I Cor 15:27 and Eph 1:20, 22 (Ps 8); Acts 13:16–41 with Luke 3:22D, Heb 1:5 and II Cor 6:18 (II Sam 7:6–16; Ps 2:7).

On the same analogy certain clustered parables of Jesus, like those in Matt 13 or Luke 15, may have been excerpted from earlier commentary formats like those of Luke 10:25–37 or Matt 21:33–44. This is suggested especially for those parables that themselves echo Old Testament passages[87] or utilize formulas customary in midrash.[88]

Perspective and Presuppositions

It has been argued above that, in terms of method, the early Christian use of the Old Testament was thoroughly Jewish and had much in common with other Jewish groups. Much more significant than method, however, was the interpretation of Scripture offered by Jesus and his followers. In some respects this also agrees with previous Jewish interpretation, but in others it displays an innovative and unique departure. Sometimes the New Testament writers (to whom we shall limit this survey), and Jesus as he is represented by them, set forth their distinctive views in a biblical exegesis; sometimes they appear, at least to us, simply to presuppose a 'Christian' exegetical conclusion. They apparently derive their particular understanding of Scripture both from Jesus' teaching and from implications drawn from his resurrection from the dead. Their perspective on the Old Testament is especially shaped by presuppositions in at least four areas: (1) eschatology, (2) typology, (3) a corporate understanding of man and of Messiah, (4) a conception of Scripture as a hidden Word of God. In the following survey their Old Testament citations and commentary (i.e. midrash), illustrative of the early Christian perspective on these issues, will be indicated in the footnotes.

Eschatology

The Old Testament prophets predicted the coming of the 'last days' (אחרית הימים) and/or 'the day of the Lord' that would bring the 'kingdom of God', together with a final judgement and a redemption of God's

---

[87] E.g. cf. Lk 15:3–7 with Zech 10–11; 13:7; Ezek 34:11f. Cf. France (note 1), 208f.

[88] E.g. οὗτός ἐστιν. Cf. Matt 13:20, 22ff., 38.

people.[89] Apocalyptic prophets, who were in important respects the mid-wives of first-century messianic Judaism, supplemented and defined these predictions by interpreting the coming kingdom in terms of a catastrophic and cosmic judgement of God followed by a renewed creation.[90] This point of view is reflected by two immediate antecedents of the Christian movement, the communities of Qumran and of John the Baptist, who consider the kingdom of God to be 'at hand.' The Baptist points to Jesus as the one through whom God will accomplish the final redemption and judgement.[91]

Jesus and the New Testament apostles and prophets are at one with apocalyptic Judaism in several respects.

1. They conceive of history within the *framework of two ages*, this world or age and the age to come,[92] and they identify the kingdom of God with the coming age.[93]

2. They view themselves to be living in *the last (ἔσχατος) days* preceding the consummation.[94]

3. They proclaim God's final redemption to be *a salvation in history*,[95] that is, a redemption of matter in time.[96]

---

[89] Num 24:14; Isa 2:2–4; Dan 10:14; Hos 3:4f.; Amos 5:18–27 (cf. Acts 7:42f.); Mic 4:1ff.; Zech 14 (cf. Matt 25:31; Rev 21:6, 25; 22:1, 17). Cf. P. von der Osten-Sacken, *Die Apokalyptik in ihrem Verhältnis zu Prophetie und Weisheit*, München 1969, 39–43; G. Kittel and G. von Rad, 'ἔσχατος,' 'ἡμέρα,' *TDNT* 2 (1964/1935), 697f., 944.

[90] Cf. P. Hanson, *The Dawn of Apocalyptic*, Philadelphia 1975, 150f. (in Isa 56–66), 371f. (Zech 14); D.S. Russell, *The Method and Message of Jewish Apocalyptic*, London 1964, 280–284; H. Ringgren, *The Faith of Qumran*, Philadelphia 1963, 155–166. But see C. Rowland, *The Open Heaven: A Study of Apocalyptic in Judaism and Early Christianity*, London 1982.

[91] Mt 3:2; cf. 1QpHab 2:7; 7:2 where the Qumran writer identifies the community with 'the last generation' (הדור האחרון). Further, cf. Mt 3:1–12; 11:2–15; Mark 1:4–7; Lk 3:1–20; 7:18–28.

[92] I.e. αἰών (Mt 12:32; II Cor 4:4; Gal 1:4f.; Eph 1:21; Heb 6:5); κόσμος (Jn 16:11; 18:36; I Cor 7:29ff.; Eph 2:2; Jas 2:5; II Pet 3:6f.); οἰκουμένη (Acts 17:31; Heb 1:6; 2:5). In rabbinic and other Jewish writings cf. Billerbeck (note 31), IV, 799–976.

[93] Cf. Mt 13:40–43; Lk 21:31; Acts 1:6ff.; I Cor 15:50; Heb 12:26ff.; II Pet 1:10f.; Rev 11:15–18.

[94] E.g. Acts 2:17 in a commentary; Heb 1:1f., introducing a *florilegium* of Old Testament texts (1:3–14) + Exposition (2:1–5) + Supporting text (2:6ff.) + Exposition (2:8b–11) + Supporting texts (2:12f.) + Concluding exposition (2:14–18). II Pet 3:3, introducing a commentary (note 81); Jude 18f. in an elaborate commentary on the theme of judgement (cf. Ellis [note 4], 221–236). Cf. also II Tim 3:1; I John 2:18.

[95] Cf. O. Cullmann, *Salvation in History*, London 1967.

[96] This stands in contrast to conceptions dominant in current Platonic thought,

Equally important, however, they modify apocalyptic ideas in four significant ways.

Christian Distinctives

1. In the teaching of Jesus and of his apostles the two-fold consummation of redemption and judgement becomes *a two-stage consummation*. As 'redemption' the kingdom of God is regarded as already present in certain respects, that is, in its manifestation through the work of Jesus the Messiah,[97] and in its 'coming in power' within the lifetime of Jesus' hearers, that is, at the transfiguration of Jesus and/or at the Christian Pentecost.[98] As 'judgement' and as final redemption the kingdom will come only at the end of this age in the second and glorious appearing of the Messiah[99] which, as in the Old Testament prophets, is represented to be just over the horizon, existentially 'near' but chronologically indefinite.[100]

---

which by the first century was influential not only among the Stoics and Pythagoreans but also in some Jewish circles and which postulated a deliverance of the 'soul' from matter and out of time. Cf. P. Perlan in *Later Greek and Early Medieval Philosophy*, ed. A. H. Armstrong, Cambridge 1967, 126–129; E. Bréhier, *History of Philosophy: The Hellenistic and Roman Age*, Chicago 1965, 137, 168–172. On body/soul dualism in rabbinic and intertestamental Jewish literature cf. R. Meyer, *Hellenistisches in der rabbinischen Anthropologie*, Stuttgart 1937; D. S. Russell (note 90), 353–390. See also O. Cullmann, *Immortality of the Soul or Resurrection of the Dead?* London 1958; idem, *Christ and Time*, London 1953, 139–143; D. R. G. Owen, *Body and Soul*, Philadelphia 1956, 33–49.

[97] E. g. Lk 10:9, 11:20; Jn 11:24f.; cf. Col 1:12f. Cf. W. G. Kümmel, *The Theology of the New Testament*, Nashville 1973, 36–39; E. E. Ellis, *Eschatology in Luke*, Philadelphia 1972, 11–14, 16f.

[98] Acts 2:16f. in a commentary (note 86). Cf. Mk 9:1f.; Jn 14:12; Acts 1:8; Rom 14:17; 15:18f. The eschatological power (δύναμις) of the Holy Spirit that was manifested in Jesus' ministry was, after Pentecost, experienced in the wider Christian community. Cf. E. E. Ellis, 'Present and Future Eschatology in Luke,' *NTS* 12 (1965–66), 27–41. Otherwise: W. G. Kümmel, *Promise and Fulfilment*, London 1957, 19–87.

[99] Lk 21:31, applying a re-worked commentary (21:8–28 = Mk 13:5–27 = Mt 24:4–31) on Daniel 7–12 (cf. L. Hartman, *Prophecy Interpreted*, Lund 1966). Cf. Mt 25:31f.; Lk 22:18, 28ff.; Jn 5:25–29; II Thess 1:5–10; 2:8; Heb 9:27f.; 12:26ff. Note the omission of Isa 61:2b in Jesus' exposition of the passage at Nazareth (Lk 4:18–21). This accords with his perception elsewhere (e. g. Lk 9:54f.; Mt 11:4ff.; 26:52ff.) of his present mission and is not to be regarded as a Lukan (or pre-Lukan) editorial even though it also serves a Lukan interest (cf. Lk 22:50f. with Mk 14:47).

[100] Mk 13:32, applying a re-worked commentary (see note 99); II Thess 2:1–7, with allusions to Dan 11:36, Ezek 28:2 and Isa 11:4; Heb 10:37, concluding a

2. The two-age, horizontal perspective of apocalyptic Judaism is also modified by *a 'vertical', heaven/earth dimension*. A vertical perspective is already at hand, of course, in that the kingdom of God is 'the kingdom of the heavens' (ἡ βασιλεία τῶν οὐρανῶν).[101] Thus, the believers' 'treasure', 'reward'[102] and 'names' are 'in heaven', or 'in God', that is, where God's rule is now manifested and from which it shall be revealed.[103] This vertical element is given a specifically Christian understanding in terms of the Messiah who has been exalted into heaven.[104] For in the resurrected body of the Messiah the world to come has been brought into being and, pending its public revelation to earth on the last day,[105] is now manifested 'in heaven.'[106]

3. Furthermore, the New Testament teachers regard this age and the age to come as standing in a *relationship of both discontinuity and continuity*, of *novum* and fulfilment. In contrast to some other Jewish views they consider resurrection life to be radically different from that of the present age.[107] They represent it, however, not as a 'non-material' life but rather as a modification of a strictly 'materialist' conception reflected in some sectors of Judaism.[108] In Paul's words the life of the age to come involves a 'Spirit-empowered body' (I Cor 15:44), that is, the present body 'transformed' to

---

commentary (see note 123); II Pet 3:8–13 in a commentary (see note 81). Cf. Isa 13:6; Joel 1:15; Luke 12:39f.; I Thess 5:10; Jas 5:7f.

[101] Mt 4:17 *et passim*. But see Billerbeck (note 31), I, 172–184.

[102] Mt 5:12; 6:19f.; 19:21; Lk 12:33f., which may have been extracted from a commentary on Zech 11 and 13; cf. F.F. Bruce, 'The Book of Zechariah and the Passion Narrative,' *BJRL* 43 (1960–61), 342–349; France (note 1), 208.

[103] Cf. Lk 10:20; Rom 1:18 and 2:5f. (see above, 102); I Cor 3:3 (see note 82); I Pet 1:4f.; 4:13; Rev 20:15; G. von Rad und H. Traub, 'οὐρανός,' *TDNT* 5 (1967/1954), 507ff., 520–535.

[104] E.g. Acts 2:34 (cf. 3:21) in a commentary (see note 86); Rom 10:6 in a commentary (?10:4–11:12) on Deut 30:12f., *etc.*; Heb 1:13 in a *florilegium* (1:3–14) including Ps 110:1; Heb 8:1 in a commentary (see note 124); cf. Acts 7:55; I Pet 3:22. Somewhat different is the commentary on Exod 16 in Jn 6:31–58 concerning the pre-existent Son, who has come down from heaven (see note 79).

[105] E.g. Mt 24:30 in a re-worked commentary (note 99); Heb 9:27f. and 10:37 in a commentary (note 124); II Pet 3:3–13 in a commentary (note 81). Cf. Acts 3:21; I Cor 15:22f.; Phil 3:21; I Jn 2:28.

[106] E.g. Gal 4:26 in a commentary; Heb 2:9 (cf. 4:14) in a commentary (1:1–2:18) on Ps 8 *etc.* Cf. Lk 24:25–27; Rev 21:1f. See note 94.

[107] Mt 22:30f. in a commentary (see note 77); I Cor 15:44–49, commenting on Gen 2:7. Cf. E.E. Ellis, 'Life,' *The Illustrated Bible Dictionary. Revised Edition*, 3 vols., ed. N. Hillyer, Leicester UK and Wheaton IL 1980, II, 901–904.

[108] E.g. in Mt 22:28 (presupposed); II Macc 7:7–29; II Baruch (Apocalypse) 50:2–51:3; Sibylline Oracles 4, 181–192.

be like Messiah's glorious body'.[109] One observes, here and elsewhere, that early Christianity defined the life of the age to come in terms of the testimony to Christ's resurrection in which the risen Messiah was seen to be both 'glory' and 'flesh,' both a new creation and the physical body of the crucified Messiah redeemed from the tomb.[110] Thus, the age to come is regarded neither as a mere extension of the present age nor as isolated from it. The future age is considered to be rather a transformation and transfiguration of the present world that is brought about by a mighty act of God.

4. Finally, unlike other Jewish groups, the pupils and first followers of Jesus teach that the age to come, the age of resurrection, would begin not at the end of the present age, as Judaism had usually believed, but in the midst of it. Already, in the resurrected Messiah, the first to rise from the dead and the firstfruits of those who have fallen asleep in death, the age to come has broken into the present age and now determines its ultimate course.[111] Again, they attribute their convictions to their experience of the resurrected Jesus who becomes the model by which their views are shaped.[112]

Typology

Typological interpretation had been employed earlier in Judaism[113] and became, in early Christianity, a basic key by which the Scriptures were understood.[114] In New Testament usage it rested upon the conviction of a

---

[109] I Cor 15:44; Phil 3:21. Cf. I Cor 15:12–18.

[110] Mt 28:8f.; Lk 24:26, 36–40; Jn 20:26f.; I Cor 15:4. The tendency to assign greater historical worth to traditions concerning the 'glory' than to those concerning the 'physical' character of the Messiah's resurrection does not appear to be justified (cf. J. E. Alsup, *The Post-Resurrection Appearance Stories of the Gospel Tradition*, Stuttgart and London 1975, 55–61, 266–274). Cf. Ellis, 'Sōma' (note 137).

[111] Cf. Acts 26:23; I Cor 15:20; Cullmann (note 95), 166–185. For the thesis that the Qumran writers also regarded the salvation of the age to come as already present cf. H. G. Kuhn, *Enderwartung und gegenwärtiges Heil*, Göttingen 1966.

[112] Jn 11:25f.; Acts 4:2; I Cor 15:12–22; Heb 2:10.

[113] The Exodus provided the model or 'type' by which the Old Testament prophets understood God's subsequent acts of redemption of Israel (Isa 40–66) and of Gentiles. Cf. M. Fishbane, 'Use, Authority and Interpretation of Mikra at Qumran,' *Compendia* II, 1 (1988), 373ff.; D. Daube, *The Exodus Pattern in the Bible*, London 1963; D. Patte, *Early Jewish Hermeneutic*, Missoula 1975, 170ff.

[114] On divergent approaches see below, 141–148. Cf. Ellis, *Paul's Use* (note 2),

correspondence between God's acts in the present age and those in the person and work of Jesus that inaugurated the age to come. From past Old Testament events and institutions it drew out the meaning of the present time of salvation and, in turn, interpreted present events as a typological prophecy of the future consummation. It may be appreciated in the framework of the following four points:

1. To summarize items discussed in the previous chapter, New Testament typological interpretation is to be distinguished from certain other approaches.[115] Unlike allegory, it regards the Scriptures not as verbal metaphors hiding a deeper meaning (ὑπόνοια) but as historical accounts from whose literal sense the meaning of the text arises. Unlike the 'history of religions' hermeneutic, it seeks the meaning of current, New Testament events not from general religious history but from the salvation-history of Israel. Unlike the use of 'type' (τύπος) in pagan and some patristic literature, which assumes a cyclical-repetitive historical process, it relates the past to the present in terms of a historical correspondence and escalation in which the divinely ordered prefigurement finds a complement in the subsequent and greater event. Like rabbinic midrash, it applies the Old Testament to contemporary situations, but it does so with historical distinctions different from those of the rabbis. Like Qumran exegesis, it gives to the Scriptures a present-time, eschatological application, but it does so with an eschatological and messianic orientation different from that at Qumran.

2. In the New Testament typology appears, broadly speaking, as *creation typology* and *covenant typology*. The former kind presents Adam as 'a type of the one to come' (Rom 5:14), that is, of Jesus the Messiah. A similar creation typology is implied in the designation of Adam, like Jesus, as 'son of God' and in the description of the age to come in terms of Paradise[116] or of a new creation.[117] Apparently, it is also reflected in Jesus' teaching on divorce: The messianic age is to fulfil the intended order of creation in

---

126–135; W.G. Kümmel, 'Schriftauslegung,' *RGG*³ V (1961), 1519; Goppelt (note 2); U. Luz, *Das Geschichtsverständnis des Paulus*, München 1968, 53–56. Otherwise: R.B. Hays, *Echoes of Scripture in the Letters of Paul*, New Haven CT 1989, 91–102.

[115] Largely following Goppelt (note 2), 17f., 29–32, 194–205 (GT: 18f., 31–34, 235–248). Cf. Luz (note 114). See above, 61 ff.; below, 141–157.

[116] Lk 3:22, 38; cf. 23:43; I Cor 15:21 f., 45–46; Rev 2:7; 22:2.

[117] Rom 8:21 ff.; II Cor 5:17; I Pet 3:20 f.; II Pet 3:13 concluding a commentary (see note 81).

which both divorce and polygamy are excluded.[118] In a word creation typology depicts the Messiah and his people as the head of a new creation in which, with a change of key, the original purposes of God are to be fulfilled.

In covenant typology various persons, events and institutions of Old Testament Israel are viewed as prophetic prefigurements of New Testament realities. The Exodus events, Paul writes, were intended as 'types for us' and 'were written down for our admonition upon whom the ends of the ages have come'[119] or, more negatively, the ritual laws from Sinai were only 'a shadow (σκιά) of the good things to come.'[120] In a typological correspondence oriented more specifically to Jesus, the royal and the servant Psalms are applied to the Messiah who represents or incorporates in himself God's servant people and who is the heir to David's throne.[121] Similarly, the Exodus 'Passover Lamb'[122] is a type of Jesus, who in his sacrificial death brings the covenant of Sinai to its proper goal and end[123] and establishes a new covenant.[124]

Since the new covenant associated with Jesus' death issues in the new creation associated with his resurrection, the two typologies may be closely intertwined. For example, the 'son of man' title given to Jesus is probably derived from typological interpretations of Dan 7:13 and of Ps

---

[118] Mt 19:8f. in a commentary. The phrase 'and marries another' (19:9) encompasses polygamy. The exception clause (19:9; contrast Mark 10:11) appears to be a postresurrection addition in which, if one accepts Matthew's prophetic credentials, the exalted Lord qualifies the principle in somewhat the same manner as God's command in Deut 24:1–4 qualifies Gen 1:27. A similar prohibition of polygamy and, probably, divorce with an appeal to Gen 1:27 is made also at Qumran (CD 4:20f.).

[119] I Cor 10:6, 11 in a commentary (see note 81). Cf. Rom 15:4.

[120] Col 2:16f. (calendrical and food laws); Heb 8:5; 10:1 (Levitical system).

[121] E.g. Luke 4:18 (Isa 61:1f.; 58:6) in a synagogue exposition; Acts 13:33 (Ps 2:7) in a synagogue exposition, 13:16–41: Theme and initial texts (16–19; cf. Deut 4:34–38; 7:1) + Exposition (20ff.) + Supplementary text (22f. cf. I Sam 13:14; II Sam 7:6–16; Ps 89:21 [20]) + Exposition (23–33) + Supplementary texts (33–35; Ps 2:7; Isa 55:3; Ps 16:10) + Exposition (36–40) + Final text (41; Hab 1:5). Cf. Ellis (note 4), 199.

[122] I Cor 5:7; Exod 12:21; cf. John 1:29; Acts 8:32; I Pet 1:19; Rev 5:12.

[123] Rom 10:4. So also, Heb 10:9f., which stands in a commentary covering Heb 10:5–39: Initial text (5–7; Ps 40:7–9) + Exposition with supplementary texts (16f., 30) and verbally linked to the initial text (8–36) + Final texts and application, verbally linked to the initial text (37–39; Isa 26:20; Hab 2:3f.). See Ellis (note 4), 155.

[124] Luke 22:20, 29. So, also, Heb 9:15, which stands in a commentary covering 8:1–10:39: Theme and initial text (8:1–13; Jer 31:31–34) + Exposition, incorporating allusions to various texts and verbally linked to the initial text (9:1–10:4) + Final 'text' (10:5–39), verbally linked to the initial text (διαθήκη, καινή, ἀληθινός). See note 123.

8:4–8 in which both covenant and Adamic motifs occur. The latter passage, apparently used in Israel's worship for the (messianic-ideal) king, also alludes to Adam.[125] In I Cor 15 and Heb 2 it is applied to Jesus, primarily as the resurrected head of a new creation, but also as 'Messiah' and 'High Priest' and 'Seed of Abraham', terms with covenantal and national connotations.[126] Dan 7:13, in imagery similar to Ps 8, seems to identify 'one like a son of man' both with 'the people of the saints of the Most High' (7:27) and with the rightful ruler of creation, who is heir to the promises given to Adam.[127] In the synoptic apocalpyse Jesus identifies this 'son of man' with his own future, glorious manifestation as Messiah.[128]

3. An Old Testament type may stand in a positive correspondence to the new-age reality or in contrast to it. This 'synthetic' and 'antithetic' typology[129] may be illustrated by two examples. Adam is like the 'eschatological Adam' in being the 'son of God' and the head of the race. But, in contrast, he brings mortality and sin while Jesus delivers man from these maladies.[130] Similarly, the law of Sinai in its ethical requirements reflects the character of God and is to be 'fulfilled' in the messianic age,[131]

---

[125] The terms 'glory' (כבוד) and 'honour' (הדר) elsewhere express the king's royal dignity (Ps 21:6[5]; 45:4f.[3f.]; Isa 22:18) and the affinities with Gen 1:26 are present in the references to dominion over the animal world. Cf. A. Bentzen, *King and Messiah*, London 1955, 41–44; C. Wifall ('Protevangelium?' CBQ 36, 1974, 365) thinks that Gen 1–3 reflects a 'messianic' framework. But see also S. Kim, *The 'Son of Man' as the Son of God*, Tübingen 1983, 31–37: With the term, Son of Man (Daniel 7:13), 'Jesus intended to reveal himself as the divine figure who was the inclusive representative (or the head) of the eschatological people of God' (36).

[126] I Cor 15:20–28; Eph 1:20–22; Heb 2:6ff. in a commentary (note 94).

[127] Gen 1:28 ('dominion'). Cf. M. Hooker, *The Son of Man in Mark*, London 1967, 11–32, 71f. For the (also probable) view that identifies 'son of man' in Dan 7 with a divine or an angelic figure cf. the discussion in S. Kim, *The Origin of Paul's Gospel*, Tübingen ²1984, 246–252.

[128] Mk 13:26f. concluding a commentary (see note 99). Cf. also Mk 14:62; Rev 1:7; 14:14ff. Cf. Grimm and Betz (note 1), II, 73–102.

[129] Cf. Luz (note 114), 59f.; Hanson, *Studies* (note 65), 151ff. Abraham represents only a positive correspondence (i. e. his faith) and not an antithetic (e. g. his circumcision); Moses (Heb 3:2–6), Jerusalem (Gal 4:25; Rev 11:8; 21:2) and the Exodus (I Cor 10:1–4; II Cor 3:7–11) may represent both.

[130] I Cor 15:21f., 45–49, commenting on Gen 2:7; 5:3; cf. Rom 5:12–21; Heb 2:6–9 in a commentary (1:1–2:18) with an unusual pattern (see note 94).

[131] Specifically, 'love' (Deut 6:5; Lev 19:18) is the command on which the whole law depends (Mt 22:40) and by which it is to be 'fulfilled' (Rom 13:8; Gal 5:14) and

but in its ritual structures and obligations it served only as a 'custodian' (παιδαγωγός), to watch over us until the Messiah came, and contained only a 'shadow' of the new-age realities.[132]

4. *A judgement typology*, in which God's earlier acts of destruction are understood as 'types' or 'examples' of eschatological judgements, also appears in the New Testament. The flood and Sodom, for example, are used in this way.[133] Likewise, the faithless Israelite is a type of the faithless Christian;[134] the enemies of Israel a type of the (religious) enemies of the eschatological Israel, that is, of the church.[135]

---

without which it is transgressed. Cf. Mt 5:17–48, where the 'fulfilment' (17) of the law is related to being 'perfect as your heavenly father is perfect' (48). Cf. the commentary in Lk 10:25–37 (see note 76).

[132] Gal 3:24; Col 2:17. In the New Testament the law is viewed from the perspective that (in Paul's words) 'Messiah is the end (τέλος) of the law' (Rom 10:4). However, as C. E. B. Cranfield (*The Epistle to the Romans*, 2 vols., Edinburgh 1979, II, 515–520; idem, 'St. Paul and the Law,' *SJT* 17 [1964], 43–68) and W. D. Davies ('Law in the NT', *IDB*, III, 100) have rightly observed, τέλος here does not mean simply 'termination' but carries connotations of 'completion' or 'goal' or 'fulfilment.' Even legal observances that stand in contrast to the new-age realities, in spite of the dangers posed by them (cf. Heb 9:9f.; 10:1; 13:9) and the prohibition of them to Gentile Christians (e.g. Gal 5:2; Col 2:13, 16f.), were not forbidden to Jewish Christians when they were practiced in the right spirit (Mt 5:23f.; 6:2ff.; Acts 2:46; 3:1; 16:3; 18:18, 20:16; 21:20–26; Rom 14; I Cor 9:19–23). When not literally observed, they continued in their antitype, transposed into a new key: *Passover* continued in the removal of unethical leaven (I Cor 5:7f.) and in the observance of Messiah's 'Passover' sacrifice of the new covenant (Lk 22:19f.; cf. I Cor 11:23–26). *Circumcision* continued in the identification of the believer with Messiah's spilt covenant blood (Col 2:11; cf. Phil 3:3). *An altar* continued in the appropriation of Messiah's sacrificial offering (Heb 13:10; cf. Jn 6:53f.) together with *sacrifices* of praise and gifts (Phil 4:18; Heb 13:15; I Pet 2:5) and of one's own life (Rom 12:1; II Tim 4:6) by which the afflictions of Messiah are 'completed' (ἀνταναπληροῦν, Col 1:24; cf. Rev 6:11). In the words of J. A. Sanders ('Torah and Paul,' *God's Christ and His People*, ed. J. Jervell, Oslo 1978, 137) the Torah was not eradicated in early Christianity but 'was caught up in Christ.' But see O. Michel, *Der Brief an die Römer*, Göttingen [5]1978, 326f.

[133] Mt 24:37ff.; Lk 17:28ff.; II Pet 2:5f.; 3:5–7 in a commentary (see note 81); Jude 7 in a commentary (see note 94). The prospect of a final divine destruction of the wicked by fire (I Cor 3:13ff.; II Thess 1:7–10; Heb 12:29; Rev 20:9–15; cf. I Pet 1.:7) and even a cosmic conflagration (II Pet 3:7, 10f.) has a part of its background in a 'Sodom' typology (II Pet 2:6–10; Jude 7). Cf. Gen 19:24; Zeph 1:18; 3:8; Mal 4:1 = 3:19; I Enoch 1:3–6; Jubil. 16:5f.; 1QH 3:28–36; C. P. Thiede, 'A Pagan Reader of 2 Peter,' *JSNT* 26 (1986), 79–96.

[134] I Cor 10:6 in a commentary (see note 81); Heb 4:11 in a commentary covering Heb 3:7–4:16: Initial text (3:7–11; Ps 95) + Exposition/application (3:12–15) +

Corporate Personality

In the Old Testament the individual (male) person may be viewed as extending beyond himself to include those who 'belong' to him. Thus, the husband (at the family level) and the king (at the national level) both have an individual and a corporate existence encompassing, respectively, the household and the nation.[136] Corporate personality also characterizes the nature of God. It is not a metaphor, as modern Western man is tempted to perceive it, but an ontological affirmation from which the biblical writers' view of reality proceeds.[137]

Man: Corporate and Individual

For Jesus and the New Testament writers this perception of man as a corporate being is determinative for the proper understanding of Scripture. It is exemplified, at its most basic level, in the interpretation of the sexual union in terms of Gen 2:24: 'The two shall be one (μίαν) flesh.'[138] At the national or covenant level it is reflected in such idioms as existence 'in Abraham' and as the nation's baptism 'into Moses' or its existence as

---

Supplementary text (3:16–18; allusion to Num 14:22f., 29) + Exposition (3:19–4:3) + Supplementary text (4:4; Gen 2:2) + Exposition with allusions to the initial and supplementary texts (4:5–10) + Concluding application and exhortation (4:11–16).

[135] Rev 11:8; Gal 4:28 in a commentary covering Gal 4:21–5:1 (Ellis, note 4, 156). Similarly, Old Testament passages originally referring to Gentiles can be applied to Jews who persecute Christians (Rom 8:36 = Ps 44:22) or who indulge in sin (Rom 2:24 = Isa 52:5). Otherwise: P. Richardson, *Israel in the Apostolic Church*, Cambridge 1969; J. Jervell, *Luke and the People of God*, Minneapolis 1972, 41–74. Cf. Ellis, *Paul's Use* (note 2), 136–139. Qumran also viewed its own community as Israel (Cross) or as the forerunner of eschatological Israel (Sanders) and regarded the current Temple authorities as Gentiles. Cf. 1QpHab 12:1–3 (on Hab 2:17); CD 3:18–4:4; 19:33f.; F. M. Cross, *The Ancient Library of Qumran*, Garden City [2]1961, 127ff. But see Sanders (note 9), 245–250.

[136] J. de Fraine, *Adam and the Family of Man*, New York 1965; A. R. Johnson, *The One and the Many in the Israelite Conception of God*, Cardiff 1961, 1–13; *Sacral Kingship in Ancient Israel*, Cardiff 1955, 2f.; J. Pedersen, *Israel*, 4 vols. in 2, London 1959 (1926), I–II, 62f., 263–271, 474–479; H. W. Robinson, *Corporate Personality in Ancient Israel*, Philadelphia 1964 (1935); R. P. Shedd, *Man in Community*, London and Grand Rapids 1958, 29–41; D. Daube, *Studies in Biblical Law*, Cambridge 1947, 154–189.

[137] See note 136. Cf. E. E. Ellis, *Pauline Theology: Ministry and Society*, Grand Rapids 1989, 8–13; idem, 'Sōma in First Corinthians,' *Int* 44 (1990), 132–144.

[138] Mt 19:5 in a commentary (see note 76); I Cor 6:16f.; Eph 5:31.

Moses' house or David's tabernacle.[139] More broadly, corporate personality of the whole of mankind appears as existence 'in Adam.'[140]

Each level of corporeity is given a Christological application. As the two in sexual union become 'one flesh,' so the believers in faith-union are 'one spirit' with Messiah or 'members of his body.'[141] In the 'new covenant' corporeity Jesus and Paul use diverse images. At the Last Supper and, according to John, in a synagogue exposition at Capernaum Jesus identifies himself with the new-covenant Passover Lamb[142] and with the manna of the Exodus[143] that his followers are given to eat. In a similar typology Paul relates Exodus events – the baptism 'into Moses' and the manna and the spring of water – to the Lord's Supper understood as a symbol of the believers' participation (μετέχειν) in Messiah's death and as an expression of their unity as 'one body', that is, the body of Christ.[144]

In closely related imagery the 'temple' (ναός) or 'house' (οἰκία, *et al.*) or 'tent' (σκῆνος, *et al.*) similarly reflects an interplay between the individual and corporate dimension of Messiah's person.[145] In the Gospels God's (new) temple[146] or the key-stone in that temple is identified as Jesus, that is, his individual body.[147] In Acts and the Epistles, as in the Qumran

---

[139] See I Cor 10:2 ('into Moses') and Heb 7:9f. ('in Abraham'), both within expository contexts (see note 81). On 'house' see Heb 3:3–6, commenting on Old Testament texts; Acts 15:16 in a commentary (see note 80). Strictly speaking, in Heb 3 it is apparently God's house of the old covenant headed up by Moses that is contrasted with God's eschatological house headed up by the Messiah.

[140] I Cor 15:22; cf. Rom 5:12, 19.

[141] I Cor 6:16f.; Eph 5:30 referring to Gen 2:24.

[142] Mt 26:27f.; Lk 22:15, 19; cf. I Cor 5:7; I Pet 1:19.

[143] Jn 6:35, 49–56 in a commentary (see note 79).

[144] I Cor 10:16f. in a commentary (see note 81); cf. I Cor 12:12f.: Here 'Christ' refers to the corporate body who 'unites the members and makes them an organic whole' (A. Robertson and A. Plummer, *First Epistle... to the Corinthians*, Edinburgh 1953 [1914], 271). Cf. J. A. T. Robinson, *The Body*, London 1952; C. F. D. Moule, *The Origin of Christology*, Cambridge 1977, 47–96. 'The body of Christ,' a frequently used Pauline idiom for the church, appears in Romans, I Corinthians, Ephesians and Colossians.

[145] Cf. Jn 2:19ff.; II Cor 5:1, 6ff.; I Cor 6:15-20; R. J. McKelvey, *The New Temple*, Oxford 1969; E. E. Ellis, 'II Corinthians V. 1–10 in Pauline Eschatology,' *NTS* 6 (1959–60), 211–224; A. Cole, *The New Temple*, London 1950. See also Ellis (note 81), 488ff.

[146] Mk 14:58; 15:29; Jn 2:19ff.

[147] Mt 21:42 (= Ps 118:22) in a commentary; cf. Acts 4:11; Rom 9:32f.; Eph 2:20ff.; I Pet 2:5, 6–8 (= Isa 8:14f.; 28:16; Ps 118:22).

writings,[148] God's temple or house[149] is the community. But it is not the community abstracted from the Messiah but rather as the corporate dimension or extension of his person. Like the 'body' imagery, these expressions sometimes go beyond a covenant corporeity to express a contrast between two creations, that 'in Adam' and that 'in Christ.'[150] The conception of a corporate Adam and of a corporate Christ underlies such Pauline expressions as 'the old (or outer) man' and 'the new (or inner) man',[151] 'the natural body' and 'the spiritual body.'[152]

The New Testament interpretation of a number of Old Testament texts is illumined by this corporate view of man. For example, within this frame of reference the promise given to King Solomon can be understood to be fulfilled not only in Christ, the messianic king, but also in his followers.[153] The 'seed of Abraham' has a similar individual and corporate reference.[154] Also, since the nation is incorporated in Israel's Messiah-king, the true Israel is constituted by all those who belong to him – Jews and Gentiles.[155]

God: Unity in Plurality

The New Testament writers' conception of corporate personality extends to an understanding of God himself as a corporate being, a viewpoint which underlies their conviction that Jesus the Messiah has a unique unity with God and which later comes into definitive formulation in the doctrine of the Trinity. The origin of this conviction, which in some measure goes back to the earthly ministry of Jesus,[156] is complex, disputed

---

[148] 1QS 8:4–10. For other passages indicating that the Qumran community regarded itself as the true Israel cf. Ringgren (note 90), 163, 188, 201–204. See above, note 135.

[149] I Cor 3:9, 16; II Cor 5:1; Heb 3:6; I Pet 2:5; cf. Acts 7:49f.; 15:16.

[150] Heb 9:11 in a commentary (see note 124); II Pet 1:13f.; II Cor 5:1; cf. Ellis (note 145).

[151] Rom 6:6; 7:22; II Cor 4:16; Eph 3:16; 4:22, 24; Col 3:9f.

[152] I Cor 15:44; cf. Rom 6:6; 7:24; II Cor 5:6, 8, 10; Col 2:11. Cf. Ellis, *Theology* (note 137), 12f.; idem, 'Sōma' (note 137), 138ff.

[153] Heb 1:5 in a commentary (see note 94); cf. II Cor 6:18 in a *florilegium*.

[154] Gal 3:16, 29 in a midrash covering Gal 3:6–29. See Borgen (note 79), 48–52.

[155] Cf. Ellis, *Paul's Use* (note 2), 136–139; Goppelt (note 2), 140–151; Lk 19:9; Acts 3:22f.; 15:14–17; Rom 9:6f.; Gal 6:16; Phil 3:3; Heb 4:9; Rev 2:9; 3:9. Otherwise: Richardson (note 135); Jervell (note 135), 41–69.

[156] E.g. certain miracles of Jesus created a sense of awe and wonder about his person, especially those in which by a word Jesus controlled nature (Mk 4:35–41 + Q;

and not easy to assess.[157] One can here only briefly survey the way in which the early Christian understanding and use of their Bible may have reflected or contributed to this perspective on the relationship of the being of God to the person of the Messiah.

Already in the Old Testament and in pre-Christian Judaism the one God was understood to have 'plural' manifestations. In ancient Israel he was (in some sense) identified with and (in some sense) distinct from his Spirit or his Angel. Apparently, Yahweh was believed to have 'an indefinable extension of the personality,' by which he was present 'in person' in his agents.[158] Even the king as the Lord's anointed (= 'messiah') represented 'a potent extension of the divine personality.'[159]

In later strata of the Old Testament and in intertestamental Judaism certain attributes of God – such as his Word (דבר/λόγος)[160] or his Wisdom

Mt 14:22–33 parr), created matter (Mk 6:32–44 + Q + Jn 6:1–15) and life (Mk 5:21–42 + Q). These miracles are in the earliest traditions and can hardly be regarded, *a la* classical form criticism, as 'mythological' accretions. Cf. Stuhlmacher (note 75), *passim*; Ellis (note 4), 43 f., 239–247; Josephus, *Ant.* 18, 63 f. = 18, 3, 3 (παραδόξων ἔργον). However, they were attributed by Jesus' opponents (Mk 3:22 + Q) and by rabbinic tradition (*B. T. Sanhedrin* 43 a, cf. 107 b) to demonic power, by rationalists to misapprehensions or trickery (cf. R. M. Grant, *Miracles and Natural Law in Greco-Roman and Early Christian Thought*, Amsterdam 1952; M. Smith, *Jesus the Magician*, London 1978). Significant also were Jesus' sovereign 'I' sayings (Mt 5:22 etc.) and his claim to forgive sins (Mk 2:5 + Q), to have a unique and reciprocal knowledge of God (Mt 11:27 par; Mk 14:36) and (implicitly) to raise himself from the dead (Mk 14:58, ἀχειροποίητος; cf. Jn 2:19ff.). Cf. E. E. Ellis, 'Background and Christology of John's Gospel...,' *SWJT* 31, 1 (1988–89), 28 f.; Kim (note 125); J. Jeremias, *Abba*, Göttingen 1966, 15–67 = *The Prayers of Jesus*, London 1976, 11–65; but see A. E. Harvey, *Jesus and the Constraints of History*, London 1982, 168 f.

[157] Cf. J. D. G. Dunn, *Christology in the Making*, London ²1989; M. Hengel, *The Son of God*, London 1976; J. Jeremias, *New Testament Theology I*, London 1971, 250–311; M. de Jonge, *Jesus: Stranger from Heaven and Son of God*, Missoula MT 1977, 141–168; Kim (note 127); I. H. Marshall, *The Origins of New Testament Christology*, Leicester 1976; C. F. D. Moule, *The Origin of Christology*, Cambridge 1977; H. E. W. Turner, *Jesus the Christ*, London 1976, 7–28.

[158] Johnson, *The One and the Many* (note 136), 16; cf. Gen 18–19; Judg 6:11–23; A. R. Johnson, *The Cultic Prophet and Israel's Psalmnody*, Cardiff 1979, 10 f., 176 f, 248 ff., 318 f.

[159] Johnson, *Sacral Kingship* (note 136), 14, 122 f.; Bentzen (note 125), 19.

[160] E. g. Isa 9:8; 55:10 f.; cf. Wis 18:15; W. H. Schmidt, 'דבר,' *TDOT* 3 (1978), 120–125. Quite different from New Testament thought is the Greek (Stoic) philosophical conception of the Logos as the divine reason, which probably lies behind Philo's identification of the wisdom (σοφία) of God with the word (λόγος) of God and his designation of the latter as 'a second God' (*Leg. Alleg.* I, 65; II, 86; *QGen* II, 62 on Gen 9:6). Cf. E. Bréhier, *Les idees philosophiques et religieuses de Philon d'Alexandrie*, Paris ²1925, 83–86; H. Kleinknecht, 'λέγω,' *TDNT* 4 (1967/1942), 88–91. Otherwise: H. A. Wolfson, *Philo*, 2 vols., Cambridge MA 1947, I, 289–294.

(חכמה/σοφία)[161] – were viewed and used in a similar manner. In some instances the usage is only a poetic personification, a description of God's action under the name of the particular divine attribute that he employs. In others, however, it appears to represent a divine hypostasis, the essence of God's own being that is at the same time distinguishable from God.

From this background, together with a messianic hope that included the expectation that Yahweh himself would come to deliver Israel,[162] the followers of Jesus would have been prepared, wholly within a Jewish monotheistic and 'salvation history' perspective, to see in the Messiah a manifestation of God. In the event, they were brought to this conclusion by their experience of Jesus' works and teachings, particularly as it came to a culmination in his resurrection appearances and commands. Although during his earthly ministry they had, according to the Gospel accounts, occasionally been made aware of a strange otherness about Jesus,[163] only after his resurrection do they identify him as God. Paul, the first literary witness to do this,[164] probably expresses a conviction initially formed at his Damascus Christophany.[165] John the Evangelist, who wrote later but who saw the risen Lord (and was a bearer of early traditions about that event), also describes the confession of Jesus as God as a reaction to the resurrection appearances.[166] Yet, such direct assertions of Jesus' deity are

---

[161] Especially Wis 7:21–27, in which Wisdom is the omniscient and omnipotent creator and is identified with the Spirit of God; cf. Sirach 24:3. Cf. Pv 8:22f.

[162] Mal 3:1: 'me' = Lord (אדון) = Yahweh (יהוה); cf. Zech 4:10 with Zech 4:14; 6:5. On this expectation in first-century Judaism cf. Ps Sol 17:36 (32); Test Simeon 6:5; Test Levi 2:11; 5:2; 8:11; Test Judah 22:2; Test Naph 8:3; Test Asher 7:3. Similarly, Mt 11:3 = Lk 7:19 (John the Baptist's disciples); cf. Lk 1:16f. with Lk 2:11 (σωτήρ... χριστὸς κύριος = משיח יהוה ... מושיע). Mk 1:2 is probably an excerpt from an antecedent midrash (cf. Ellis, note 4, 150f., 161f.) that expounded Mal 3:1 in terms of Isa 40:3 (Lord = Yahweh = Elohim) and applied the text to Jesus the Messiah (see note 167).

[163] See note 156; cf. Mk 4:41 + Q; Mk 9:2f. + Q; Lk 5:8.

[164] Rom 9:5f.; cf. Cranfield (note 132), II, 464–470; Tit 2:13. The argument of the 'history of religions' school that Jesus was perceived in the earliest Palestinian church solely as a human figure and was given the status of deity only later in the diaspora is an artificial construct and is not supported by the sources. Cf. Hengel (note 157), 3–6, 17ff., 77–83.

[165] I Cor 9:1; 15:8; Gal 1:12, 16; Acts 9:3ff., 20; 22:14; 26:19; cf. Ezek 1:26ff.; Kim (note 127), 193–268; M. Thrall, 'The Origin of Pauline Christology,' *Apostolic History and the Gospel*, ed. W. W. Gasque, Grand Rapids 1970, 311–315.

[166] Jn 20:28f.; cf. 1:1, 14, 18; I Jn 5:20. A 'circle' or perhaps amanuenses participated in some manner in editing the finished and published Gospel. But the Beloved Disciple, who is explicitly identified as an eyewitness (Jn 19:35; 21:24) and very probably as John the Son of Zebedee (Robinson), is represented by the Gospel to be the real author. Both internal and external evidence support the Gospel's representa-

exceptional in the New Testament[167] and could hardly have been sustained among Jewish believers apart from a perspective on the Old Testament that affirmed and/or confirmed a manifestation of Yahweh in and as Messiah.

The New Testament writers usually set forth Messiah's unity with God by identifying him with God's Son[168] or Spirit[169] or image or wisdom[170] or by applying to him biblical passages that in their original context referred to Yahweh.[171] They often do this within an implicit or explicit commentary (midrash) on Scripture and thereby reveal their conviction that the 'supernatural' dimension of Jesus' person is not merely that of an angelic messenger[172] but is the being of God himself.

The use of Scripture in first and second century Judaism, then, marked a watershed in the biblical doctrine of God. At that time it channeled the imprecise monotheism of the Old Testament and early Judaism in two irreversible directions. On the one hand Jewish-Christian apostles and prophets, via 'corporate personality' conceptions and Christological exposition, set a course that led to the trinitarian monotheism of later Christianity. On the other hand the rabbinic writers, with their exegetical

---

tion. So, D.A. Carson, *The Gospel accordingto John*, Leicester 1991, 68–81; J.A.T. Robinson, *The Priority of John*, London 1985, 36–122; Ellis (note 156), 24f.; but see M. Hengel, *The Johannine Question*, London 1989; R. Schnackenburg, *The Gospel according to St. John*, 3 vols., New York ²1990, I, 75–104.

[167] Χριστὸς κύριος in Lk 2:11 may also represent 'Messiah Yahweh' and refer to Jesus' birth as an epiphany of Yahweh. See above, note 156; cf. Ps Sol 17:36 (32); H. Sahlin, *Der Messias und das Gottesvolk*, Uppsala 1945, 217f., 383ff.

[168] Mt 11:27; Mk 1:2; Lk 1:35; Rom 8:3; Heb 1:2; Kim (note 127), 109–136; O. Cullmann, *The Christology of the New Testament*, London ²1959, 270–305.

[169] II Cor 3:16 (= Exod 34:34) in a commentary (3:7–18) on Ezek 34. 'The Lord' (II Cor 3:16ff.), who is the Spirit, refers to Jesus as (the messianic manifestation of) Yahweh: Paul makes no distinction between the Spirit of God, the Spirit of Christ (Rom 8:9) and the Holy Spirit. See especially Kim (note 127), 11ff., 231–239. Cf. Ellis (note 4), 63, 67f. But see C.F.D. Moule, 'II Cor 3:18b,' *Neues Testament und Geschichte*, ed. H. Baltensweiler, Zürich 1972, 231–237.

[170] On 'image': II Cor 4:4; Col 1:15 (εἰκών); Heb 1:3 (χαρακτήρ); cf. Kim (note 127) 137–141, 229–268; U. Wilckens, 'χαρακτήρ,' *TDNT* 9 (1974), 421f. On 'wisdom:' I Cor 1:24; cf. Lk 11:49 with Mt 23:34. Cf. C.F. Burney, 'Christ as the ΑΡΧΗ,' *JTS* 27 (1926), 160–177 (on Col 1:15–18); A. Feuillet, *Le Christ Sagesse de Dieu...*, Paris 1966. Otherwise: J.N. Aletti, *Colossiens 1, 15–20*, Rome 1981, 148–176.

[171] E.g. Rom 10:13 (= Joel 3:5); II Cor 3:16ff. (= Exod 34:34); Eph 4:8 (= Ps 68:19); Heb 1:6 (= Ps 97:7); 1:10 (= Ps 102:25); probably I Cor 10:26 (= Ps 24:1).

[172] Cf. P.J. Kobelski, *Melchizedek and Melchiresa*, Washington DC 1981, 99–141; L.W. Hurtado, *One God, One Lord*, Philadelphia 1988, 71–92. But see D.B. Capes, 'Paul's Use of... Yahweh Texts,' Ph.D. Diss., Ft. Worth, Texas 1990, 284–295.

emphasis on God's unity, brought into final definition the unitarian monotheism of talmudic Judaism.[173]

Charismatic Exegesis

Some New Testament writers, particularly the Evangelists and Paul, represent the Old Testament as a hidden word of God, a divine mystery whose interpretation is itself a divine gift (χάρισμα) and act of revelation. For this viewpoint they appear to be dependent in the first instance on Jesus and, more generally, on prior Jewish apocalyptic conceptions.

Jesus

Jesus argues against the Sadducees that they 'do not know (εἰδέναι) the Scriptures'[174] and against other religious opponents that by their traditional interpretations they 'make void the word of God.'[175] Since he used methods of interpretation similar to theirs, his criticisms give rise to a question: How does one 'know' the true meaning of a biblical passage, that is, its 'word of God' import? Jesus gives no direct answer to this question, but he appears to connect it with his role as a prophet, a role that others ascribe to him[176] and that he himself affirms.[177] Unlike the profes-

---

[173] For rabbinic references to disputes with heretics over the unity of God cf. H. L. Strack, *Jesus, die Häretiker und die Christen nach den ältesten jüdischen Angaben*, Leipzig 1910, 70*–74*. More generally, cf. A. F. Segal, *Two Powers in Heaven*, Leiden 1977, 33–155. However, even into the second century some mystical Jewish writings apparently continued to identify Yahweh, in some sense, with other beings. Cf. H. Odeberg, *3 Enoch*, Cambridge 1928, 82 (Introduction), 32f. (Text): Metatron, the exalted Enoch, has divine glory conferred on him and is called 'the lesser Yahweh' (III Enoch 12:5). See also P. Alexander, '3 Enoch,' *The Old Testament Pseudepigrapha*, 2 vols., ed. J. H. Charlesworth, Garden City NY 1985, I, 243, 265 n. Cf. G. G. Strousma, 'Form(s) of God: Some Notes on Metatron and Christ,' *HTR* 76 (1983), 269–288; M. Hengel, *Judaism and Hellenism*, 2 vols., Philadelphia 1974, I, 153–162; W. O. E. Oesterley and G. H. Box, *The Religion and Worship of the Synagogue*, London ²1911, 195–221. But see J. Klausner, *The Messianic Idea in Israel*, London 1956, 293, 466; E. E. Urbach, *The Sages, Their Concepts and Beliefs*, 2 vols., Jerusalem 1975, I, 19–36, 135–138, 207f.

[174] Mk 12:24, in a *yelammedenu*-type commentary (Mk 12:18–27 + Q); cf. Mt 12:7; see note 77.

[175] Mt 15:6, in a *yelammedenu*-type commentary (15:1–9 par). See note 76. Perhaps the pericope extends to Mt 15:1–20; cf. Daube, *New Testament* (note 7), 143.

[176] Mk 6:15 par; 8:28 parr; cf. 14:65 parr; 8:11 + Q; Lk 7:39.

[177] Mk 6:4 parr; Lk 13:33; Jn 4:44. His disclosure of visions in Lk 10:18; cf. Mt

sionally trained Scripture-teachers of his day, the scribes (γραμματεῖς), Jesus is said to expound the Old Testament with an authority (ἐξουσία)[178] that in the Gospels is related to his claim to possess the prophetic Spirit.[179] Likewise, he attributes the response to his 'kingdom of God' message and to his messianic signs, both of which are rooted in the interpretation of Old Testament promises, to the fact that God revealed (ἀποκαλύπτειν) it to some and hid (ἀποκρύπτειν) it from others.[180] This is evident, for example, in his response to the Baptist as well as in his sermon at Nazareth.[181]

In similar imagery Jesus describes his parables as a veiling of his message from 'those outside' but as an aid to understanding for his disciples because 'to you it is given [by God] to know the mysteries (γνῶναι τὰ μυστήρια) of the kingdom of God.'[182] As has been observed above, Jesus uses 'parable' in the sense of 'mystery' or 'dark saying', the meaning that the term carries in some other Jewish literature.[183] He also employs such veiled meanings in his exposition of Scripture.[184]

There is then a paradox about Jesus' biblical exposition. He follows exegetical methods that were current in Judaism and regards them as a useful means to expound the biblical passages. Nevertheless, he recog-

---

4:2–11 (Q) falls into the same category. Cf. M. Hengel, *The Charismatic Leader and his Followers*, New York 1981, 63–71.

[178] Mk 1:22 par, in the context of synagogue teaching, i.e. of biblical exposition. Cf. Mt 7:29. On the definition of γραμματεῖς and the distinction between the scribes and the Pharisees cf. J. Jeremias, *Jerusalem in the Time of Jesus*, London 1969, 233–245, 252–259; J. Neusner, *Early Rabbinic Judaism*, Leiden 1975, 66ff.; Safrai (note 84), 149–150.

[179] Cf. Lk 4:18, 21, 24, in a commentary (see note 121).

[180] Mt 11:25, as a sequel to the identification of his message (11:5) and of the role of the Baptist (11:10–14) with the fulfilment of OT promises; similarly, in Lk 10:21 f. the same saying is placed after the preaching of the seventy that the kingdom of God promised in the Scriptures has come in Jesus (10:5 f., 9). Cf. Mt 16:16 f.; Lk 9:45; 19:42; 22:32, 45.

[181] Lk 7:22 f. (Q); 7:35; 4:18 f., 21, 25 f.; cf. Isa 29:18 f.; 61:1 f.; cf. E. E. Ellis, *The Gospel of Luke*, London and Grand Rapids ⁵1987, 120.

[182] Mt 13:11 (Q); cf. Mk 4:11. The passive form veils a reference to deity; cf. F. Blass, A. de Brunner, R. W. Funk, *A Greek Grammar*, Cambridge 1961, 72, 164 f., 176.

[183] Jeremias (note 28), 16. Cf. Ezek 17:2; Hab 2:6; Ps 49:5; 78:2; I Enoch 68:1; Sirach 47:17; Barn 6:10; 17:2. See above, 86 f.

[184] Cf. Mt 15:12, 15–20, explaining the exposition at 15:1–9 (see note 76); Mk 12:1–12 + Q, in a commentary (cf. Ellis, note 4, 157 f.). Cf. Mk 12:12 with 12:36 f.; Jn 7:38 f. Certain assertions about his relationship to God, his messiahship and other matters also have this veiled character. Cf. Mk 4:33 f. par.; 8:15–18 parr; 14:58 with Jn 2:19 ff.; Lk 9:45; Jn 4:13 f.; 12:32 ff.; 16:25.

nizes that the meaning of Scripture – even his exposition of it – remains hidden from many and, at least in the latter part of his ministry, he seems deliberately to veil the presentation of his message. The acceptance of his exposition, and of his teaching generally, depends in his view on a divine opening of the minds of the hearers:

He who has ears to hear let him hear...
Blessed are your ears because they hear.[185]

Paul and Peter

In the writings of Paul and of Peter[186] there is the same conception of the Old Testament as a hidden divine wisdom. This wisdom was long concealed but is now revealed in the teachings of the Apostles. In Paul's case the particular task of his ministry is 'to make known the mystery (γνωρίσαι τὸ μυστήριον) of the gospel,' namely, the inclusion of the Gentiles in eschatological Israel.[187] This purpose of God is a divine mystery or wisdom (σοφία) that was not made known (οὐκ γνωρισθῆναι) and indeed was hidden (σιγᾶν, ἀποκρύπτεσθαι) for ages but is now (νῦν) revealed (ἀποκαλύπτεσθαι), made known (γνωρισθῆναι) and manifest (φανερωθῆναι). It is revealed especially in the writings of Paul (and other pneumatics),[188] in his preaching 'by the Spirit'[189] and in his messianic/eschatological exposition of Scripture.

In I–II Corinthians and in the Pastorals[190] Paul describes the broader gospel message in a similar way. In II Cor 3 he likens the hiddenness of the word of God to a veil on the mind of (Jewish) unbelievers that keeps them from understanding the meaning of the Scriptures read in the synagogue, a veil that is taken away when they turn to the Lord, i.e. to the Messiah. More often he represents the unveiling as a revelatory understanding of Scripture gifted to the pneumatics (πνευματικοί) who, in turn, disclose its meaning by inspired exposition to the Christian assembly and to interested outsiders.[191]

---

[185] Mt 13:9, 16; cf. Mk 4:9, 12 + Q; Mt 11:15; 13:43; Lk 24:32.

[186] I Pet 1:11 f., 20.

[187] Rom 16:25 f.; Eph 3:2 f., 5 f., 9 f.; Col 1:25 ff. The theme is present also in the cited (εἰδότες ὅτι) hymn in I Pet 1:18–21 if, as is probable, I Pet 1:18 identifies the audience as Gentiles, i.e. God-fearers. So, W.C. van Unnik, *Sparsa Collecta*, 3 vols., Leiden 1973–83, II, 3–82, 32 f., 81.

[188] Rom 16:26.

[189] Eph 3:3, 5; cf. Col 1:28 ('in wisdom').

[190] II Tim 1:9 f., 11, in a (preformed) hymn; Tit 1:2 f. Cf. Ellis (note 18).

[191] II Cor 3:14 ff., in a commentary embracing II Cor 3:7–18 (see note 169); cf. II

In I Cor 2:6–16, a proem-type midrash,[192] and in I Cor 12–14 he discloses his rationale for this view of God's revelation.[193] He argues that certain believers are given a gift of divine wisdom (12:8), a prophetic endowment that enables them to speak 'the wisdom that has been hidden in a mystery' (2:7) and, indeed, 'to know (εἰδέναι) all mysteries' (13:2; cf. 2:12) because 'God has revealed (ἀπεκάλυψεν) them to us through the Spirit' (2:10). They are called pneumatics (2:13, 15; 12:1 ff.), a term that is probably equivalent to 'man of the Spirit' in Hos 9:7, that is, a prophet (14:37). As recipients and transmitters of divine mysteries and of wisdom, they are the 'mature' (τέλειοι) believers who 'have the mind of Christ' (2:16) and who rightly interpret (συνκρίνειν) the things of the Spirit to others (2:6, 13), expounding the Scripture and affirming or testing (διακρί-νειν) the exposition of other prophets (14:29, 37).[194] Such a pneumatic interpreter of the word of God is best exemplified by Paul himself. What is the background of his perception of Scripture as a hidden wisdom requiring a charismatic, revelatory exposition?

The Maskilim

Various parts of the Old Testament[195] as well as some rabbinic writings[196] speak of divine wisdom and knowledge as God's secret and his gift to selected individuals. However, it is the teaching of Jesus and conceptions current in the contemporary Qumran community which provide the more immediate and significant antecedents for Paul's thought. Tradi-

---

Cor 4:3; I Tim 4:13. On the reading of Scripture in Paul's churches cf. Ellis, *Theology* (note 137), 137 f.

[192] I Cor 2:6–16: Theme and initial texts (6–9; Isa 64:4; 65:16) + Exposition (10–15) + Concluding text and application (16a; Isa 40:13). Cf. Eph 3:3 ff. Ellis (note 4), 155 ff., 213 ff.

[193] For the detailed argument see Ellis (note 4), 45–62. Somewhat differently, P. Stuhlmacher, 'The Hermeneutical Significance of 1 Cor 2:6–16,' *Tradition and Interpretation in the New Testament*, ed. G. F. Hawthorne with Otto Betz, Grand Rapids and Tübingen 1987, 334–339.

[194] I Cor 14:37 concludes a section concerned with *inter alia* the regulation of the conduct of wives (14:34 f.) that is partly based on an interpretation of Gen 3:16. Cf. E. E. Ellis, 'The Silenced Wives of Corinth,' *New Testament Textual Criticism*, ed. E. J. Epp, Oxford 1981, 213–220; idem, *Theology* (note 137), 67–71.

[195] E. g. Gen 41:38 f. (Joseph); Num 24:15 f. (Balaam); Deut 34:9 (Joshua); Dan 1:17; 2:21 f. (Daniel); G. von Rad, *Wisdom in Israel*, London 1972, 55–68.

[196] Cf. Jeremias (note 178), 235–242 re esoteric traditions. Cf. *M. Megillah* 4:10; *Hagigah* 2:1; *B. T. Pesahim* 119 a; *Sanhedrin* 21 b; *T. Hagigah* 2:1, 7. Further, IV Ezra 14:45 f.

tions of Jesus' teaching were certainly known to Paul and to his church-es,[197] and they may have included some traditions on this theme. But the Dead Sea Scrolls, which have affinities with Pauline thought and her-meneutic in several areas,[198] display on this subject a greater number of parallels with the Apostle's writings.

The wise teachers or *maskilim* (משכילים) at Qumran, including the Teacher of Righteousness, understand their role to be like 'the wise' in Dan 12:9f. Indeed, they may take as their paradigm Daniel himself, whose gifts of wisdom (שכל, חכמה/σοφία) and knowledge enable him to understand sacred writings and interpret (פשר/συγκρίνειν) them, i. e. to reveal the mystery (למגלא רזא /ἀποκαλύψαι τὸ μυστήριον).[199] The same gifts of wisdom enable Daniel to understand and expound the prophecy of Jeremiah and, by implication, they will also give understanding to the 'wise teachers' (משכילים) at the time of the end.[200]

The *maskilim* at Qumran consider themselves to have these gifts and the role arising from them. They confess to God that 'by your Holy Spirit' you opened knowledge 'in the mystery (רז) of your wisdom' (שכל).[201] They are 'to test' (לבחן; cf. LXX διακρίνειν) those in the community[202] and guide them with knowledge and wisdom (שכל) in the mysteries (רזי)... so that they may walk maturely (תמים; cf. LXX τέλειοι) with one another in all that has been revealed (גלה) to them.[203] The *maskilim* probably regard the Teacher of Righteousness, 'to whom God has revealed all the mysteries of his servants the prophets,'[204] as the leading representative of their own ministry.[205] If so, they would also have emulated his exposition of Scrip-

---

[197] I Cor 7:10; 9:14; 11:23; 15:3; I Tim 5:18; D. Dungan, *The Sayings of Jesus in the Churches of Paul*, Oxford 1971; Ellis (note 75), 46; idem (note 81), 485–490. Otherwise: N. Walter, 'Paulus und die urchristliche Jesustradition,' *NTS* 31 (1985), 498–522.

[198] Cf. J. Murphy-O'Connor, ed., *Paul and Qumran*, London 1968; Ellis (note 4), 33f., 173–181, 188–197; R. E. Brown, *The Semitic Background of the Term 'Mystery' in the New Testament*, Philadelphia 1968, 24–27.

[199] Dan 1:17; 5:12; 2:47. Cf. F. F. Bruce, 'The Book of Daniel and the Qumran Community,' *Neotestamentica et Semitica*, edd. E. E. Ellis and M. Wilcox, Edinburgh 1969, 225ff.; O. Betz, *Offenbarung und Schriftforschung in der Qumransekte*, Tübingen 1960, 73–98, 110–142.

[200] Dan 9:2, 22f.

[201] 1QH 12:12f.

[202] 1QH 2:13f.

[203] 1QS 9:12, 17ff.

[204] 1QpHab 7:4f.

[205] This follows if the Teacher is the author of (some of) the Hymns, as is argued by G. Jeremias (*Der Lehrer der Gerechtigkeit*, Göttingen 1963, 176f., 264). But see M. Man-soor, *The Thanksgiving Hymns*, Leiden 1961, 45–49; Dimant (note 20), 523 n. 199.

ture. Both in their gifts and in their ministry the *maskilim* bear a striking resemblance to the pneumatics in the Pauline churches, and they shed considerable light on the background of the charismatic exegesis of the early church.

Conclusion

Biblical interpretation in the New Testament church shows in a remarkable way the Jewishness of earliest Christianity. It followed exegetical methods common to Judaism and drew its perspective and presuppositions from Jewish backgrounds. However, in one fundamental respect the early Christian hermeneutic differed from that of other religious parties and theologies in Judaism, that is, in the christological exposition of the Scripture totally focused upon Jesus as the Messiah. This different focus decisively influences both the perspective from which they expound the Old Testament and the way in which their presuppositions are brought to bear upon the specific biblical texts. Their perspective and presuppositions provide, in turn, the theological framework for the development of their exegetical themes and for the whole of New Testament theology.

First-century Judaism was a highly diverse phenomenon, as becomes apparent from a comparison of the writings of Philo, Josephus, Qumran, the (traditions of the) rabbis and the early Christians. The New Testament, which as far as I can see was written altogether by Jews,[206] is a part of that diversity but also a part of that Judaism. Its writers were Jews, but Jews who differed from the majority of the nation and who in time found the greater number of their company of faith not among their own people but among the Gentiles. And still today, apart from a continuing Judeo-Christian minority, the church remains a community of Gentiles, but Gentiles with a difference. For as long as Gentile Christians give attention to their charter documents, they can never forget that as those who are joined to a Jewish Messiah they are in a manner of speaking 'adopted Jews' or, in Paul's imagery, branches engrafted into the ancient tree of Israel and a people who have their hope in the promise given to Abraham. The centrality of the Old Testament in the message of Jesus and his apostles and prophets underscores that fact.

---

[206] Luke is the only New Testament author whom many scholars identify as a Gentile. But see Ellis (note 181), 51 ff.; idem, 'St. Luke,' *Encyclopedia Britannica III*, Chicago 1974.

Appendix I

Jesus and his Bible

Christians have always taken the Gospels as a trustworthy guide to the teachings of Jesus. Today they have considerable historical and literary grounds to support their confessional commitment[1] and are able, with the appropriate analysis, to synthesize from the Gospels Jesus' views and teachings on a number of issues. These issues include (1) the identification of the books composing our Lord's Bible, (2) his attitude toward these writings and (3) the methods and emphases of his biblical interpretation.

What was the Bible of Jesus?

As has been related in detail in chapter one above, about a hundred years ago a particular theory about the origin of the Old Testament canon gained popularity. It posited that the Jewish Bible – our Old Testament – was canonized, that is, given recognized acceptance as a divinely inspired and normative authority, in three stages: the Pentateuch about 400 B.C., the Prophets about 200 B.C. and the Writings, including the Psalms and wisdom literature, at the Council of Jamnia about A.D. 90. This theory left the content of the Hebrew Bible in Jesus' day an uncertain quantity as far as its third division was concerned.

While the three-stage canonization theory continues to be widely followed, in the past two decades it has been seriously critiqued by Jewish and Protestant scholars and, in my view, has now been effectively demolished.[2] The theory failed primarily for three reasons. (1) It was not based on specific evidence but rather on inferences, none of which were proven and some of which were clearly mistaken.[3] (2) For certain Old

---

[1] I have addressed this matter elsewhere, in particular the mistaken confessional assumptions and the literary analysis of the classical form criticism that led to skeptical conclusions about the historicity of the Gospels. For a critique and correction of the classical form-critical approach see the literature below, note 27.

[2] See above, 37–44. Cf. S. Z. Leiman, ed., *The Canon and Masorah of the Hebrew Bible*, New York 1974, 254–261 (J. P. Lewis); idem, *The Canonization of Hebrew Scripture*, Hamden CT 1976; R. T. Beckwith, *The Old Testament Canon of the New Testament Church*, Grand Rapids 1985.

[3] For example, the testimony of Josephus (c. A.D. 90; *c. Apion.* 1, 38–42) to a long-

Testament books it assumed a late dating, for example, for Ecclesiastes and Daniel, that can no longer be entertained. (3) It assumed without justification that the Council of Jamnia acted to canonize certain books, but the evidence suggests that Jamnia at most only reaffirmed books that had been long received but were later disputed by some Jews.[4]

It is significant that the Old Testament apocryphal books, received by Roman Catholics as canonical (or deuterocanonical), were never included in Jewish canonical designations and are never cited in the first-century writings of Qumran, Philo or the New Testament. However, all the Old Testament books appear at Qumran except Esther, a book that also is lacking in one early Christian canonical list. Esther also is not cited in the New Testament and was questioned by some rabbis and by a few Christian writers.[5] To summarize briefly, one may say with some confidence that the Bible received and used by our Lord was, with the possible exception of Esther, the Old Testament received today as sacred Scripture by Jews and Protestants.

Jesus' Attitude Toward his Bible

Jesus' use of the Old Testament rests on his conviction that these writings were the revelation of God through faithful prophets, a conviction that is decisive for his interpretation of Scripture and that surfaces explicitly in a number of places in the Gospels. Let us look at four examples of this: Matt 19:4f., Mark 12:24, Matt 5:17f., and John 10:35 (cf. Luke 4:3–12).

Two examples of Jesus' attitude to his Bible appear in his debates with rabbis of other Jewish religious parties. In a question on divorce posed by the Pharisees Jesus cites Gen 1:27 and 2:24 as the conclusive texts:

---

settled, universally recognized Jewish canon of Scriptures cannot simply be dismissed as a sectarian viewpoint. See above, 39.

[4] Cf. Leiman (note 2); R. C. Newman, 'The Council of Jamnia and the Old Testament Canon,' *WTJ* 38 (1976) 319–349. See above, 40.

[5] Lacking Esther is the list of Melito, Bishop of Sardis (c. A.D. 170), cited in Eusebius, *HE* 4, 26, 13f. For criticisms of Esther among the rabbis, cf. *B. T. Megillah* 7a; *Sanhedrin* 100a; among a few Christian groups, cf. T. Nöldeke, 'Esther,' *EB* II, 1407.

The one who created them from the beginning
Made them male and female
And said, '... The two shall be one flesh.'

Matt 19:4f.

Noteworthy for our purposes is the fact that, according to Matthew, Jesus identified the editorial comment of the author of Genesis as the utterance of God. That is, the 'word of God' character of Scripture is not limited to 'thus says the Lord' passages.

In a debate with the Sadducees on the resurrection[6] Jesus identifies their error thus:

You err
Not knowing the Scriptures
Nor the power of God

Matt 22:29 = Mark 12:24

Two points are to be observed here. First, since these trained theologians memorized the Bible by the book, Jesus is not ascribing their theological error to an ignorance of the words of the Bible but to a lack of understanding of its meaning. That is, the 'word of God' character of Scripture, its divine truth, is not to be found merely by quoting it but by discerning its true import. Second, the Sadducees' ignorance of the Scripture is bound together with their skepticism about the power of God to raise to life those who have returned to the dust in death. Not unlike some liberal Christians today, they apparently allowed (Epicurean) philosophical dogmas to shut their minds to the teaching of the prophets.[7]

In the Sermon on the Mount Jesus contrasts his teaching with what his audience has heard before. For example,[8]

---

[6] Matt 22:23–33 = Mark 12:18–27 = Luke 20:27–40. Assuming Luke's independence of Matthew, those two Gospels rely on a second source, a Q tradition, in addition to their (presumed) use of Mark. This is evident from the agreements of Matthew and Luke against Mark in this episode. But see below, notes 28, 31.

[7] The rabbinic tradition associates the Sadducean denial of the resurrection with Epicurean philosophy. Cf. *M. Sanhedrin* 10:1; *B. T. Rosh Hashanah* 17a; K. G. Kuhn, ed., *Sifre zu Numeri*, Stuttgart 1959, 328 (Section 112 on Num 15:31); J. Neusner, ed., *The Fathers According to Rabbi Nathan*, Atlanta 1986, 47f. = *ARN* 5. Further, cf. M. Hengel, *Judaism and Hellenism*, 2 vols., London 1974, I, 143; (H. L. Strack and) P. Billerbeck, *Kommentar zum Neuen Testament*, 4 vols., München 1922–28, I, 885; IV, 344. *Pace* E. Schürer (*The History of the Jewish People in the Age of Jesus Christ. New Edition*, 3 vols. in 4, ed. G. Vermes, Edinburgh 1973–87, II, 391f.), the Sadducean denial of resurrection was no mere retention of Old Testament conceptions, not even of Ecclesiastes (cf. Eccl 12:14).

[8] Cf. Matt 5:21, 27, 31, 33, 38, 43.

You have heard that it was said to those of old
You shall not kill...
But I say to you
That everyone who is angry with his brother
Shall be liable to judgement

Matt 5:21 f.

Jesus is thought by some to be setting his authority against that of the Old Testament,[9] but several considerations exclude this understanding of the matter. First, as we have seen in the illustrations above, Jesus never understands Scripture (γραφή) as words of the Bible in the abstract but as the message in its true meaning and application. Thus, in the debate on divorce (Matt 19:3–9), which is also one of the antitheses in the Sermon (Matt 5:31 f.), he counters the Pharisees' appeal to Deut 24:1, 3 by arguing that Gen 1:27 and 2:24 are the governing texts for the principle involved. In doing this, he follows good rabbinic practice, not denying the 'word of God' character of either passage but arguing against the traditional use of Deuteronomy 24 as the regulative passage for the marriage relationship.[10]

So also in the command, 'You shall not kill,' Jesus argues not against God's command through Moses but against the traditional limitation of that command to literal murder. If someone objects, 'But the text says "kill,"' I shall reply as a certain rabbi once did to his pupil: 'Good, you have learned to read. Now go and learn to interpret.'[11]

A second objection to taking the antitheses in the Sermon to mean that Jesus opposed or disparaged the Old Testament is the introductory formula used to introduce the biblical texts: 'You have heard that it was said to those of old.' As far as I know, this formula is never used in Christianity or Judaism to introduce Scripture as such, that is, in its true force as the word of God.[12] The words, 'You have heard,' point to the oral reading and interpretation of the Old Testament that the audience of

---

[9] So, apparently, R. A. Guelich, *The Sermon on the Mount*, Waco 1982, 182–185.

[10] It is not that one passage is right and the other wrong but that both are right in different senses. The permission of divorce (Deut 24:1, 3) was God's word to a particularly evil situation, because of 'the hardness of your hearts;' but to employ it as a regulative principle for marriage was a misuse of the text.

[11] Cf. D. Daube, *The New Testament and Rabbinic Judaism*, London 1956, 428 ff. He notes a number of sayings that are similar to this although not the one that sticks in my memory and that I cannot now locate.

[12] The term, 'it was said' (ἐρρέθη) at Matt 5:31 is so used elsewhere (Rom 9:12) but the preceding clause, 'you have heard that,' makes clear that here the word is only an abbreviation for the longer formula. Cf. Daube (note 11), 62.

Jesus heard regularly in synagogue,[13] and they show that in the Sermon Jesus is contrasting his teachings with traditional interpretations of the Bible that were known to his hearers. This is a characteristic feature of Christ's teachings that perhaps reached its highpoint in his accusation against certain Jewish churchmen and theologians: 'For the sake of your traditions you have made void the word of God.'[14] This conclusion is reinforced by the fact that the quotations in the Sermon sometimes include an explicit non-biblical teaching, for example,

You shall love your neighbor
And hate your enemy
        Matt 5:43

The second command is not found in the Old Testament but is part of the interpretation of the Bible at Qumran.[15]

A third and perhaps the most important objection to setting Jesus' teachings in opposition to the Old Testament is the passage at Matt 5:17f., which is prefaced to this section of the Sermon:

Do not suppose that I have come
To annul the law and the prophets
I have not come to annul (καταλῦσαι)
But to fulfil [them]
Truly I say to you
Until heaven and earth pass away
Not one jot or tittle shall pass from the law
Until all things be accomplished

Matthew doubtless knew that some readers could misunderstand the antitheses in the Sermon as setting Jesus over against the holy Scriptures. To preclude that, he includes this explicit declaration of the Lord on the inviolate character of the biblical teaching. This verse is very similar to Christ's word in the exposition at John 10:35: 'The Scripture cannot be broken of its force' (λυθῆναι).[16]

---

[13] Cf. Daube (note 11), 55: 'In Rabbinic discussion, *shomeʻa ʼani*, "I hear," "I understand," or rather "I might understand," introduces an interpretation of Scripture which, though conceivable, yet must be rejected.'

[14] Matt 15:6 = Mark 7:13. Possibly (but not likely) Jesus here also rejects a view expressed by some later rabbis that the oral tradition originated at Sinai and thus was a divinely sanctioned interpretation of Scripture. Cf. W.D. Davies, 'Canon and Christology,' *The Glory of Christ in the New Testament*, edd. L.D. Hurst and N.T. Wright, Oxford 1987, 19–36, 30f.

[15] 1QS 1:3f., 10.

[16] The term 'broken' (λυθῆναι, John 10:35) has this significance. Cf. Billerbeck (note 7), II, 542f.; C.K. Barrett, *The Gospel According to St. John*, London 1956, 319f.

'The law and the prophets' represent here, as elsewhere,[17] the whole Old Testament. Jesus is revealed not only as the proclaimer of God's word but also as the proclaimer of himself as the one in whom that Old Testament word is to find fulfilment.

In these texts Jesus fulfils the Old Testament in two ways. By his interpretation of it he unveils its true and final (eschatological) meaning. In his person and work he fulfils the true intention of its prophecies and the goal of its history of salvation.

Jesus' Method of Interpretation

The Use of Hillel's Rules

The great rabbi Hillel († c. A.D. 10), who taught Scripture about a generation before our Lord's ministry, used seven rules or principles for interpreting the Bible. Some of them, for example, interpreting according to context (Rule 7), come down to us today virtually unaltered. Hillel's Rules drew inferences and analogies from Scripture, and some of them were employed by Christ in his interpretation of his Bible. From those mentioned above in chapter three, let us consider in more detail the following examples:[18]

Rule 1: קל וחומר, inference from minor and major, *a fortiori*.

Consider the ravens they neither sow nor reap...
And God feeds them (Ps 147:9)
Of how much more value are you
Than the birds
           Luke 12:24

---

[17] Cf. Rom 3:21 with 4:7; 'The law' can refer to the whole Old Testament (cf. Rom 3:19 with 3:10–18; I Cor 14:21); so also 'the prophets' (cf. Acts 13:27; 26:27).

[18] See above, 87–91. For Hillel's Rules and their exposition by the rabbis cf. *T. Sanhedrin* 7:11; *ARN* 37, 10. Cf. *The Tosefta*, 6 vols. ed. J. Neusner, New York 1977–86; Neusner (note 7); M. Mielziner, *Introduction to the Talmud*, New York 1968 ([1]1894), 123–129; H. L. Strack, *Introduction to the Talmud and Midrash*, New York [5]1959 ([1]1887), 93–98. For other New Testament examples, see above, 89f.; cf. E. E. Ellis, *Paul's Use of the Old Testament*, Grand Rapids [5]1991, 41 f.

Is it not written in your law
'I said you are gods' (Ps 82:6)
If [God] called 'gods' those to whom the word of God came...
Do you say, 'You blaspheme'
Because I said, 'I am "the Son of God"' (Ps 2:7)
John 10:34 ff.

From the biblical verse teaching that God cares for the least of his creatures, Jesus infers *a fortiori* that the passage also applies to his disciples. From the verse addressing as 'gods' the whole people of God, he infers *a fortiori* that the title 'Son of God' is appropriate for the One God has sent into the world.[19]

Rule 2: גזירה שוה, an equivalent regulation, an inference drawn from a similar situation (words and phrases) in Scripture.

On the sabbath... [Jesus'] disciples plucked and ate grain...
The Pharisees said, 'Why do you do that which is not lawful' (Exod 20:10)...
Jesus said,... '[David] took and ate the bread of the Presence
And gave to those with him (I Sam 21:1–6)
Which is not lawful to eat except for the priests (Lev 24:9)...
The Son of Man is lord of the Sabbath'
Luke 6:1–5

David, who received a kingdom from God (I Sam 15:28), was blameless when he and those with him violated the law in eating the bread of the Presence. Therefore, the Son of Man, who has also received a kingdom from God (Dan 7:13f.), is equally blameless when those with him violate the sabbath law in similar circumstances.

Rule 3: בנין אב מכתוב אחד, constructing a family from one passage, a general principle inferred from the teaching contained in one verse.

Moses showed that the dead are raised...
He calls the Lord 'the God of Abraham'... (Exod 3:6, 15)
He is not the God of the dead but of the living
Luke 20:37 f.

God is not the God of the dead, yet he affirmed his covenant relationship with the dead Abraham. Therefore, Jesus concludes, he must intend to

---

[19] That Jesus had (reportedly) identified himself as 'the Son of God,' that is, the Messiah, is also presupposed by the high priest's question at Mark 14:61f. = Matt 26:63f. Peter's confession of some similar teaching of Jesus to disciples had apparently become common knowledge. Cf. S. Kim, *The 'Son of Man' as the Son of God*, Tübingen 1983, 1–6.

raise Abraham out of death. From this one passage one may infer the resurrection of all the dead who have a similar covenantal relationship with God.[20]

Rule 7: דבר הלמד מעניינו, an interpretation of a word or a passage derived from its context.

He who made them from the beginning,
'Made them male and female' (Gen 1:27)
And said, ... '[A man] shall be joined to his wife
And the two shall be one flesh' (Gen 2:24)
Therefore, what God has joined, let no man separate
[The Pharisees said], 'Why then did Moses command
That he give her a bill of divorce...' (Deut 24:1-4)?
[Jesus said], 'For the hardness of your hearts...
But from the beginning it was not so'
                                        Matt 19:4-8

At the creation God established marriage as an indissoluble union. This context, Jesus concludes, takes priority over the later provisions for divorce and provides the regulative standard by which other biblical teachings on this subject are to be understood and applied.

We have given no examples of a general principle derived from the teaching of two verses (Rule 4), of an inference drawn from a general principle to a specific example and vice versa (Rule 5) or of an inference drawn from an analogous passage (Rule 6). But the above examples are sufficient to show how Jesus employed, for the most part implicitly, Hillel's Rules in his exposition of Scripture. Not all of Hillel's Rules are clearly attested in the Gospels, and the Rules in Jesus' usage appear less stylized than in the later rabbinic writings. But they are present, and they form a part of the hermeneutical framework for our Lord's biblical interpretation.

The Use of Commentary Patterns

Much of the older form criticism of the Gospels assumed that Jesus uttered pithy pronouncements and that his scriptural references and expositions almost always represented postresurrection creations of the church.[21] In this respect it read the historical development precisely

---

[20] Further, cf. E. E. Ellis, *The Gospel of Luke*, Grand Rapids [5]1987, 234–237.

[21] For example, R. Bultmann, *History of the Synoptic Tradition*, Oxford 1963 ([1]1921),

backwards. In part the early form criticism reflected a mistaken dichotomy between Jesus the apocalyptic prophet and Jesus the teacher; in part it simply lacked an understanding of the Jewish context of Jesus' ministry.

For example, Jesus' teaching against divorce would have no force with his hearers unless he could establish it exegetically from Scripture and could thus successfully counter the traditional interpretation of Moses' teaching on the matter. Like anyone else, Jesus had to meet the standard imposed by Deut 13:1–5 (cf. 30:10) with its implied requirement that succeeding prophets be in accord with Moses' teaching:[22]

If a prophet arises among you...
And he gives you a sign... and [it] comes to pass...
And if he says, 'Let us go after other gods...'
You shall not listen...
You shall... keep [God's] commandments...
[That] God commanded you [by me].

With such texts as a part of Jewish consciousness Jesus, or any other prophetic teacher, could not hope to persuade the nation only by signs and wonders or by wandering about the country uttering pronouncements or even by quoting isolated biblical texts. He was required to support his views by expounding Scripture, by a midrash, an exposition, in which various passages were called upon to aid in understanding a particular text.[23] That Jesus did this, and did it with an authority that exceeded that of the usual scribe or 'Bible teacher,' evoked the astonishment of his hearers.[24] Thus, it is, for example, the exposition at Matt 19:3–9 that represents the authoritative foundation of Jesus' teaching on divorce

---

46–50; cf. 16f., 26f., passim. Cf. J. W. Doeve, *Jewish Hermeneutics in the Synoptic Gospels and Acts*, Assen 1954, 178: '[The] classifications used by Dibelius and Bultmann... are not cognate to the material. For they are derived from the Greek world and not from the Jewish...' See below, note 27.

[22] Deut 13:1–5 and the judgment on false prophets invoked there is reproduced in the Temple Scroll (11QTemple 54:8-18) and referred to in CD 12:2f.; *M. Sanhedrin* 7:4 and applied to Jesus in *B. T. Sanhedrin* 43a; cf. Justin, *Dialogue* 69. Cf. Billerbeck (note 7), I, 1023f.; A. Strobel, *Die Stunde der Wahrheit*, Tübingen 1980, 81–94; W. A. Meeks, *The Prophet-King*, Leiden 1967, 47–57. The demand by the Jewish churchmen for 'a sign' from Jesus (Mark 8:11) also presupposes a suspicion or conviction that he is a false prophet and his miracles the work of demons (Mark 3:22). Cf. W. L. Lane, *The Gospel According to Mark*, Grand Rapids 1974, 277f.

[23] Doeve (note 21), 115f.: To the Jewish mind it 'is not the detached passage, the separate text, that has weight, that proves something...' See above, 100f.

[24] Cf. Daube (note 11), 212–223. Matt 7:29; 22:33.

which the pronouncement at Matt 5:31 f. summarizes and on which it depends. The biblical expositions of Jesus elsewhere are likewise the bedrock of his teaching and of the Synoptic tradition,[25] and from a critical perspective they cannot be regarded as creations of the Gospel traditioners.

Two commentary patterns found in rabbinic writings also appear in expositions of Jesus which are, in fact, the earliest extant examples of this form of exegetical discourse. They are the *proem* midrash and the *yelam-medenu* midrash.[26] They were significant for Christ's teaching in at least two ways. Like Hillel's Rules (or like the sermon outline of a modern preacher), they provided a framework for communicating his message that would be familiar to his audiences in the synagogue and in other places. And they could be easily summarized for memorization by Jesus' pupils.[27]

An Exposition on the Kingdom of God and the Messiah

An example of a *proem*-type midrash, which has been noted in chapter three, appears at Matt 21:33–46:[28]

---

[25] A number of Christ's expositions are found in both Mark and Q traditions, for example, Mark 4:10–12; 12:1–12; 12:18–27; 12:28–34; 12:35–37. But see below, notes 28, 31.

[26] See above, 96–100. For rabbinic examples of these two types of midrash, see *Pesikta de Rab Kahana*, ed. W.G. Braude and I.J. Kapstein, Philadelphia 1975, xf., xxviii–xxxvii, xlix, passim; *Pesikta Rabbati*, 2 vols., ed. W.G. Braude, New Haven CT 1968, I, 3–5, 17, 26, passim. Although collected later, these midrashim are largely the work of third- and fourth-century rabbis. Cf. S. Maybaum, *Die ältesten Phasen der Entwicklung der jüdischen Predigt*, Berlin 1901, 1–27.

[27] On the manner of Jesus' training of his disciples and of their transmission of his teachings cf. R. Riesner, *Jesus als Lehrer*, Tübingen ³1988; B. Gerhardsson, *The Gospel Tradition*, Lund 1986; idem, *The Origins of the Gospel Traditions*, Philadelphia 1979; E. E. Ellis, 'New Directions in Form Criticism,' *Jesus Christus in Historie und Theologie*, ed. G. Strecker, Tübingen 1975, 299–315 = idem, *Prophecy and Hermeneutic in Early Christianity*, Tübingen 1978, 237–253; idem, 'Gospels Criticism,' *The Gospel and the Gospels*, ed. P. Stuhlmacher, Grand Rapids 1991, 37–43 (GT: 38–45); idem, *The Making of the New Testament Documents*, forthcoming.

[28] See above, 98. Assuming their mutual independence, Matthew and Luke (20:9–19) utilize both Mark 12:1–12 and a Q tradition, as their agreements against Mark show. But see below, note 31; T. Zahn, *Introduction to the New Testament*, 3 vols., Grand Rapids 1953 (³1909), II, 601–612; III, 107–114; idem, *Das Evangelium des Matthäus*, Wuppertal 1984 (⁴1922), 10–32.

33   – Initial text: Isa 5:1 f.
34–41   – Exposition by means of a parable, linked to the initial and/or final texts by the catchword λίθος (42, 44, cf. 35; Isa 5:2, סקל); cf. οἰκοδομεῖν (33, 42).
42–44   – Concluding texts: Ps 118:22f.; Dan 2:34f., 44f. and application.

The opening *(proem)* text has been reduced to an allusion and the key word ('stone') omitted, but the reference to Isaiah 5 is clear. In Mark one of the concluding texts (Daniel 2) has been omitted, but it is retained from the Q *Vorlage* (also as an allusion) by Matthew and Luke. The commentary pattern in the Gospels is looser than in the later, more stylized *proem* midrashim in the rabbinic writings, but a common root underlying the New Testament and the rabbinic usage is quite evident.

Jesus expounds Isa 5 in terms of the religious leaders' rejection of his person and his teachings. With the parable of 'the wicked vinedressers' he shifts the focus of the parable in Isa 5 from God's vineyard, allegorically indentified there as the unrighteous nation, to the vineyard keepers, that is, the nation's unrighteous religious authorities. He specifies their sin as the killing of the vineyard owner's messengers, allegorically identified with God's prophets and with himself, God's son. While Jesus veils the reference to himself, for the perceptive hearer he makes via the parable both a messianic claim and a prediction of his violent death.

More clearly, with the concluding texts of the exposition Jesus interprets Isa 5 in terms of 'the rejected stone' of Ps 118 and 'the crushing stone' of Dan 2, both of which were interpreted in Judaism of the Messiah. With these texts Jesus warns the Jewish churchmen that they will be replaced by the One they have rejected, and at Messiah's parousia they will be destroyed.[29]

In his exposition of Isa 5 Jesus tied eschatology to christology, his message of the coming kingdom of God to his own person and role. When he sent out the missions of the Twelve and the Seventy (Luke 9–10), it is altogether likely that, in their preaching of the kingdom of God, they transmitted the memorized summaries of such expositions.

An Exposition on Right Interpretation

Many of Jesus' expositions of Scripture occurred in debates with opposing religious teachers. They were summarized in a pattern later known as the

---

[29] Cf. Ellis, *Prophecy* (note 27), 205–208; J. Jeremias, 'λίθος,' *TDNT* 4 (1967/1942), 271–275: 'Jesus directs [Ps 118:22] against his opponents as a word of eschatological threat and a summons to repentance' (275).

yelammedenu rabbenu[30] midrash, which is similar to the *proem* pattern except that the opening is formed by a question and counter-question. An example is found in Matt 15.1–9:[31]

1f.	– Theme and Pharisees' biblical question (Lev 15:11; 22:6f. and similar texts as traditionally interpreted).[32]
3–6	– Jesus' biblical counter-question, with texts and commentary (Exod 20:12; Deut 5:16; Exod 21:17; Lev 20:9), verbally linked to the theme, commentary and final text (παράδοσις, 2, 3, 6; τιμᾶν, 4, 6, 8).
7–9	– Concluding text: Isa 29:13, with application.

Summarized here, using a *yelammedenu*-type commentary pattern, is a debate between Jesus and other Jewish churchmen about the true meaning of Scripture for present conduct.

The original debate may have been restricted to Matt 15:1–9. If so, the question about eating with unwashed hands was only introductory, and the counter-question put by Jesus was the center of the debate. It concerned the Pharisees' traditional biblical interpretation in which the

---

[30] ילמדנו רבנו, 'may our rabbi teach us.' For a discussion of the origin of the pattern cf. J.W. Bowker, 'Speeches in Acts: A Study in Proem and Yelammedenu Form,' *NTS* 14 (1967–68) 96–111.

[31] The expository, *yelammedenu*-type pattern is more original in Matthew and has broken down in Mark (7:5–13). This could be explained (1) if Mark is dependent on Matthew (Farmer) or (2) if Matthew has retained more closely the order of a proto-Mark (cf. Schmithals) or of a proto-Matthew (cf. Zahn). Of these Zahn's reconstruction seems to have the best historical basis. Cf. W.R. Farmer, *The Synoptic Problem*, Macon GA [3]1982, 243f.; W. Schmithals, *Das Evangelium nach Markus*, Gütersloh 1979, 48, 57f.; Zahn (note 28). Cf. also Matt 12:1–8, where the parallels at Mark 2:23–28 and Luke 6:1–5 have lost a part of the commentary pattern, indicating that Matthew is (or has retained) the earliest form of the tradition. See above, 98. For further examples cf. Matt. 19:3–9; Luke 10:25–37; Ellis, *Prophecy* (note 27), 158f. For rabbinical examples cf. Braude, *Pesikta* (note 26), I, 3, and the Piskas cited. In the Gospels the *yelammedenu*-type pattern is usually employed in Jesus' debates with opponents, but it can also be used, as it is in the rabbinic writings, for the instruction of his hearers; cf. Matt 11:7–15.

[32] So, H.A.W. Meyer, *Gospel of Matthew*, New York 1884, 279; Zahn, *Matthäus* (note 28), 516f. Otherwise: A. Plummer, *S. Matthew*, London [5]1920, 211. Cf. G. Bornkamm – G. Barth – H.J. Held, *Tradition and Interpretation in Matthew*, London 1963, 88f.: 'The interpretation of the law is… the deciding criterion.' 'In the interpretation, however, the love-commandment is decisive…; with this critical attitude… the Rabbinical tradition is… broken through' (Barth). On the rabbinical discussion cf. J. Lightfoot, *A Commentary on the New Testament from the Talmud and Hebraica*, 4 vols., Grand Rapids 1979 ([1]1684), II, 223–226 (on Matt 15:2); Billerbeck (note 7), I, 695–704.

command concerning 'vows' (Num 30:2; Deut 23:21) took precedence over the command to honor one's parents (Exod 20:12; 21:17).[33]

With his critique Jesus sets forth two important principles of his biblical interpretation. First, he subordinates external commands concerning the 'lips' to those commands touching the 'heart' (cf. Isa 29:13) and, thereby, implicitly cuts through all legalistic interpretations of the Bible that cause a violation of the supreme commandments, love for God and for one's neighbor.[34] Second and equally important, Jesus condemns such wrong interpretations of Scripture as 'commandments of men' that 'make void the word of God' (15:9, 6).[35] As he does elsewhere, Jesus here also identifies the 'word of God' character of Scripture with its true interpretation and application.

The following section (15:10–20), which both Matthew and Mark join to the biblical debate, presents Jesus' teaching on true defilement to the crowds and the disciples.[36] It elaborates the point made in the citation at 15:7 ff. from Isaiah by explicitly distinguishing internal attitudes and acts arising out of them from external observances that have no necessary connection with one's heart-attitude. With this distinction Jesus, in Mark's (7:19) comment, 'declared all foods clean.' In principle, Matthew and Paul agree with this, but they do not make the point so bluntly. They know that external observances sometimes serve the law of love and that, with that proviso, they may be meaningful and appropriate.[37]

In his exposition of the Old Testament in Matt 15:1–9 and 21:33–44, Jesus underscored two important features of his teaching generally:[38] (1) He showed that his christological and eschatological hermeneutic was at the center of his understanding of the Old Testament and of his conflict with traditional Jewish biblical interpretations. (2) Also against some

---

[33] The issue is raised again in *M. Nedarim* 9:1, where a somewhat different point of view is offered. Cf. D. Hill, *The Gospel of Matthew*, London 1972, 251.

[34] See above, note 32.

[35] 'The tradition of men' (Mark 7:8) or 'of the fathers' (Gal 1:14) stands in contrast to the 'tradition of Christ' (Col 2:8). Cf. I Cor 11:1.

[36] Matt 15:10–20 = Mark 7:14–23. It is difficult to say whether the whole episode Matt 15:1–20 was formulated as a unit from the beginning (Daube) or whether the debate (15:1–9) had an independent usage and was later joined to Jesus' further teaching on defilement. Certainly, the Evangelists present the whole as a unit, joined by catchwords ('heart,' 'defile;' Matt 15:18ff.; Mark 7:21ff.).

[37] Cf. Matt 5:23f.; 23:2f.; Rom 14; I Cor 8:13; 9:20.

[38] For example, the exposition at Matt 12:1–8 (see above, 98) also combined Jesus' christological hermeneutic (12:6, 8) with his subordination of ritual to moral law (12:4f., 7).

traditional views, ✓ Jesus subordinated and relativized ritual and cultic observances vis-à-vis the moral law that was rooted in the great commandments of love toward God and love toward one's neighbor.[39] He thereby initiated a distinction that was to be taken up by Paul and James and to become a permanent feature of a truly Christian hermeneutic of Scripture.[40]

Conclusion

Jesus' interpretation of his Bible proceeds from his recognition of the canon of sacred books accepted by the mainstream Judaism of his day and from his settled conviction that these writings, rightly understood, were the expression of the mind of God through faithful prophets. The exposition of the received Scripture is, then, the sum and substance of Jesus' message, both in teaching his followers and in debating his opponents. This is true even when the Gospel traditioners and Evangelists, because *inter alia* of the limits of space, have summarized, compacted or omitted the express biblical references that originally formed the basis of Jesus' teachings.

Contrary to some misguided modern interpreters, there is never any suggestion in the Gospels of Jesus opposing the Torah, the law of God, the Old Testament. It is always a question of Jesus' true exposition of Scripture against the misunderstanding and/or misapplication of it by the dominant biblical scholars of his day. This becomes apparent in Jesus' encounters with such rabbis in numerous debates, a number of which the Evangelists have been careful to retain.

The Judaism of Jesus' day was a Torah-centric religion. To gain any hearing among his people Jesus' teaching also had to be Torah-centric. Thus it was necessary, not only from his own conviction of the Law as the word of God and of himself as the fulfilment of that Law but also from practical considerations, that our Lord show by his teachings as well as by his acts that his message and his messianic person stood in continuity with and in fulfilment of Israel's ancient word from God. It is in this frame of reference that one finds the meaning of Jesus' interpretation of his Bible.

[39] Luke 10:25–37; Matt 22:34–40 par. See above, 98.

[40] Cf. Rom 13:8ff.; Gal 5:6, 14; 6:2, 15; Jas 2:8. Cf. J.B. Mayor, *The Epistle of St. James*, London 1892, lxxxii ff., 84f. In the light of Paul's use of Jesus-traditions elsewhere, it is probable that his teaching here also rests upon that of Jesus. Cf. E.E. Ellis, 'Traditions in 1 Corinthians,' *NTS* 32 (1986), 485–490.

Appendix II

Typological Interpretation – and its Rivals

Early Christianity and Judaism

As has been observed in the pages above, the typological interpretation of the Old Testament has an important place in the history of research as well as in current biblical studies. Nevertheless, it has not been universally affirmed, and it has had to contend with a number of rival approaches. Indeed, the interpretation of the Old Testament in the church has been a matter of controversy almost from the beginning. As a number of writers have argued,[1] a typological understanding of the Bible was fundamental for the New Testament apostles and prophets, and it continued to be followed, more or less closely, by Irenaeus of Lyons (c. A.D. 125–195)[2] and by the patristic school of writers associated with Antioch.[3] There were, however, other views bidding for acceptance. Most prominent among them was an allegorical approach, fostered by Origen (c. A.D. 185–254) and the School of Alexandria,[4] which largely dominated the church's exposition of the Old Testament during the Middle Ages.[5]

In addition to allegory and typology[6] two more extreme interpretations of the Scriptures appeared in early Christianity. Marcion (c. A.D. 100–160) rejected the Old Testament altogether, regarding it as the

---

[1] See above, 105f. Cf. also G.R. Osborne, 'Type,' *ISBE*[2] 4 (1988), 930ff.; L. Goppelt, *TYPOS. The Typological Interpretation of the Old Testament in the New*, Grand Rapids 1982 ([2]1969); E.E. Ellis, *Prophecy and Hermeneutic in Early Christianity*, Tübingen 1978, 165–169; D.L. Baker, *Two Testaments: One Bible*, Downers Grove IL 1977, 239–270; R.T. France, *Jesus and the Old Testament*, London 1971, 38–80; W.G. Kümmel, 'Schriftauslegung,' *RGG*[3] 5 (1961), 1519; W. Eichrodt, 'Is Typological Exegesis an Appropriate Method?' *Essays in Old Testament Hermeneutics*, ed. C. Westermann, Atlanta 1979 (1960), 224–245.

[2] His doctrine of ἀνακεφαλαίωσις is not mere 'recapitulation' but, like typology, contains elements of both correspondence and escalation. Cf. G. Wingren, *Man and the Incarnation. A Study in the Biblical Theology of Irenaeus*, Edinburgh 1959, 125f., 192ff.

[3] Cf. R.M. Grant, *A Short History of the Interpretation of the Bible*, London [2]1965, 69–79; H.B. Swete, 'Theodore of Mopsuestia,' *DCB* IV, 946f.; F.W. Farrar, *History of Interpretation*, New York 1886, 210–219.

[4] Cf. H. Crouzel, *Origen*, San Francisco 1989, 61–84; R.P.C. Hanson, *Allegory and Event: Origen's Interpretation of Scripture*, Richmond 1959; B.F. Westcott, 'Origenes,' *DCB* IV, 131 ff.

[5] Cf. Grant (note 3), 94–101; B. Smalley, *The Bible in the Middle Ages*, Oxford 1952, 360, 372f.; Farrar (note 3), 239–242, 248–300.

[6] On the distinction between them see above, 106.

instrument of an evil deity.[7] According to Clement of Alexandria some of Marcion's followers or a similar sect urged that whatever the Old Testament taught, one should do the opposite.[8] This attitude, however, was not present in the first-century church.

At the other extreme was the biblical interpretation of the Judaizers (Gal 2:14, ἰουδαΐζειν) and that of Jewish political messianism. The Judaizers surface in the New Testament as a faction within the 'Hebraists,' that is, the ritually strict Jewish Christians sometimes known as 'the circumcision party.'[9] Unlike others in their party, they were not content with a 'live and let live' attitude toward ritually lax Jewish and Gentile believers but demanded that Gentiles be circumcised and observe the Mosaic ritual laws. Apparently, they rejected the distinction made by Jesus between Old Testament ritual and moral commandments[10] as well as the typological fulfilment of the Mosaic worship-system is taught (especially) by Paul and by the book of Hebrews.[11] Because of their insistence on literal interpretation and the universal observance of the Old Testament regulations, the Judaizers sought to undermine and at length adamantly opposed and were opposed by the allied missions of James, Peter, Paul and John,[12] that is, the missions whose prophetic writings make up our New Testament.[13]

In the Judaism of the first and second centuries a political interpretation of Old Testament messianic texts was popular[14] and was an impor-

---

[7] Irenaeus, *Haereses* 1, 27, 2.

[8] Clement of Alexandria, *Stromata* 3, 4, 34f. (on Exod 20:13), cited by Hanson (note 4), 138, although it is not clear to me that the reference ἄλλοι τίνες is to Marcionites.

[9] Cf. Acts 6:1; 10:45; 11:2; II Cor 11:22; Gal 2:12; Col 4:11; Tit 1:10.

[10] For example, in Matt 15:1–20, as has been observed above, 135–138.

[11] See above, 105–112. Cf. Goppelt (note 1), 127–178, passim (GT: 152–215).

[12] The following passages from the several apostolic circles appear to be *inter alia* directed against Judaizers: Matt 15:17–20 (Jacobean-Matthean); Mark 7:18f. (Petrine); Galatians (Pauline). The same seems to be the force of Rev 2:9, 14 when it is compared with I Cor 10:19f.; II Cor 11:13f., 22; Phil 3:2f.

[13] For a criticism of the Baur-tradition, which sets Peter and James against Paul on this issue, and for an alternative understanding of these Judaizers cf. Ellis (note 1), 89–95, 103–115, 116–128, 230ff., 235ff.; idem, 'Gospels Criticism,' *The Gospel and the Gospels*, ed. P. Stuhlmacher, Grand Rapids 1991, 43–52 (GT: 45–54); idem, 'Foreword,' to H. Harris, *The Tübingen School*, Grand Rapids ²1990, vii–xv. Cf. F. C. Baur, *Paul*, 2 vols., London 1876 (1845), I, 120–128, 256f.; idem, *The Church History of the First Three Centuries*, 2 vols., London ³1878 (1853), I, 53–55.

[14] E.g. Jn 6:15; Acts 5:36ff.; 21:38; Josephus, *Ant.* 20, 97–99; 20, 167–172; 1QM

tant factor leading to the Jewish revolts against Rome in A.D. 66–70 and A.D. 132–135.[15] It was an interpretation that brought disastrous results and one that Jesus clearly rejected.[16] However, it may have influenced some of his followers, who apparently sought to make him a political Messiah.[17] A few scholars have argued that a kind of 'political Judaizing,' that is, an interpretation of the kingdom of God in terms of Israel's liberation from Rome, was promoted by some early Christians. But there is little evidence for it.[18]

A Judaizing hermeneutic of the Old Testament, whether of ritual laws or of a (less evident) political messianism, sought to make a one-to-one equation or correspondence between the Old Testament and the messianic community of the kingdom of God. Unlike a typological interpretation, it failed to understand the principle of escalation or change of key between Old Testament institutions and promises and their New Testament fulfilment. In particular it failed to recognize the church as the 'true' Israel that was both in continuity with and also distinct from national Israel.[19]

The Modern Church

For at least two reasons typological interpretation continues to be significant for current biblical studies. First, it is essential to the broader issue of biblical hermeneutics, which remains at the forefront of scholarly interest.[20] Second, and perhaps more important, competing alternatives to

---

5:1; 1QSb 5:20–28; *P. T. Taanit* 4:5; CD 7:19ff.; 4QTest 9–13; 1QM 11:6f.; Test Judah 24:1–6.

[15] There were doubtless other factors as well; cf. M. Goodman, *The Ruling Classes of Judea: The Origins of the Jewish Revolt Against Rome*, Cambridge ²1988.

[16] Matt 4:8ff.; 12:28; 26:51f.; Jn 18:36; cf. 6:15. Cf. J. P. M. Sweet, 'The Zealots and Jesus,' *Jesus and the Politics of His Day*, ed. E. Bammel, Cambridge ²1988, 1–9; M. Hengel, *Was Jesus a Revolutionist?* Philadelphia 1971. Otherwise: S. G. F. Brandon, *Jesus and the Zealots*, Manchester 1967.

[17] Jn 6:15.

[18] Cf. the intensely argued albeit unsuccessful thesis of S. G. F. Brandon, *The Fall of Jerusalem and the Christian Church*, London ²1957. But see B. Reicke, 'Judeo-Christianity and the Jewish establishment, A. D. 33–66,' in Bammel (note 16), 145–152.

[19] Cf. C. F. D. Moule, 'Jesus, Judaism, and Paul,' *Tradition and Interpretation in the New Testament*, ed. G. F. Hawthorne with O. Betz, Grand Rapids and Tübingen 1987, 43–50; Goppelt (note 1), 17f., 140–151, 199 (GT: 18ff., 169–182, 240f.).

[20] E.g. B.S. Childs, *Introduction to the Old Testament as Scripture*, Philadelphia 1979;

typological exegesis that were present in early Christianity and in the surrounding Judaism are again, under other names, bidding for acceptance in the church today.

Allegorical interpretation is not currently advocated under that label. But contemporary scholars who depreciate the historical meaning of the text and who use biblical words, concepts and stories as symbols, metaphors or myths for deeper meanings, manifest essential features of an allegorical approach to the Bible.[21]

A second and more curious phenomenon in the modern church is the revival of a Marcionite attitude toward the Old Testament, an attitude that has apparently arisen from a distortion of the law/gospel dialectic of traditional Lutheranism.[22] It first came to extensive expression in Adolf von Harnack's book on Marcion.[23] Harnack, a leading representative of the older liberal theology, called for an outright ejection of the Old Testament from the Christian canon. At about the same time but for other reasons the history-of-religions school, with which Harnack had his differences, also tended to give the Old Testament a secondary role and to disparage its significance for understanding the origin of New Testament teachings.[24] Through Wilhelm Heitmüller, Johannes Weiss and William Wrede this school decisively shaped the thought of Rudolf Bultmann and his pupils. Bultmann was not far from Harnack's viewpoint, writing that

'to the Christian faith the Old Testament is no longer revelation as it has been, and still is, for the Jews.' It 'is not in the true sense God's Word. So far as the church proclaims the Old Testament as God's Word, it just finds in it again what is already known from the revelation in Jesus Christ.'[25]

Goppelt (note 1); P. Stuhlmacher, *Vom Verstehen des Neuen Testaments*, Göttingen [2]1986; idem, *Historical Criticism and Theological Interpretation of Scripture*, Philadelphia 1977.

[21] Cf. the criticisms of psychological and structural exegesis by O. C. Edwards, Jr., 'Historical-Critical Method's Failure of Nerve...,' *ATR* 59 (1977), 115–134; A. C. Thistleton, 'Structuralism and Biblical Studies: Method or Ideology?' *ET* 89 (1978), 329–335; B. C. Lategan, 'Directions in Contemporary Exegesis: Between Historicism and Structuralism,' *JTSA* 25 (1978), 23–29; of existentialist demythologizing by K. Frör, *Biblische Hermeneutik*, München 1961, 326. Cf. B. Stancil, 'Structuralism and New Testament Studies,' *SWJT* 22 (1980), 41–59.

[22] Cf. C. E. Braaten, *History and Hermeneutics*, London 1968, 121–125.

[23] A. v. Harnack, *Marcion. Das Evangelium vom fremden Gott*, Leipzig [2]1924 (ET: 1990).

[24] E. g. W. Bousset, *Kurios Christos*, Nashville 1970 ([2]1921), 149; W. Wrede, 'The Task and Methods of "New Testament Theology"' (1897) in R. Morgan, *The Nature of New Testament Theology*, London 1973, 99, 184.

[25] R. Bultmann, 'The Significance of the Old Testament for the Christian Faith,' *The Old Testament and the Christian Faith*, ed. B. W. Anderson, New York 1963, 31f. On

This confessional attitude, in turn, was not without its effect on Bultmann's reconstruction of the Gospel traditions, which largely determined the direction of the early form criticism and in which Old Testament quotations were regularly regarded as secondary accretions.[26]

One of Bultmann's pupils, Gunther Klein, approaches even more closely the ancient Marcionite attitude when he describes Moses the lawgiver as 'the functionary of antigodly powers' and the historical realm based on him as 'not merely profaned but flatly demonized.'[27] Other heirs of the history-of-religions school are generally more moderate. But it is, I think, not unfair to say that in their thorough and minute attention to Greco-Roman parallels to the New Testament – a necessary and important task – they are often correspondingly weak in their perception of its Old Testament and Jewish antecedents.[28] Such scholarship is not necessarily Marcionite. But it does, at the least, risk losing sight of the fundamental importance of the Old Testament and of post-Old Testament Judaism for understanding the New Testament. One of the values of studies on typology is to demonstrate vis-à-vis the history-of-religions school the priorities and the more significant conceptual background of the New Testament writers.[29]

Judaizing interpretations of Scripture did not disappear with the opponents of Paul. In a general way they are implicitly present in all movements in the church that seek to achieve salvation by human endeavor. They appear, for example, in the imposition of regulations about food and drink and days or in attitudes toward ministries and sacraments that do not recognize the proper distinctions – the escalation – between Old Testament orders and rituals and their New Testament counterparts.[30] Such efforts to facilitate redemption by human achievements were pretty

---

the philosophical background cf. H.J. Kraus, *Geschichte der historisch-kritischen Erforschung des Alten Testaments*, Neukirchen 1956, 175–179. For a criticism cf. R.N. Longenecker, 'Three Ways of Understanding Relations Between the Testaments...,' in Hawthorne (note 19), 22f., 28.

[26] R. Bultmann, *History of the Synoptic Tradition*, New York 1963, 16ff., 26f., 47–50, 125, passim. In important respects this approach can now be seen to have been mistaken.

[27] G. Klein, *Rekonstruktion und Interpretation*, München 1969, 210.

[28] E.g. H.D. Betz's *Galatians* (Philadelphia 1979) reflects this imbalance, as C.K. Barrett (*Int* 34 [1980], 417) has noted.

[29] See above, note 1.

[30] Cf. Gal 2:14; 4:10; Matt 12:5f.; Rom 2:28f.; 14:3ff.; Col 2:16; E. Hatch, *The Organization of the Early Christian Churches*, Oxford 1881, 137ff.; T. Greenwood, *Cathedra Petri*, 8 vols. in 3, London 1856–59, I, 147–152, 159.

effectively addressed at the individual level by the *sola fide, sola gratia* theology of the Reformation, however one may judge the acceptance and implementation of Reformation insights in the doctrine and praxis of various sectors of the post-Reformation church. But at the societal level they continue to be pursued both in Roman Catholic and in Protestant denominations.[31]

Somewhat different is the phenomenon that we have termed political Judaizing, the attempt to facilitate societal salvation, the coming of the kingdom of God, along the lines of the Jewish 'messianic' revolt under Bar Cochba and similar figures in the first and second centuries. This understanding of the Bible also fails to observe the proper distinctions between the acts and ordinances of God in the Old Covenant and those in the New. Certain elements in the medieval church and in the modern 'social gospel' movement have affinities with political Judaizing but cannot really be identified with it. The political status, the papal armies and the Crusades of the institutional church in the Middle Ages did rest in part on earlier Old Testament analogies between the church and the institutions of Israel.[32] But they were not aimed toward achieving eschatological salvation. Conversely, the social gospel of American liberalism, which did promote a salvation by works with eschatological goals,[33] had little direct connection with any Old Testament hermeneutic known in Judaism, but was more an amalgam of the messianic ideals of the Puritans and the scientific, evolutionary optimism of the Victorians.[34] These two phenomena fall short, then, of reflecting a truly Judaizing interpretation. However, in the contemporary 'liberation theology' one does encounter what may be properly termed a Judaizing tendency in the modern church.

Attempts to hasten the coming of the kingdom of God by political revolution were initiated by the Münster Rebellion (1535) during the

---

[31] Cf. E.E. Ellis, *Pauline Theology: Ministry and Society*, Grand Rapids and Exeter 1989, 18–23, 151–155.

[32] Cf. A.D. Nock, 'The Development of Paganism in the Roman Empire,' *CAH* 12 (1939), 445f.; Hatch (note 30), 138; Greenwood (note 30); *Apostolic Constitutions* 2, 25, middle: '[Bishops] are to the laity prophets, rulers, governors and kings.'

[33] Cf. W. Rauschenbusch, *The Righteousness of the Kingdom*, Nashville 1968; K. Cauthen, *The Impact of American Religious Liberalism*, New York 1962, 84–107, 147–168. In criticism cf. H.J. Cadbury, *The Peril of Modernizing Jesus*, New York 1937; J.G. Machen, *Christianity and Liberalism*, Grand Rapids 1946 (1923), 117–156.

[34] Representative were, for example, the writings of G.A. Coe, 'Salvation by Education,' *American Protestant Thought: The Liberal Era*, ed. W.R. Hutchison, New York 1968, 117–126; idem, *A Sociological Theory of Religious Education*, New York 1917, whose index has the entry, 'Kindom of God, see *Democracy*' (359).

Reformation and again by the Fifth Monarchy Men of Oliver Cromwell's England.[35] In the present century they have been based upon Marxist analysis[36] and accompanied by a passion to obtain 'economic justice' for the poor. Our concern here is not to query the methods or the general theological implications of liberation theology[37] but, much more limited, to contrast briefly its biblical interpretation with that of typology.

'The distinctively Jewish... element in the traditional religious inspiration of Marxism is the apocalyptic vision of a violent revolution... [Marx's] messianic kingdom is conceived as a Dictatorship of the Proletariat. But the salient features of the traditional Jewish apocalypse protrude through this threadbare disguise, and it is actually the pre-Rabbinical Maccabaean Judaism that our philosopher-impressario is presenting in modern Western costume...'[38]

This incisive summation by Arnold Toynbee of the influence of Marx's Jewish heritage strikes, I believe, close to the mark even though it is not a matter that can be specifically documented. Marx's latter-day disciples among the liberation theologians are in this respect not untrue to their mentor when they use Marxist ideology to interpret the Old Testament.[39] In doing so, they suppose that they have discovered a new thing. The question arises, however, whether they have not in fact fallen back essentially into a Jewish political hermeneutic already current in the first century that, from the standpoint of Jesus and of the New Testament, would be regarded as a Judaizing interpretation of Scripture.

The 'horizontal' interpretation of liberation and the minimizing of God's intervention to achieve it, writes Andrew Kirk, 'overestimates man's unaided capability to effect real and lasting change... and ends, not infrequently, in an illusory "triumphalism."'[40] This is a fair characterization of liberation theology. Its concern for subjugated people, like that of the messianic pretender Bar Cochba, is entirely to be commended. But in

---

[35] They formed their views on an interpretation of Dan 2:44.

[36] Or, in the view of some, they replaced the Gospel of Mark with the gospel of Marx. Cf. Cadbury (note 33), 203. Expressing this view more precisely, they read Mark through Marxist spectacles and used it to serve Marxist ideology.

[37] For an appreciative analysis and critique cf. J.A. Kirk, *Liberation Theology*, London 1979, esp. 143–208; more critically, H.T. Hoekstra, *The World Council of Churches and the Demise of Evangelism*, Wheaton 1979, 63–131; E.R. Norman, *Christianity and the World Order*, Oxford 1979.

[38] A.J. Toynbee, *A Study of History*, 10 vols., London 1939–54, V, 178f.

[39] E.g. G. Gutierrez, *A Theology of Liberation*, Maryknoll NY 1973, 153–212; J.P. Miranda, *Marx and the Bible*, Maryknoll NY 1974. For more moderate expressions cf. J.E. Weir, 'Liberation Theology Comes of Age,' *ET* 98 (1986–87), 3–9.

[40] Kirk (note 37), 152.

terms of its biblical hermeneutic it must be classified as a reactionary, philosophical manifestation of an ancient error of salvation by works. For that the words of Augustine are not inappropriate:

'It is because the philosophers will not believe in this beatitude [of eternal life] which they cannot see that they go on trying to fabricate here below an utterly fraudulent felicity built on virtue filled with pride and bound to fail them in the end.'[41]

In contrast to a Marxist approach typological exegesis explains the New Testament fulfilment of Old Testament promises of liberation as acts of God within history that, at the same time, sovereignly select and go beyond the human political processes of this age. It thus implicitly distinguishes between 'salvation history' and 'general history,'[42] a distinction that liberation theology rejects. The rejection is perhaps best expressed in the words of Gustavo Gutierrez:

'[There] are not two histories, one profane and one sacred, "juxtaposed" or "closely linked." Rather there is only one human destiny, irreversibly assumed by Christ, the Lord of history.'[43]

Typological exegesis, however, recognizes the two dimensions of history and a relationship between them.[44] In this frame of reference it poses an alternative to Judaizing exegesis, no less than to allegorical and Marcionite interpretations of the Bible, and it offers a much better foundation that will be of interest to all who are concerned to structure their theology within biblical categories.

Criticisms of Typological Interpretation

The typological approach has encountered a number of criticisms of its attitude toward history. First, it is suggested that the New Testament's typological interpretation of the Old is not a true 'historical' understanding but only a 'reading back' of the interests of the New Testament writers.

---

[41] Augustine, *City of God* 19, 4, end (ET: *Fathers of the Church. Vol. 24*, ed. J. De Ferrari, New York 1954, 201 f.).

[42] Cf. O. Cullmann, *Salvation in History*, London 1967, 150–166; L. Goppelt, *Theology of the New Testament*, 2 vols., Grand Rapids 1981, I, 276–281.

[43] Gutierrez (note 39), 163.

[44] Cf. Cullmann (note 42); briefly, Ellis (note 1), 163–169; idem, *The Gospel of Luke*, Grand Rapids ⁵1987, 15–18.

The criticism immediately gives rise to a further question, the nature of historical knowledge. During the eighteenth and nineteenth centuries it was thought that the study of history, including biblical history, was an objective science and that the past could be reconstructed 'as it actually happened.' Today there is a greater recognition of the subjective factors that influence every historian's representation of the past.[45] As the reconstruction of a scholar, history *is* interpretation since any reading, say, of an Old Testament text, no less than a typological reading, is done through interpretive spectacles. While it can be plausibly argued that the biblical writers themselves had in view a future significance of the things that they were relating,[46] this is not necessary for the argument that such a significance was placed in them by God as the New Testament claims.[47] Typological exegesis assumes a divine sovereignty over history, an assumption that admittedly not everyone is prepared to accept. But it may, nonetheless, be a defensible assumption.

A second criticism of a typological approach addresses this presupposition of divine sovereignty. Karl Popper labels as 'historicism' the doctrine that 'there are specific historical laws which can be discovered, and upon which predictions regarding the future of mankind can be based.'[48] He brilliantly critiques this view of history as it is expressed in Hegelianism and Marxism, a critique that is pertinent to modern biblical studies. As we have seen above, a Marxist historicism heavily influences the biblical views of the liberation theologians. Also, through the theories of J. Wellhausen and F. C. Baur, a kind of Hegelian captivity has long afflicted the scholarly study of the Bible.[49] Indeed, virtually no nineteenth-century Continental theology escaped the pervasive influence of the Berlin master. Even those who reacted against Georg Hegel's philosophy, such as Søren Kierkegaard and Karl Marx, were in some respects influenced by him.[50]

---

[45] Cf. B. J. F. Lonergan, *Method in Theology*, New York [2]1973, 197–234; A. Richardson, *History, Sacred and Profane*, London 1964, 83–183.

[46] Cf. G. von Rad, *Old Testament Theology*, 2 vols., London 1962–65, II, 319–429.

[47] E. g. Matt 4:14; John 13:18; Acts 13:27; Rom 15:4; I Cor 10:11; Gal 4:24ff.; Heb 8:5; 10:1. Cf. E. E. Ellis, *Paul's Use of the Old Testament*, Grand Rapids [5]1991, 126–135.

[48] K. R. Popper, *The Open Society and its Enemies*, 2 vols., London [5]1980, I, 8f.

[49] Cf. Kraus (note 25), 178f. 239f.; W. F. Albright, *History, Archaeology and Christian Humanism*, London 1965, 36f., 136–140; E. E. Ellis, 'Dating the New Testament,' *NTS* 26 (1980), 494ff.; Harris (note 13), 25ff., 155–158; W. G. Kümmel, *The New Testament: The History of the Investigation of its Problems*, Nashville 1972, 132f.

[50] Cf. N. Thulstrup, *Kierkegaard's Relation to Hegel*, Princeton 1980; Popper (note 48), II, 318f.

The theology of 'salvation history,' as represented by J.C.K. von Hofmann,[51] was also not unaffected. But does a theistic, biblical view of history, which affirms a divine purpose and sovereignty in human affairs and which is assumed by a 'salvation history' typological interpretation of the Old Testament, as such, fall under the strictures upon historicism?

Professor Popper thinks that it does and, unlike C.S. Lewis,[52] he seems to make no distinction between the two situations of divine sovereignty and historicism. In his comments on the topic, he reflects a shift in his definition of historicism and a misunderstanding of the relationship between divine sovereignty and human freedom as it is represented by the Scriptures and by more perceptive Christian theologians. As a rationalist – or what Helmut Thielicke and Leonard Goppelt call a Cartesian[53] – thinker Popper has no place for revealed truth, much less for the truth of logical antinomies. He apparently is not aware that in a theistic view of history divine sovereignty and human freedom and responsibility operate as a *concursus* in which neither is sacrificed and neither forcibly conformed to the other. For him 'the rationalist attitude toward history in its emphasis on our supreme responsibility for our actions' on the one hand, and the conception of divine purpose and predetermination of the course of history on the other, are mutually exclusive.[54] But a proper Christian attitude toward history affirms the biblical revelation that both are true and that here, as in other matters, reality transcends the reasoning of autonomous man.[55]

As Popper initially defined historicism – 'historical laws which can be discovered' by human reason – it does not apply to a theology of salvation history or to a typological interpretation of Scripture. For in such a case the plan of history is in the hands of God and is not subject to human discovery or prediction. Even God's decisive act in sending Jesus the

[51] J.C.K. von Hofmann, *Interpreting the Bible*, Minneapolis 1972 (1880); cf. Kraus (note 25), 207f.

[52] C.S. Lewis, 'Historicism,' *Christian Reflections*, London 1967, 100–113.

[53] Goppelt (note 42), I, 272; cf. H. Thielicke, *The Evangelical Faith*, 3 vols., Grand Rapids 1974–82, I, 30–65, for a critique of an epistemology controlled by Cartesian assumptions and for its implications for biblical interpretation (esp. 64f.).

[54] Popper (note 48), II, 259–280, 279.

[55] Cf. M. Luther, *The Bondage of the Will*, Westwood NJ 1957 (1525), 74–108, and the translator, J.I. Packer's introduction, 45–57; B.B. Warfield, 'Predestination,' *HDB* IV, 47–63 = *Biblical and Theological Studies*, Philadelphia 1952, 270–329; G. Florovsky, 'The Predicament of the Christian Historian,' *God, History and Historians*, ed. C.T. McIntire, New York 1977, 428–442.

Messiah is perceived only by a divine disclosure.[56] Furthermore, except in its broadest outline the plan is revealed only in retrospect. Only in the light of the New Testament fulfilment is the typological significance of an Old Testament personage, event or institution made clear. Equally, only as the events of the consummation of the age occur will the relevant prophecies concerning them be fully understood. If in the light of the ministry, death and resurrection of the Messiah gifted Christians are able to perceive these events somewhat more specifically than the faithful of the Old Testament, they can do so only in general terms such as those in the Apostles' Creed. Certain current events and anticipations may signal fulfilments of prophecies.[57] But the pages of church history encourage the prudent Christian more to hopeful expectation than to flat affirmations about them. The fulfilment of God's purpose, like the gradual focusing on a screen of a previously unseen picture, always brings surprises even as it unveils its perfect correspondence and coordination with the foregoing reality and plan.

Typology and the Unity of the New Testament

When typological interpretation is pursued throughout the New Testament, it illumines the writers' wide-ranging unity in their understanding of the Old Testament.[58] On this account also it has been criticized by those who view the New Testament as a collection of competing and even contradictory theologies. Since typology and, indeed, any approach to the Bible as a unified body of teaching has been criticized rather broadly in this respect, it may be worthwhile to look at the source and the validity of the criticism.

The loss of a sense of the unity of the New Testament has been characteristic of some circles of scholarship for over two centuries. In part it was the result of the general 'secularization of the European mind'[59] with a consequent rejection of the revelatory character of Scripture or, in

---

[56] Matt 16:17; 11:25ff.; 13:11; cf. Luke 9:45; 24:31; Rom 10:17; 16:25f.; I Cor 2:9f.; I Pet 1:10ff.; II Pet 1:20f.

[57] E. g. the return of Jerusalem to the Jews (cf. Luke 21:24) and their turning en masse to the Messiah (cf. Rom 11:25–32).

[58] E. g. Goppelt (note 1), 194f.

[59] Cf. O. Chadwick, *The Secularization of the European Mind in the Nineteenth Century*, Cambridge 1975, esp. 179–188, 193–197, 212–226; P. Gay, *The Enlightenment: An Interpretation. The Rise of Modern Paganism*, New York 1966; Ellis in Harris (note 13), viii.

the words of T.W. Manson, with a consequent failure to interpret the Bible as the word of God.[60] The determination to treat the Bible as a purely human product, combined with the self-assurance of the eighteenth century's 'absolute man,'[61] produced not only antipathetic interpretations of biblical texts but also the conviction that these interpretations were 'scientific' results that had virtually the character of facts. Largely unrecognized was what the rabbis long before knew and, indeed, developed into a fine art:[62] Contradictions in Scripture are the result of interpretation (or of superficial reading), and what one interpreter could bring forth another could resolve. The meaning of ancient texts no less than other aspects of historical knowledge is never free from the subjective factors, including a confessional *a priori* world-view, with which the interpreter comes to and pursues his task. What appears probable to one interpreter will be improbable to another. The failure of the historical-critical method, after two hundred years, to achieve an agreed meaning for any substantive biblical passage underscores that fact and makes a more modest attitude incumbent upon all biblical scholars.

Perhaps more important in promoting the tendency to set one New Testament passage or writer against another was a dialectical *Denkmethode* that became an important factor in Continental biblical criticism in the nineteenth century. In modern theology biblical interpretation by dialectical antitheses may, like Marcionite tendencies, have some roots in the law/gospel dichotomy of traditional Lutheranism.[63] However, it appears to be largely the legacy of the philosophy of Georg Hegel, who by 'his powerful dialectical methods [was able] to draw real physical rabbits out of purely metaphysical silk hats.'[64] Clearly, dialectic can be an important tool, as it is in Plato's *Dialogues*, for defining an issue. And it can be useful in highlighting the unique contribution of a biblical passage or writer vis-à-vis another. But the highly antithetical Hegelian form in which it appears, implicitly or explicitly, in many New Testament studies often

---

[60] Cf. T.W. Manson, 'The Failure of Liberalism to Interpret the Bible as the Word of God,' *The Interpretation of the Bible*, ed. C.W. Dugmore, London 1944, 92–107.

[61] Cf. K. Barth, 'Man in the Eighteenth Century,' *Protestant Theology in the Nineteenth Century*, London 1972, 33–79, esp. 37–41.

[62] Cf. N.A. Dahl, 'Contradictions in Scripture,' *Studies in Paul*, Minneapolis 1977, 159–177.

[63] E.g. Galatians against James; cf. Braaten (note 22), 107f. Luther, however, apparently did not regard James as a part of his New Testament canon. Cf. M. Reu, *Luther and the Scriptures*, Columbus OH 1944, 38–48.

[64] Popper (note 48), II, 27.

exaggerates and distorts the texts and ignores the (far more likely) complementary character of the different perspectives that biblical writers bring to an issue.

The unity of the New Testament writings does not exclude their manifold diversity. If one is prepared to grant the prophetic credentials of the authors, the unity may be attributed to the Holy Spirit who speaks his message through their various voices, giving different responses to different situations. However, even if one takes a different confessional attitude, the unity of these documents is quite in accord with their historical origin. For they are the product of a cooperative and relatively close-knit segment of early Christianity.

In the first two centuries after Christ a stream of writings poured forth from those professing to be followers of Jesus. They represented the most diverse interpretations of the Old Testament and of the meaning of Christianity itself. Apart from the New Testament all writings that are extant were, with a few exceptions,[65] written after the first century, and the hypothesis that some had (Christian) *Vorlagen* contemporary with the canonical writings has thus far not been established.[66] Nevertheless, other contemporary Christian writings of various sorts are alluded to by the New Testament authors.[67] One or two of them are attributed to a competing Judaizing-gnosticizing mission,[68] and probably others from that or similar groups can be inferred. Supporting this inference is the vast literary output of a similar and contemporary Jewish apocalyptic sect, the Qumran community. Unknown until 1947, the Qumran writings raise the probability of an extensive literary activity also among the first followers of Jesus. It is not unlikely, then, that the canonical New Testament documents represent a select portion of a larger and more diverse body of Christian literature from the apostolic period.

Considerable evidence both from the New Testament and from second-century witnesses suggests that four or five apostolic circles – Pauline, Petrine, Johannine, Jacobean-Matthean – produced the whole canonical

---

[65] E. g. I Clement; The Didaché; perhaps Barnabas, Shepherd of Hermas and Odes of Solomon. See the discussion in J. A. T. Robinson, *Redating the New Testament*, London 1976, 312–335; J. H. Charlesworth, ed., *The Old Testament Pseudepigrapha*, 2 vols, Garden City NY 1985, II, 726f. (Odes of Solomon).

[66] E. g. Gospel of Thomas; cf. C. Tuckett, 'Thomas and the Synoptics,' *NT* 30 (1988), 132–157; E. Yamauchi, *Pre-Christian Gnosticism*, Grand Rapids 1973, 89ff.; Ellis (note 1), 206, 251 n. 57.

[67] Cf. Luke 1:1; Acts 18:27; Rom 16:26; I Cor 7:1; Eph 5:14; Jas 4:5.

[68] II Cor 3:1; cf. II Thess 2:2; 3:17; Ellis (note 1), 101–115, 122–128, 226–236.

corpus within a generation or two of the resurrection of Jesus.[69] The individual authors led or worked within one or more of these allied circles and, for their mutual benefit, gave and received and used (oral and) written traditions from other circles.[70] The New Testament representation that the leaders of these groups cooperated with each other, even as they pursued their separate missions and their distinctive emphases, is historically entirely credible.[71] However, for some the letter of James has long been regarded as a glaring exception to this.

James, like Jesus, ignores the cultic and ceremonial laws and, like Paul, gives pre-eminence to the law of love.[72] Thus he has some teachings quite in accord with Paul's as well as some that appear to be contrary to those of the Apostle to the Gentiles. With respect to the latter the letter of James has posed a problem for advocates of the theological unity of the New Testament. For example, James speaks against a 'faith without works' (2:20f.) and uses Abraham as a type of one who 'is justified from works and not from faith only' (2:24). In this matter he is thought to be in conflict with Paul, for whom Abraham is a type of the Christian who 'is justified by faith apart from the works of the law' (Rom 3:28; 4:3ff.). The letter of

---

[69] From the Pauline circle come Luke, Acts, Paul's thirteen letters, Hebrews; from the Petrine circle, Mark, I Peter, II Peter; from the Johannine circle, John, I-III John, Revelation; from the Jacobean-Matthean circle, Matthew, James, Jude. The Gospel of Matthew or its *Vorlage* is closely associated with, if not a part of the Jacobean mission. Cf. J. B. Mayor, *The Epistle of James*, London 1892, lxxxii ff. for the parallels. Cf. Ellis, 'Gospels' (note 13), 45–54; idem, *The Making of the New Testament Documents*, forthcoming.

John Robinson (note 65; idem, *The Priority of John*, London 1985, 67–93) makes a strong case from historical (external) evidence for dating all of the New Testament documents before A. D. 70, even if a question mark may be placed at a few points in his argument. Cf. Ellis (note 49). Also still in point is J. B. Lightfoot's perceptive critique of a Scottish devotee of F. C. Baur's school in *Essays on ... Supernatural Religion*, London 1893, 90–96, 101f., 251–271.

[70] E.g. common traditions behind the four Gospels and behind letters from different apostolic missions; common traditions in the Gospels and in I Corinthians; common elements of church order in the Jerusalem church and in the Pastoral Epistles; common traditions on the regulation of wives in the Pauline and in the Petrine missions; common traditions on wisdom in I Cor 2:6–16 and in Jas 3:13–18. Cf. Ellis (note 69); idem (note 31), 72f.; idem, 'Traditions in 1 Corinthians,' *NTS* 32 (1986), 481–502.

[71] This representation of the matter appears, for example, in Acts; Gal 1:18f.; 2:1, 9; I Cor 3:22–4:1; 9:5; II Pet 3:15. Cf. Ellis (note 1), 3–22, 122–128, 235f.; idem, 'Church Order in the Pastoral Epistles,' (note 31), 109ff.

[72] Goppelt (note 1), 125f. Cf. Jas 2:8; Rom 13:8ff.

James was written during Paul's mission, indeed, before A. D. 62,[73] and it includes a polemic against those who downplay or reject the role of works in salvation. But is the polemic directed against Paul's teaching or against those who have gone beyond Paul and whom Paul himself rebukes?

As has been observed above,[74] the ritually-strict Jewish Christians, the circumcision party, included two factions, non-Judaizing and Judaizing. So also the ritually-lax believers, those who saw themselves as free from the law, included non-libertine and libertine factions. The libertine attitude appeared among the Corinthians[75] and was later reinforced by Paul's opponents in II Corinthians and in other Pauline letters, gnosticizing Judaizers who combined ritual observance with moral abandon.[76] This attitude was strongly censured by Paul in both his early[77] and later letters and also by James.[78]

Paul has a rather complex attitude toward the law, as a number of writers have pointed out.[79] He affirms both justification apart from works of law[80] and, at the same time, a judgement by works[81] in which 'justification' language also appears.[82] Like James and Jesus, he gives pre-eminence to the law of love and asserts that the true believer does fulfil through the Spirit the just requirements of the law.[83]

In the light of these factors, the targets of James' polemic are not Paul[84]

---

[73] Rightly, M. Hengel, 'Der Jakobusbrief als antipaulinische Polemik,' in Hawthorne (note 18), 248–253 (A. D. 58–62). I would not rule out a date in the forties, before the Council of Jerusalem, but a date in the fifties seems better to fit the issues addressed. Cf. P. Davids, *Commentary on James*, Grand Rapids 1982, 22.

[74] See above, 142.

[75] I Cor 5–6.

[76] Cf. Ellis, 'Paul and His Opponents' (note 1), 101–115.

[77] E. g. Rom 3:8, where libertines have claimed Paul's support for their views; I Cor 5:11; II Cor 12:21; Phil 3:19.

[78] E. g. II Tim 3:4ff.; Tit 1:10–16. On James, see below, notes 84, 85.

[79] E. g. S. Westerholm, *Israel's Law and the Church's Faith*, Grand Rapids 1988; Moule (note 19); P. Stuhlmacher, *Reconciliation, Law and Righteousness*, Philadelphia 1986; H. Hübner, *Law in Paul's Thought*, Edinburgh 1984; E. P. Sanders, *Paul, the Law and the Jewish People*, Philadelphia 1983; J. Weima in *NT* 33 (1990), 219–235.

[80] Gal 2:16; Rom 3:20–31.

[81] I Cor 4:4; II Cor 5:10; cf. Rom 2:6ff.; Eph 2:8–10.

[82] Cf. C. H. Cosgrove, 'Justification in Paul,' *JBL* 106 (1987), 653–670; K. P. Donfried, 'Justification and Last Judgment in Paul,' *ZNTW* 67 (1976), 90–110.

[83] Rom 6:22; 8:4; 13:8ff.; Eph 2:10; Phil 1:6–11; I Tim 1:8ff. Cf. J. G. Lodge, 'James and Paul at Cross-Purposes? James 2:22,' *Bib* 62 (1981), 195–213.

[84] *Pace* Hengel (note 73). But see Peter H. Davids, *The Epistle of James*, Grand Rapids 1982, 19ff.: Jas 2:14–21 may attack 'a misunderstood Paulinism,' but more

and his faithful followers but rather the same kind of libertine elements, in Paul's churches and elsewhere, whom Paul himself condemns. These people are not only without good works but also manifest jealousy (ζῆλος), strife (ἐριθεία), boasting (κατακαυχᾶσθαι), lying (ψεύδειν) and an egoistic human wisdom (ψυχικὴ σοφία), the same vices that Paul rebukes his own congregations about.[85] It is true, of course, that Paul and James approach these questions from different perspectives. But when one observes carefully the characteristics of the practices that each attacks, they appear to be essentially in agreement and to oppose basically the same kind of theological and ethical aberrations.

Current reconstructions that view the circles of Paul, Peter, John and James, and the New Testament writings coming from them, as antithetical expressions of Christian theology are largely echoes of F. C. Baur's Hegelian model, interpretations that in my view wrongly identify the opponents and that mold the texts to accord with a preconceived philosophical mindset.[86] Against this approach, a reconstruction is quite justifiable that, with Leonard Goppelt, presents the New Testament's teachings, including its explanation of the Old, as a cohesive and compatible theological unity.

The New Testament's use of the Old Testament lies at the heart of its theology, and it is primarily expressed within the framework of a typological exposition. It unfolds a hermeneutical perspective that will deepen one's understanding of the biblical message, and it offers important

---

likely it stands in the tradition of I Macc 2:52 and is 'refuting a Jewish Christian attempt to minimize the demands of the gospel...' (21); W. Schrage, 'Der Jakobusbrief,' *Die 'katholischen' Briefe*, edd. H. Balz and W. Schrage, Göttingen 1973, 35: James probably has 'in his sights a crude and wild-growth Paulinism;' similar, P. Stuhlmacher, *Gerechtigkeit Gottes bei Paulus*, Göttingen 1966, 193 n; J. H. Ropes, *Epistle of St. James*, Edinburgh 1916, 35: James addresses the possible misuse 'of Paul's doctrine of justification... to excuse moral laxity.'

[85] Jas 3:14f.; 4:16; cf. Rom 13:13; I Cor 2:4, 13; 3:3; II Cor 12:20. Libertine distortions of Paul's teaching by some in his congregations may have occasioned the false report mentioned in Rom 3:8: 'Some even affirm that we say, "Let us do evil that good may come."' Cf. I Cor 5:1–6; Schrage (note 84), 35; C. K. Barrett, *Romans*, London 1957, 65; J. B. Lightfoot, *Notes on the Epistles of Paul*, London 1895, 266.

[86] Cf. J. B. Lightfoot's criticism of Baur's approach in 'St. Paul and the Three' *Galatians*, London 1896, 295 n, 309 n, 334 n, 354 n, 355, 363 n; idem, *The Apostolic Fathers*, 3 vols. in 5, London 1890, I, i. 357 f.; II, i, xi f.; idem (note 69), 24 f., 64, 82, 90–96, 101 f., 151, 251. Cf. Ellis (note 1), 86–95. For a broader analysis and critique cf. Harris (note 13). For a contemporary defense of the Baur-tradition cf. G. Lüdemann, *Opposition to Paul in Jewish Christianity*, Philadelphia 1989.

insights into the way in which Jesus and his apostles and prophets interpreted his acts and teaching. And their interpretation, I believe, is the foundation and the key to any legitimate contemporary expression of Christianity.

Index of References

I. Old Testament

7:13	93	61:1f.	91, 107, 117
7:14	55, 93	61:2b	103
8:14	91	61:9	96
8:14f.	111	62:2	96
9:2f.	94	62:11	91, 94
9:6f.	93	64:4	119
9:8	113	65:1–5	67
9:11	48, 93	65:16	119
9:12	66	65:17	47, 99
9:14f.	69, 83	66:1f.	81
11:1	47, 93f.	66:22	47
11:4	103		
11:6–9	47	*Jeremiah*	
11:15f.	47		
13:6	104	4:3	67
19:19–22	92	7:21f.	66
19:20	92	16:14f.	47
19:20ff.	92	23:5	93f.
22:18	108	31:15	93
25:8	91	31:31	77
26:20	91, 107	31:31f.	47
28:11f.	3	31:31ff.	89
28:16	71, 91, 95, 111	31:31–34	90, 107
29:13	97, 136f.	31:33f.	98
29:18f.	117	32:18	66
40–66	105	48:45	66
40:3	91, 114		
40:9	91	*Ezekiel*	
41:8	89, 91		
42	65	1:26ff.	114
43:16–21	47	5:5	83
45:21	91	16	49
48:20f.	47	17:2	117
49:6	93	28:2	103
51:3	47	34:11	67
51:9ff.	47	34:11f.	101
52:5	110	36:8	47
52:11	57	36:35	47
52:13	93	37:24	47
53	65	40–48	47
54:1	99	47:7–12	47
54:10	47	47:13	47
54:11f.	47		
54:13	98	*Daniel*	
55:3	107		
55:10f.	113	1–6	43
56–66	102	1:17	119f.
58:6	91, 107	2	69, 135
59:7f.	99	2:4b–7:28	41
		2:21f.	119

III. Apocrypha and Pseudepigrapha

V. Early Jewish Writings

VI. Apostolic Fathers

II Clement

11:6	82

Ignatius

To the Smyrnaeans

1:1	80

To the Trallians

13:3	82

Barnabas

3:1	81
4:3	24
6:2 ff.	71

6:8	81
6:10	117
6:13	63
6:14	81
9:1	81
12:1	71
16:5	34
17:2	117

Shepherd of Hermas

Mandates

1,1	24

Visions

2,3,4	24

VII. Ancient Christian Writings

Amphilocius

Iambi ad Seleucum

319	3

Apostolic Constitutions

2,25	146
2,57,2	23
5,20	14 f.

Athanasius

De Decretis Nicaenae

18	3

Easter Letter

39	21

Augustine

De Civ. Dei

15,23	29
17,20	29
18,36	29

18,42 ff.	55
18,43	25, 50
19,4	148

De Doct. Christ.

2,12	29
2,12 f.	23
2,13	29

Letters (= Epistulae)

71,5	25
82,35	30, 32

On the Soul

3,2	29

Clement of Alexandria

Stromata

1,21	24
3,4,34 f.	142

VIII. Mishnah, Tosefta, and Babylonian and Palestinian Talmuds

IX. Other Rabbinic Writings

X. Greco-Roman Writings

Index of Modern Authors